Remorse and Reparation

Forensic Focus

This series takes the currently crystallizing field of Forensic Psychotherapy as its focal point, offering a forum for the presentation of theoretical and clinical issues. It also embraces such influential neighbouring disciplines as language, law, literature, criminology, ethics and philosophy, as well as psychiatry and philosophy, as well as psychiatry and psychology, its established progenitors.

Forensic Psychotherapy
Crime, Psychodynamics and the Offender Patient
Edited by Christopher Cordess and Murray Cox
ISBN 1 85302 634 4 pb
ISBN 1 85302 240 3 hb 2 vols
Forensic Focus 1

The Cradle of Violence
Essays on Psychiatry, Psychoanalysis and Literature
Stephen Wilson
ISBN 1 85302 306 X
Forensic Focus 2

A Practical Guide to Forensic Psychotherapy
Edited by Estela Welldon and Cleo Van Velsen
ISBN 1 85302 389 2
Forensic Focus 3

Prison Theatre
Practices and Perspectives
Edited by James Thompson
ISBN 1 85302 417 1
Forensic Focus 4

Challenges in Forensic Psychotherapy
Edited by Hjalmar van Marle and Wilma van der Berg
ISBN 1 85302 419 8
Forensic Focus 5

Managing High Security Psychiatric Care
Edited by Charles Kaye and Alan Franey
ISBN 1 85302 581 X pb
ISBN 1 85302 582 8 hb
Forensic Focus 9

Forensic Focus 7

Remorse and Reparation

Edited by Murray Cox

Jessica Kingsley Publishers
London and Philadelphia

First published in the United Kingdom in 1999 by
Jessica Kingsley Publishers Ltd,
116 Pentonville Road,
London N1 9JB, England
and
325 Chestnut Street,
Philadelphia, PA 19106, USA.

www.jkp.com

Copyright © 1999 Jessica Kingsley Publishers

Library of Congress Cataloging-in-Publication Data
Remorse and reparation / edited by Murray Cox.
p. cm. -- (Forensic focus ; 7)
Includes bibliographical references and index.
ISBN 1-85302-451-1 (hc. : alk. paper). -- ISBN 1-85302-452-X (pbk. : alk. paper)
1. Criminal psychology. 2. Remorse. 3. Reparation. I. Cox, Murray. II. Series.
HV6105.R45 1998
364.3--dc21

British Library Cataloguing in Publication Data
Remorse and reparation. - (forensic focus ; 7)
1. Remorse 2. Criminal psychology
I. Cox, Murray
152.4

ISBN 1-85302-452-X pb
ISBN 1-85302-451-1 hb

Printed and Bound in Great Britain by
Athenaeum Press, Gateshead, Tyne and Wear

Contents

Part II: Legal Perspectives

Part III: Remorse and Reparation from Other Perspectives

Publisher's Note

Murray Cox died suddenly just a few weeks before the manuscript for this book was due to be delivered. Although some chapters were still missing, he had read all those he had received, and had drafted the Introduction. The last time I spoke to him, he told me how much he was looking forward to working on the book during his convalescence. We were both looking forward to discussing it when he had finished, and he had dropped enough tantalising hints during the spring of 1997 for me to know that he had something very interesting indeed.

We began discussing the book in the autumn of 1995. What Murray had originally envisaged as a book on psychiatry and the criminal justice system became much larger as the lack of written material became increasingly apparent and we began to look outwards to other disciplines. This proved so interesting that at one point we even talked about putting the other disciplines first, and enlarging the scope of the book.

The book in its final form is not how he had planned it. There are several chapters that never were delivered, for one reason or another, and rather than attempt to fill the gaps I realized in the end that the book stood as it was. Murray's Introduction is clearly unfinished, but I know that he felt that this book represented a first step towards an understanding of remorse and its related topics – regret, apology, guilt, shame, repentance and reparation to name only a few.

No one *wants* to feel remorse; it is not a light thing. Not only does it carry with it all the baggage of a dreadful act committed, but it is an unpleasant feeling in itself, as Sophocles and his successors show us. What I have come to understand over the last year, reading the manuscript and Murray's notes, and mulling over the central issue, is just what a deep and difficult topic remorse is, and how writing about it requires quite a difficult level of self examination. Murray's absence has been extremely sorely felt.

In the last year the newspapers seem to have been full of news items with a bearing on remorse and its paler shadows. 'Apology' has featured again and again, frequently for venial sins where its use seems appropriate, but also for dark and intractable acts, where to speak of apology seems wholly out of place. Is it really appropriate to *apologise* for war crimes? Even more, what is the value of an apology for torture, which has been made because someone has demanded that it be made? In what sense can this be either an expression of remorse or an attempt at reparation? The conductor Christophe Eschenbach recently spoke of the power of music to convey these things, saying that Beethoven's Ninth Symphony expresses the aims of the UN, while an apology exacted under duress can be

summed up as 'nya nya ne nya nya' which has everything to do with power and
nothing to do with remorse. I think this has much to say of what remorse is about,
and I know that Murray, who loved music, would have been much taken with it.
What the news items show, however, is that these issues are part of the Zeitgeist.

I think this must be the last of Murray's 'works in progress' to be published. It
was a project very close to his heart, so I hope that what I have done to it in his
absence does him, and the book, justice. Without question, if it had not been for
Alice Theilgaard's generous and extensive help it would not be the book it is. Alice
has been a tower of strength – not just as 'technical advisor' but as moral support
and interpreter of Murray's intentions and handwriting. Murray's finishing
touches for all his books seem, by chance (or perhaps not) to have been written on
significant days: St Catherine's Day; Easter Day; Christmas Eve. So perhaps it is
not inappropriate, given the subject matter of the book, that this is written on
Armistice Day. I wish he were here to write it himself.

Jessica Kingsley

11th November 1998

Remorse and Reparation

'To Double Business Bound'

Murray Cox

An introductory editorial usually assumes one of two forms. It either offers a brief explanation of the book's *raison d'etre*, explaining how and why it came into being. Or it serves to tune the reader's receptivity, in preparation for the ensuing ebb and flow of debate. Within the compass of a few pages this editorial attempts to serve both ends, under the commanding rubric of being 'To Double Business Bound'.

It would be as absurd to expect an identical format for each chapter, as it would be to welcome a level playing field for competitive downhill skiing – to use the current idiom. Numerous fields of specialist endeavour are represented in these pages, yet they are all linked by the fact that each contributor received an identical letter of invitation. This is obviously not a systematic textbook. On the contrary, it takes the form of a number of variations on the theme of Remorse and Reparation. It is for this reason that a certain degree of repetition is not only inevitable, it is welcome. Editorial scissors have not necessarily been at work pruning comments in one chapter which have already appeared in a previous contribution. Confluence, especially when evident in an interdisciplinary study such as this, carries its own credentials. Several authors have referred to the etymology of remorse (Latin: *re-modere*) but the 're-biting' is a theme in several keys. In addition to the pangs of remorse, there are the nagging gnawing doubts of inadequate conceptualization, and the provocative stimulation of being bitten and bitten again by the possibility of fresh opportunity. To be offered a second bite at the cherry is not an entirely alien metaphor in the present circumstances. Or even a third.

Ibsen's play *Little Eyolf* is woven of remorse which colours much of the 'double density dialogue' (Meyer 1994). There is even a rat-wife who asks if there is 'anything that gnaws in the house'.

So kaleidoscopic is the structure of this volume, that a strong case could be made for reading Part III on complementary perspectives first. This would set the scene and provide the background for current clinical and legal debate.

With the shaking of the thematic kaleidoscope, hitherto confused thoughts on remorse and reparation have been jolted. The theme is tantalizingly elusive, provocative and frustrating. In many ways it is not surprising that so little has been written on it. This volume could not possibly be the last word on the subject. Neither is the first. But it is not unreasonable to hope that the next word on the subject will take the form of a better informed debate.

CONFLUENT PERSPECTIVAL WORLDS

This book brings together three realms of discourse: the clinical, the legal, and those complementary subjects which include areas of professional enquiry without which this exploration would be incomplete. Each major section finds itself confronting unsparingly ultimate questions and, in one way or another, is 'to double business bound'.

Writing as a clinician, it is tempting to set the scene by delineating the broad range of clinical presentations in which remorse may feature. Its apparent presence may be bona-fide and *en route* to attempts at reparation, although in the world of forensic psychiatry the possibility of spurious pseudo-remorse, which is nothing other than instrumental and attention-seeking, must never be forgotten. Yet again, the patient suffering from endogenous depression may feel vicariously remorseful and over-responsible for all the ills and sins that flesh is heir to.

Nevertheless, I sense that the more distant horizon offered by the broad landscape of the arts may give the reader more bias-free interdisciplinary air to breath, before settling down to reflection upon the sombre substance which follows. Our attention therefore turns to the remorse experienced and voiced for us by Claudius, who feels that he is 'to double business bound'.

TO DOUBLE BUSINESS BOUND

With that immediacy of contact which the arts and clinical encounter share, Shakespeare enables us to overhear Claudius speaking to himself 'like a man to double business bound' (*Hamlet* III. iii.41). His remorse is such that he cannot pray. And the connotation of being 'bound' to double business implies both being fettered by, and destined for, inherent conflict.

> Try what repentance can. What can it not?
> Yet what can it, when one cannot repent?
> O, wretched state! O, bosom black as death!
> Oh liméd soul, that struggling to be free
> Art more engag'd! Help, angels! Make assay.

The 'liméd soul' is a powerful image. It is taken from a method of trapping birds which landed on adhesive lime from which it was impossible to struggle free.

Claudius is trapped in the double business of remorse. He wishes to repent while retaining 'those effects for which I did the murder'.

In a lecture on Yeats and Remorse, McDonald (1996) writes:

> In a prose draft [of *The Man and the Echo*] Yeats pictures himself 'worn down by my self-torturing search', and wrote how 'Among this solitude I seek remorse', but struck out 'remorse' to replace it with 'escape'. The words are true alternatives: one precludes the other, and Yeats' decision to choose 'escape' is what causes this poem's creative heart to beat... The remorselessness of the poem's self-interrogations is the guarantee of its escape from the deathwards pull of remorse. The extraordinary conclusion in which 'I have lost the theme', takes the poem to places wholly unprepared for its initial scenario of unsparingly ultimate questions:

> > But hush, for I have lost the theme,
> > Its joy or night seem but a dream;
> > Up there some hawk or owl has struck
> > Dropping out of sky or rock,
> > A stricken rabbit is crying out
> > And its cry distracts my thought.
> >
> > (*The Collected Poems 'W.B. Yeats'* 1950, p.395)

McDonald's comment about true alternatives, in which one precludes the other, offers this editorial writer a thought provoking launching pad from which it requires little or no struggle to be free. It encourages the free flight of associative ideas. For whereas 'remorse' and 'escape' are true alternatives, the words of the title of this present volume, *Remorse and Reparation*, are not. Many of the ensuing essays explore their degree of reciprocity and their etymological sources crop up in several places. Reparation has a much gentler, restorative or renewing ethos than the ominous gravitas conveyed in the sheer implicatory weight of remorse. Cordelia says:

> Oh my dear father! Restoration hang
> Thy medicine on my lips: and let this kiss
> Repair those violent harms that my two sisters
> Have in thy reverence made! (*King Lear* IV. 7. 26)

This is in marked contrast to the cry of a stricken rabbit, which so distracts thought that recall is blocked, and amnesia – 'for I have lost the theme' – temporarily prevails.

It is within the experience of the forensic clinician to learn that it is not just the stricken rabbit which is crying out. The memory of human victims, whose cry distracts attempted sequential thought, may lead to incipient narrative failure within therapeutic space. 'Of all the screams I've heard, this has so much on top of it' (Therapeutic Space). Certain groups of homicidal assailants exhibit what could be called 'species escalation', whereby the early experimental killing of unknown animal victims progresses, via pets to random killing of human strangers, to 'familiar' target victims. As a note of editorial caution at this point, I would emphasize that one needs to retain the highest degree of vigilance (and an enhanced capacity) to be surprised by surprise. Almost to the extent of expecting the unexpected. It is a self-confirming fact that until one knows the inside story, one does not know.

By 'the inside story' I do not refer to the story which an individual may 'know' but 'refuse' to tell. I also imply that through the unconscious defence of repression, the patient, himself, is not aware of what has taken place in all its fullness. Unconscious defences do defend! This has an important corollary in terms of the capacity to develop remorse. In the early days of therapy, before the necessary unforgetting or *anamnesis* which is a *sine qua non* of forensic psychotherapy has taken place, an individual may scarcely 'know' of the stark horrors about which he will subsequently experience remorse. Those familiar with psychodynamic attempts at working with psychopaths, and other excessively narcissistic individuals, will be alert to the possibility of pseudo-disclosure and its corollary of pseudo-remorse. One of the issues which arises in the following pages is the ironic juxtaposition of a defendant who one moment denies that he was involved in a particular assault and then, within minutes, is expressing profound remorse for his participation!

In his single phrase 'unsparingly ultimate questions' McDonald takes us to the heart of the matter. Remorse is about that which is felt to be directly linked to the 'unsparingly ultimate', however inaccessible or conceptually ungraspable it may be. Trivial remorse is a contradiction in terms. And when the clinician or the lawyer senses this, it is likely to be trailing clouds of strategy as it comes, perhaps deliberately designed to encourage lenient disposal. It brings with it an ethos of ulterior motives. True remorse, *per se*, is invested with harsh self-disposal of which Judas Iscariot is paradigmatic. I use this term in the theological sense (Torrance 1969, 16), as meaning that which 'points beyond itself', rather than being merely a normative exemplification. Indeed, in the recently published version of *The Mysteries: The Passion*, Kemp and Mitchell (1997, 52) entitle one whole section 'Judas' Remorse'. There is a primordiality about the self-addressed reference of true remorse and its gravitas is no less than that of the question asked in the garden of Eden:

> 'What is this that thou hast done?' (*Genesis* 4,10)

There is a widely accepted convention about the structure of the introduction to a multi-authored, inter-disciplinary volume. It is expected to say something to the effect that the theme under discussion is so all-embracing that no single discipline could possibly have a monopoly of access to the material, even though, within the boundaries of each discipline, there may be well established, authoritative monographs. It is therefore the bringing together of hitherto clearly demarcated, well recognized authorities which would be the main *raison d'etre* and justification of a current publishing enterprise.

These, at least, were some of my expectations in the early days when the preliminary outline of this book began to take shape. This was before the paradoxical, pervasive-yet-ungraspable capacity of remorse as a central theme began to assert itself. It seems to have an in-built capacity for de-railing conceptual organization, particularly if it involves engagement with those from other disciplines. This is part of its fascination, which generates both perplexity and interest. So that in place of the customary 'so far so good' comment, I found myself floundering in conceptual quick-sands, for which 'so far so bad' seemed an apt description. I suspect that even at this stage the reader's initial sweeping glance at the list of contributors, and the disciplines they represent, will have made him aware that many fields of study and professional expertise have been called upon. Since its inception, it had been my expectation that the major contribution of this symposium would have been the bringing together of major, heavyweight established works which were familiar to the specialist in his field, but which were unfamiliar to those outside. The surprise, the joker in the pack, which seemed to evoke an almost identical response wherever I turned, and whoever I asked, took something of the following form:

> Yes, remorse is an important topic. – It pops up here and there – but at the moment, I can't think of a single publication – at least in my field – in which it is the predominant theme. Interesting. Food for thought. I wonder why –.

If this was the response evoked from representatives of each individual field, it is not unexpected that the non-existence of an inter-disciplinary monograph meant that potential contributors were 'to double business bound' with a difference. All agreed it would be worth doing, was much needed and would prove challenging to all who were eventually involved in the project, whether as contributor, editor or reader.

Remorse is a feeling-laden concept and therefore evokes a powerful affective penumbra. This may be one of the reasons why poetry, recently defined as a way of expressing what cannot be expressed directly, often takes us closest to its core. It is therefore somewhat surprising that the poetry of A.E. Housman, which is so often heavy with implicit remorse and regret never uses the word itself. But the sour–salt–fault echo stays in the taste buds of nagging memory.

> When the bells justle in the tower
>   The hollow night amid,
> Then on my tongue the taste is sour
>   Of all I ever did.

> The word unsaid will stay unsaid
>   Though there was much to say.
>
> The toil of all that be
>   Helps not the primal fault;
> It rains into the sea,
>   And still the sea is salt.

I cannot find the word remorse in any of his poems, but I have come across one mention of 'the remorseful day'.

> Ensanguining the skies
> How heavily it dies
>   Into the west away;
> Past touch and sight and sound
>   Not further to be found,
> How hopeless underground
>   Falls the remorseful day. (*The Collected Poems of A.E. Houseman* 1939)

This is in marked contrast to the numerous direct references in the work of Yeats, so helpfully delineated by McDonald: 'The body calls it death,/The heart remorse.'

Let me end this introduction under a somewhat ironic heading 'Remorse starts here' – fortunately, so does Reparation.

REMORSE STARTS HERE

Remorse may have been too strong a word, but I certainly felt bad when I was unable to answer a question posed by Andrew Horne, a consultant colleague at Broadmoor.

> Murray, could you give me a research reference on the relationship between the expression of remorse and the diminished likelihood of re-offending?

After 25 years in the field I surely ought to have been able to do so 'off the cuff'. But the only phrase that jumped into my mind was:

> Stop up the access and passage to remorse. (*Macbeth* I. iv. 45)

It is one of my life's journeying mercies that, poetic cadence and rhythm seem to have an intrinsic capacity to lock into registration and to rebound on recall. This is in such contrast to the way in which statistics always seem to scatter before me and figures invariably fail. It is one of the values of working alongside others in a team who have complementary characteristics! However helpful Lady Macbeth's injunction may have been on the spur of the moment, I returned to my office and quickly thumbed through the indexes of the major edited works – representing, *in toto,* a battalion of expert contributors – on forensic psychiatry and psycho-therapy, such as Bluglass and Bowden (1990), Gunn and Taylor (1993) and Cordess and Cox (1996). It was to my great surprise (and partial chagrin) that such references as there were were scant, almost to the point of non-existence. There were numerous references to guilt, fewer to shame but virtually no secondary references to remorse. Reparation is an easier theme to conceptualize and references were consequently somewhat more copious, but relatively few – considering the importance of the topic.

My surprise grew, almost by logarithmic proportions, when all searches in specialist libraries, depending on appropriate databases, were only slightly more productive. There were a few obscure references awaiting translation, but no major publications were unearthed.

Virtually all the experts, representing the wide variety of disciplines included in this book, came up with much the same reply. Nevertheless, it still seems scarcely credible that the word does not feature in the index of any standard books on criminal law or even in the guidelines submitted to the Parole Board. There was however one single exception to the named 'authorities' who was mentioned in many of my initial exploratory discussions. In one way or another, many said: 'Of course one has to start with Kierkegaard.' It is for this reason that a single chapter is devoted to the study of Søren Kierkegaard, the brilliant, enigmatic, existential Danish philosopher.

REMORSE AND THE SPACE BETWEEN

Sooner or later the penny drops. We come to realize that remorse is, by definition, a perpetually interim, never-to-be-satisfied restless state. It seems to lie between categories of thought, or clinical diagnostic categories. For example, it is both cognitive and affective. As the above discussion has shown, it is certainly inter-disciplinary and not the exclusive prerogative of any single field of enquiry. Its inbuilt successiveness is diachronic, so that the individual experiencing remorse feels bitten again and again. It is also synchronic, as the chapters on sociology and anthropology vividly demonstrate.

Even so, I suspect that part of the ubiquitous difficulty of grappling with the concept is that it has some of the qualities which Jungians attribute to archetypes; in that they are larger than we are so that we have difficulty in discerning the qualities on the far side of remorse.

I want to conclude this final section on the space between by concentrating on a particular space between two stage directions in Act I of *Macbeth.* It occurs in Scene v between 'exit messenger' and 'enter Macbeth'. Lady Macbeth is alone. The invocation to the spirits is ominously ambiguous as we are told that they tend on thoughts which are 'mortal' – thus implying either human or fatal. Or both.

She addresses the 'murdering ministers' in the their 'sightless substances' and implores them to:

> Stop up the access and passage to remorse. (I. v. 44)

Such proleptic activity when planning homicide is not unusual. But this is drama and the criminal justice system is 'out there' in the world of another reality. Lady Macbeth did not ask for access to memory to be stopped. It was the access to remorse that needed blocking, because ineffective semi-permeable partial access might hinder homicide and render it semi-performable. Subsequently there were partial killings, a 'botching' and the accumulating impact of rooted sorrows. So that it was not heaven which peeped at her through the blanket of the dark, but the doctor of physic and the waiting gentlewoman who observed her saying:

> What's done cannot be undone. (V. ii. 74)

And these words bring us abruptly face to face with the fulcrum of this volume. For remorse is the re-biting of experience following a doing which cannot be undone. It may be an act which brings an individual within the orbit of the criminal justice system. It may be a fantasy confined within the inner world and so bring him within the orbit of a therapeutic or confessional system. Finally, it may of course start as an unconscious phantasy, which eventually erupts into an assaultative constellation, so that he reaches forensic psychotherapeutic asylum via the criminal justice system.

But if remorse is linked to that which cannot be undone – a dead victim cannot be brought to life again, neither can a raped victim be unraped – what frame of reification carries reparation? Or is remorse always an experience within one frame of reference and reparation an experience in another? Is transference, in a psychoanalytic sense, evidence of a flow of energy and feeling in one direction as remorse which, after mutation and modulation in the inner world of the therapist, is returned and received as creative reparative energy? If so, the interesting question arises as to the nature of counter-transference phenomena. This raises a third meta-conceptual question as to the therapist's resources of creative presence replenishment. Such concerns are beyond the scope of the present volume but certainly feel at home under the rubric of the space between.

This all points to the key words which Lady Macbeth etches into our conceptual vocabulary. In order for change to occur there must be 'access to remorse'.

Let one Broadmoor patient, who had killed a child, speak for all those who ultimately reach the remorse-laden, painful point of auto-transparency. Once initial denial and protectively defensive amnesia had been, like curtains, drawn aside, he said:

> I've done a terrible thing and I want nothing to do with anything [even 'therapy'] that might make it not a terrible thing.

And let one para-clinical vignette convey the intensity of being in the presence of 'a terrible thing' – which is so terrible that full understanding may never be reached. The words of Titus can stand vicariously for all those in the presence of the extremity of psychological or physical dismemberment. It is the depths of horror and shock, mingled with remorse, in the untidy amputations that psyche flesh and blood are heir to. Titus is speaking to his daughter, Lavinia, 'her hands cut off, and her tongue cut out, and ravish'd'. These are his words:

> Thou shalt not sigh, nor hold thy stumps to heaven,
> Nor wink, nor nod, nor kneel, nor make a sign,
> But I of these will wrest an alphabet,
> And by still practice learn to know thy meaning.
>
> (*Titus Andronicus* III. ii. 44)

This a capacious and elaborate metaphor which implies the long-term struggle to 'wrest an alphabet' and the attention over time necessary to 'learn to know thy meaning' from someone who is unable to speak or write.

I suggest that this image can carry every inflection of remorse – even though Titus had not been directly responsible for his daughter's abuse. And his intention to 'learn to know [Lavinia's] meaning' is reparative energy on behalf of others, which is intrinsic to the process of therapy.

> Whatever our final aesthetic judgement concerning the merits of *Titus Andronicus*, we must understand that we are dealing, not with a paucity of imagination, but with an excess of dramatic witness.' (*Tricomi* 1974, p.19).

And from the clinical forensic arena, comes this codicil:

> But NOT with an excess of CLINICAL witness. (Cox and Theilgaard 1994, p.359)

A POST-SCRIPT ON HEADLINES

If an academic journal on *Titus Andronicus* can carry an article entitled 'A Footnote on Hands', I think we can end with a post-script on headlines.

Probably the most frequently read mention of the word 'remorse' comes as a banner headline reporting the result of a trial in which a defendant was described as being

EVIL AND SHOWING NO REMORSE

on account of which he would receive a long custodial prison sentence.

The disturbing fact is that there appears to be no firm evidence that had he shown remorse, there is less likelihood of him re-offending. Indeed, he might do so and show even greater remorse. Such matters raise deep and disturbing questions which, in one way or another, make an impact on every strand of society.

This book is unlikely to contain all the answers, though it probably asks most of the questions. We all have a vested interest because we know from our own experience how disturbing it is to be 'to double business bound'. And we need no convincing of the pain of having to confront unsparingly ultimate questions.

PART I

Clinical Perspectives

Ethical Perspectives

CHAPTER 1

Reflections on Remorse in Forensic Psychiatry

Andrew S. Horne

INTRODUCTION

Remorse is of interest to psychiatrists because it is a psychological phenomenon that they need to understand in order to be able to understand their patients – in the same way that they need to understand shame or grief. Psychiatrists are primarily concerned with helping people who are in an abnormal mental state to achieve a normal mental state. Forensic psychiatrists deal mainly with people who have come into conflict with the criminal law, and because a fair proportion of their patients have committed serious violence against another person, they are frequently in contact with people who experience remorse. Moreover, their work brings them into regular contact with the criminal justice system where there is a particular interest in remorse in offenders. Remorse is therefore of particular concern to forensic psychiatrists. Discussion of reparation is more likely to be heard in the criminal justice system. The courts have long had the power to order financial compensation in certain circumstances and in recent years there has been interest in reconciliation and in offenders providing a service of some kind to their victims by way of reparation.

As a person moves between his solicitor's office, prison, court, and hospital his status changes – client, prisoner, defendant, patient. I hope the reader will not find these changes of name confusing; it would be confusing without them. The term 'psychopath' is used loosely by those working with mentally disordered offenders to denote people whose primary problem is a personality disorder rather than a mental illness. I will avoid the term because of its varying usages and derogatory connotations, preferring the expression 'personality-disordered'; and where there may be confusion because many mentally ill forensic patients also have personality disorders, 'primarily personality-disordered'.

FORENSIC PSYCHIATRY

Forensic psychiatry springs from two roots: the needs of the criminal justice system for advice and assistance and the particular practical difficulties of treating mentally disordered offenders. Judges and other members of the criminal justice system are not generally well-informed about mental disorder and therefore obtain a report from a psychiatrist when they encounter it in a defendant. For the defence lawyer, psychiatric evidence occasionally offers a defence to the charge, often provides evidence that can be used in mitigation and sometimes provides access to a hospital order or probation order with a condition of psychiatric treatment; disposals which are often far more attractive than those the defendant would otherwise receive. If the defendant is sent to hospital on a hospital order he can appeal to the mental health review tribunal to be discharged. The psychiatrist prepares a detailed report on the case for the tribunal and is closely questioned at the hearing by the tribunal members and the patient's solicitor about whether the patient is yet fit to be discharged.

The aim of forensic psychiatry in relation to the patient is to relive his distress, improve his mental state and reduce the risk of further offending. In this the 'index offence' – the offence which brought about the current period of detention – is crucially important. It is usually the patient's most serious offence and it gives a crucial insight into the ways in which that particular patient can run into trouble and the severity of what can go wrong. An adequate understanding of the index offence is essential if there is to be any attempt at modifying the factors contributing to the patient's offending and so reducing the risk of further offending. This often requires the patient to participate in a very detailed and painful examination of the offence and the details of how it arose.

In many cases the offence is the most dreadful disaster that the patient has ever been involved in. Often the victim is a member of the offender's family, and the offence has the effect of alienating the people to whom he or she is closest and to whom he or she might wish to turn for support. The stigma of having a close relative who is a 'violent madman' is not to be under-rated. The situation is further complicated by the fact that many forensic patients come from disturbed families and have suffered very unsatisfactory parenting and have difficulty in maintaining relationships. Often other family members as well as the patient have very limited relationship skills, which makes the repairing of relationships very difficult for all concerned.

Examining the patient's offending, and the allied process of helping the patient to come to terms emotionally with what he or she has done, inevitably involve the patient experiencing remorse but, rather curiously, forensic psychiatrists do not normally use that expression in this context. They do, however, often include statements in their court reports about whether or not the defendant 'shows remorse', and sometimes in reports for the mental health review tribunal. Such comments are usually very terse, conveying little, if anything, of the observations which lead to the conclusion that the defendant was or was not remorseful; and I have never seen a discussion in a report of the different interpretations the observations might support. It thus appears that the concept of remorse has crept into the thinking and habits of forensic psychiatrists from the criminal justice system and is used by them only in that context.

REMORSE AND REPARATION

Remorse is one concept in a constellation of functionally related concepts which include guilt, shame, regret, repentance, reparation, and more peripherally accusation, apology, culpability, punishment, justice, and many others. The phenomena to which they refer are to do with what happens when one person wrongs another. To investigate the logic of this area thoroughly would take a whole volume. Here I have space only for an outline of the argument.

The *Oxford English Dictionary* (OED) describes remorse as 'a feeling of compunction, or deep regret and repentance, for a sin or wrong committed'. If we turn to 'compunction' we find 'the pricking or stinging of the conscience or the heart; regret or uneasiness of mind consequent on sin or wrongdoing; remorse, contrition.' If we look to its roots we find that it derives from *re-* and *mordere*, to bite, sting or attack. Remorse is therefore a repetitive or perhaps recurrent experience rather than something transient. It follows serious rather than trivial wrongdoing. For reparation the OED gives three related meanings: 'the action of restoring something to a proper or former state'; 'the action of repairing or mending something'; and 'the action of making amends for a wrong or loss; compensation'. I shall argue below that remorse probably occurs mainly in situations in which irreparable harm has been done.

Consider what happens when one person is thought to have wronged another and a dispute arises. To give an adequate account we need to consider what goes on between those two, but we also need to include the onlookers because morality is essentially to do with shared ways of behaving and feeling. (Onlookers who are not directly involved in a dispute show great interest in the way the dispute is handled and the outcome and tend to have strong feelings about it. Consider the television news: great effort goes into reporting criminal trials, discussion about drug use, scientific advances that have ethical implications and similar things – and always there is also reporting of other people's reactions to the news.) The person offended against challenges the offender, who then states whether or not he accepts the accusation. If he does admit it, the matter is soon sorted out. Admitting the offence, taking responsibility for what happened, making an apology (which is best done promptly and with an appropriate show of emotion, because everyone knows that our non-verbal behaviour is a better guide to our true feelings than our words are) all serve to reduce the victim's anger and so reduce his calls for punishment. They also reduce the onlookers' anger and make them see the perpetrator as deserving less punishment. In addition, an apology, if accepted, makes all involved feel better, including making the perpetrator feel less guilty. Forgiveness, like the acceptance of an apology, makes all feel better. Sometimes something more tangible than an apology is appropriate. The perpetrator may make reparation by replacing the glass in the window that he broke or compensating the victim financially. Such reparation, if properly negotiated, leaves both sides feeling better. Punishment, where it occurs, is behaviour intended to hurt and deter the offender and to emphasize to him the seriousness of what he has done. In so doing it provides satisfaction to the victim and the onlookers: 'Justice has been done.' Perhaps because of this, punishment makes the offender feel better in the long run, relieving him of feelings of guilt. All these things help to draw a line beneath the offence. They assist in the process of resolving feelings of anger, guilt, outrage and distress on all sides. The people involved can forget about the offence, and so can face each other again as if the offence had not happened.

If the offender does not accept the accusation the matter is argued out. The accused may reject the charge or make an excuse, such as 'I did not know what I was doing' or 'I did not intend to do it' or any other excuse he can think of – the list of possible excuses is endless. A very few excuses exonerate the offender completely, but most are partial excuses which serve to reduce the offender's blameworthiness only somewhat.

The shape of the process of resolving the dispute is essentially the same whether the offence is an insult or a serious assault, and whether it is handled spontaneously and informally, or follows the slow formal processes of the law. However, for very serious offences the system does not work well. The weight of an excuse has to match the gravity of the offence (Austen 1961) and there are very few excuses that are weighty enough to balance against a serious offence. Apologies, forgiveness and reparation are similarly inadequate. Thus the offender is left full of regret and guilt which he is unable to deal with, ruminating painfully on what he has done, wishing he could put the clock back, being pricked by his conscience, wishing he could make everything all right again – in other words experiencing remorse. If he were able to resolve his predicament he would of course do so, if only to escape his distress. It would appear therefore that remorse occurs mainly after serious offences and probably particularly where irreparable harm has been done.

So much for the philosophy. But what are the detailed features of remorse in mentally normal people? What, in practice, does and does not provoke it? What course does it follow once it occurs and what influences that course? Does the intensity of remorse decline as time passes, and does its severity and duration depend on the extent of the harm that the offender has caused and how close he was to the victim? These are empirical questions that are yet to be studied. Longitudinal studies of people who were involved in road accidents and felt partially responsible might be of some help here.

MENTAL DISORDER

Mental disorders are divided into two broad categories: mental illnesses and personality disorders. The paradigm of a mental illness is a condition in which a previously normal person changes and functions in an abnormal fashion for a while, and then, perhaps with treatment, returns to normal; whereas the paradigm of a personality disorder is a life-long condition in which one can see the features of the disorder developing as the person grows into adulthood. Many of the symptoms of mental illness can be seen as arising because normal functions are temporarily not working properly; whereas the symptoms of personality disorders tend to be the life-long lack or excess of skills and personality characteristics. For example, someone who is depressed may complain of low mood, anxiety, poor concentration, lack of appetite, weight loss and many other symptoms. His spouse can describe how his state has changed and has at least a rough idea of when the change began. With treatment he will almost certainly return to normal. We know that in depression there are abnormalities of neurotransmission in the brain and that antidepressant drugs affect these. In contrast, someone with a personality disorder might complain of difficulties in getting on with people, lack of confidence, feeling awkward in social situations and a feeling that he has always been different from other people. A careful history reveals long-standing difficulties. At school he had no close friends and was bullied. He has always lead a solitary existence and enjoyed solitary activities. Thus he appears to lack certain skills and abilities, and to have done so all his life.

Mental illnesses are divided into neurotic and psychotic types. In simple terms, in psychotic illness the patient is out of touch with reality, whereas in neurotic illness he is not. Depression is the only condition which is commonly thought of as spanning the neurotic–psychotic divide. Our depressed patient above is likely to tell us that he finds it very hard to think about the future because it all seems pointless and he cannot conceive of getting better. He feels (often quite wrongly) that he is a failure in his career and he is letting his family down by letting himself get into this state and cannot imagine ever getting better. The only sensible solution is suicide. We can see that his perception of his situation and his thinking about it are extremely distorted by his illness.

If he receives no treatment and his illness gets worse he may reach the point where he becomes deluded and hallucinates. He may become convinced that he is so useless that he deserves to be killed, and through brooding and worrying about this come to believe that he is going to be killed. He may hear voices of people talking about his worries, perhaps discussing killing him or the repossession of his house as a result of his (imagined) non-payment of his mortgage. He is now frankly psychotic. It is impossible to argue him out of his false beliefs.

I have described depression in some detail because it is relatively easy to understand, as there is a gradual progression through the degrees of severity to the psychotic state. However the commonest kind of mental illness that forensic psychiatrists have to treat is schizophrenia. Whereas in very severe depression the delusional beliefs and other psychotic symptoms can be seen as arising out of the depressed mood, in schizophrenia the psychotic experiences manifest themselves differently. Patients describe phenomena which are clearly gross distortions of their mental processes. They often describe hearing the voices of other people talking. The sound appears to come from a discernible direction and the experience is convincing. Usually there are several voices and they talk to each other in derogatory terms, abusing the patient and running him down, and this distressing and distracting experience continues for much of the time. The voices may tell him to do things, or that people are against him or planning to kill him. The patient often misconstrues events around him. When he sees two strangers laughing he may suddenly become convinced that they are laughing at him, and he may be convinced that articles in the newspapers or programmes on the television are about him, or have been produced in order to convey a particular message to him. Many patients develop delusional belief systems. For example, one patient, an intelligent, educated man, asked me in all seriousness: 'Which planet are we on?' He then talked about the difficulty of keeping track of events when he was moving frequently from one planet to another, and said that he would like to be discharged to his own hospital. Asked where this was, he said it was on a different planet whose name I could not catch, giggled, said he had said too much already, and declined to discuss the matter further. Antipsychotic medication helps considerably by damping down and often eliminating the psychotic phenomena, but the illness usually damages the patient's personality leaving him emotionally flat and apathetic, so that he tends to lose his interests and neglect himself and spends much time doing nothing. Patients tend to lose their social skills and often slide down the social scale, ending up in menial employment or unemployed and living in the poor areas of big cities, with their attendant problems.

MENTAL DISORDER AND OFFENDING

Contrary to popular belief, people who are mentally ill are only very slightly more prone to acting violently than is the rest of the population, but sometimes the illness is clearly the cause of violence. Sometimes someone who is severely depressed may kill his spouse and children in order to save them from the pain his own suicide would have caused them, but then stop short of killing himself. Such a person will soon come under the care of a forensic psychiatrist, whilst on remand for murder. Some patients hear hallucinatory voices telling them to attack or kill and feel unable to resist the compulsion; some act on what they believe to be the instructions of God. The majority, however, act violently as a result of the fear, confusion, and panic caused by their symptoms, often in misguided pre-emptive self-defence.

The downward social drift into poverty in inner city areas and the apathy that schizophrenia causes probably increase the risk of non-violent crime. Living in an area where drug abuse is rife makes it easy for patients to obtain illicit drugs which some find give them temporary relief from their symptoms (though in the long run they tend to make the psychotic symptoms worse). They may then resort to property crime to pay for the drugs.

There is very often an element of acting out a fantasy in the crimes of the mentally ill. In a few cases that is essentially what the offence is about. For example, a severely personality-disordered man, who cannot relate to women, develops a fantasy of taking a woman to a deserted house and keeping her there whereupon she falls in love with him and they live happily ever after. He then tries to act this out in real life. Even in crimes of violence there is often a considerable element of fantasy. We are not accustomed to attacking or killing, and in our fantasies, as in films, the victim tends to fall down dead at the first blow. The reality is horribly different from what the aggressor imagined. The victim fights back so that the aggressor fears he is going to be killed, and the knife will not penetrate. When it does, blood goes everywhere and the victim still stubbornly refuses to die. The aggressor is often severely traumatized by such experiences.

COMING TO TERMS WITH THE OFFENCE

The offender's response to the offence usually begins with a period of numbness and disbelief. This may last hours, days or years and it may develop into a state of frank denial, such that the patient says that he did not commit the offence at all. The stage of denial gives way to a partial acceptance in which the patient gradually acknowledges more clearly and accurately what he did. Cox (1986) described the following progression in one case: 'I don't know what you are talking about' to 'I didn't do it' to 'I did it, but I was mentally ill at the time' (which excuses me) to 'Even though I was mentally ill, I did it' (acknowledging some personal responsibility in spite of the illness) to 'I did it' to 'I murdered a 65-year-old woman'. That is a bare outline of the process. Having a mental disorder is only a partial excuse for offending. Most mentally disordered people do not offend in any serious way, so the patient inevitably asks himself 'How is it that I did this?' He has to examine every detail of what happened and his intention at every moment in order to make sense of it and form a view about the extent to which he was at fault and accept that.

Those patients whose illness is first diagnosed only after the offence have to come to terms with having a mental illness at the same time as coming to terms with the offence. Schizophrenia is a chronic debilitating distressing illness from which the majority never make a full recovery. That is hard enough to accept, but it is a *mental* illness as well, with all the stigma and loss of face that that implies.

GRIEF

Those mentally disordered offenders who kill a person who is 'important' to them have to grieve. But their grieving is complicated by their responsibility for the death. The process of grieving normally follows a predictable pattern. It begins with a stage of shock, numbness and disbelief. This is followed by a period of anger (at the person for dying, at others and perhaps the whole world for letting it happen); and then a period when thoughts about the dead person trigger waves of distress which may be uncontrollable. The bereaved person is intensely preoccupied with the deceased and goes through a period of blaming himself for little ways in which he imagines that he let the deceased down or wronged him. The waves of distress gradually decline in frequency and intensity over a period of months. The bereaved may idealize the deceased for a period. The process normally proceeds to its conclusion, but sometimes there is an abnormal grief reaction where the process is delayed or stops prematurely. This is most striking when it happens at the very beginning of the process, and perhaps years after the death we find the bereaved talking and carrying on living as if the deceased were still alive, setting a place for him at table and so on. Someone who is grieving for a person that they have killed has a much greater risk of having an abnormal grief reaction.

Mentally disordered offenders suffer many losses as a result of their offending. Psychiatrists have stretched the concept of grieving to include grieving for losses other than people. It is commonplace to hear talk of grieving for one's lost freedom, for one's damaged identity, and so on. This usage of the concept of grieving is useful, but it is difficult to see how it relates to the concept of remorse; indeed, remorse could almost be subsumed under it. This point will need to be born in mind by researchers.

POST-TRAUMATIC STRESS DISORDER (PTSD)

The experience of committing the offence causes PTSD in a significant proportion of those mentally disordered offenders who offend seriously. PTSD is a psychiatric condition which sometimes arises following severe emotional trauma. The patient suffers intrusive distressing memories ('flashbacks') of the event which are often so vivid that they can be difficult to distinguish from reality. He tends to withdraw somewhat from his normal activities, complain of feeling detached from others, and be emotionally unresponsive. Many suffer difficulties in concentration and memory, or feel guilty about having survived while others died. They tend to avoid activities which precipitate the intrusive memories, and it can be an extremely disabling condition. It makes it very difficult for the patient to talk about the traumatic experience with any vividness. Though he can often give a narrative account, it comes across in an emotionless way. In the case of an offender, this can give the impression that he does not experience remorse for the offence, which may not in fact be the case.

A NOTE ON VICTIM EMPATHY

Victim empathy is a concept that has been formulated as part of the study of sex offenders (Hildebran and Pithers 1989). Many sex offenders are oblivious to the suffering that they cause their victims, and they often claim that their victims enjoy being victimized. In many cases the offender was himself once a victim and the denial derives from this. It is unfortunate that the specialized term 'victim empathy' is increasingly used in connection with other kinds of offending, in which the psychological processes are different.

FACTORS AFFECTING THE EXPRESSION OF REMORSE

For a person to express remorse he must both feel that he has done harm, and feel that it was a very wrong thing to do. We also need to distinguish between the experiencing of remorse and the expression of it. *There are no studies of the features of remorse or its course in the mentally abnormal,* but some observations from clinical experience shed a little light on the area.

It seems likely that extreme anger can prevent the patient feeling that what he did was wrong, and so prevent him feeling remorse. It is quite common to see a very angry young patient, with a long history of abuse, who experiences everything as someone else's fault, and expresses little or no remorse for his offences.

An acute psychotic illness can make the patient feel that the offence was justified and therefore not experience or express remorse.

> A woman killed her two young children because she heard the voice of God telling her to do so. She was reluctant, but felt she had no alternative. Subsequently, in hospital, her symptoms fluctuated. At times when she was actively psychotic and her delusions had returned to their full strength she would justify the offence, explaining that she had had no alternative. When she was less ill she was full of guilt and remorse and would lie awake in bed weeping about the offence.

An acute psychotic illness can make the patient feel that he had not committed the offence, and therefore not experience remorse.

> A man in his thirties had a fist fight with another man in a lodging house and shortly afterwards was seen to attack him with a knife. He was found to be suffering from schizophrenia. He consistently denied the offence, whilst admitting all the circumstances. Following a marked improvement in his mental state owing to treatment with medication, he admitted the offence. Asked why he had only just admitted it, he said in puzzled tones 'Until very recently I didn't feel as if I had done it'.

Other aspects of the patient's mental state may limit the extent to which he can express remorse for the offence.

> A young man of low intelligence, illiterate and suffering from schizophrenia, killed a close relative because he experienced her as interfering with his brain. In hospital his positive psychotic symptoms resolved with medication, but he could not accept that he was suffering from a mental illness. Whilst he agreed that he had committed the offence he complained angrily at being kept in hospital, asserting: 'There's nothing wrong with me, I'm not on any medication, and anyway there's people being discharged from here who have killed three people and I only killed one.' When he was reminded of the evidence in the notes and the fact that he was receiving weekly injections he said that the injections had no effect on him and the symptoms of mental illness described in the notes were all lies. Asked about a nurse that he had attacked for no apparent reason and injured seriously earlier on, he declared that the nurse had deserved it, but could not say why. A series of interviews with a psychologist assessing his suitability for psychotherapy produced a marked improvement in his surly behaviour around the ward. It was soon apparent that he was unable to face up to the significance of the illness and the offence because his self-esteem was unbearably low, and work on that was required before further progress could be made.

THE USE OF REMORSE IN THE CRIMINAL JUSTICE SYSTEM

Reference is made to remorse in the criminal justice system in various contexts. Judges comment on it when sentencing, barristers point to it in pleas in mitigation, and the Parole Board is reluctant to grant parole until the prisoner shows some remorse for his offence. The reason for this interest in unclear, as the legal textbooks do not discuss remorse at all. If we look to the above account of what happens when one person wrongs another, three possible reasons for legal interest in the *presence* of remorse come to mind. First, to show remorse for an offence is very close to apologizing, and apologizing makes all involved feel better and so reduces the need for punishment. Second, experiencing remorse is painful and that pain might be thought to substitute for part of the punishment, so making a reduced sentence appropriate; and third, the experience of remorse might make further offending less likely, so suggesting a reduced sentence. This last possibility is an empirical matter. But the extent to which the offending of the mentally disordered is emotionally driven suggests that, though the experience of remorse may deter in certain special cases, it is most unlikely that it has much effect in the general run of cases. The *absence* of remorse is likely to be taken to mean that the defendant does not care about what he has done, or, even worse, does not appreciate the significance of it. This may be taken to imply that he deserves more punishment than he would otherwise deserve, in order to impress upon him the seriousness of the offence. Alternatively he may be seen as morally defective or evil in which case he may be considered to deserve extra punishment or to be so dangerous as to require longer incarceration in order to protect the public.

CONCLUSION

Remorse refers to an experience which often follows doing serious harm to another person. It is of great importance in forensic psychiatry and criminal law, but little is known about it empirically. Its features and cause need to be studied in normal and mentally disordered people. Grief may provide a useful model for this work. In forensic psychiatry the process of coming to terms with the offence is intimately associated with experiencing remorse and this needs systematic study.

The reasons for the interest of the courts and Parole Board in whether the defendant shows remorse are unclear, and until they become clear psychiatrists advising them will need to be extremely careful to ensure that their advice is understood properly and incorrect inferences are not drawn. Psychiatrists should maintain a clear distinction between their observations of the patient and the conclusions that they draw from them.

A number of factors including PTSD, mental illness, extremely low self-esteem and probably also personality disorder can cause the patient to show little, or in some cases, no remorse. It is very difficult to be sure in any particular case that these factors are all absent. In view of this uncertainty, and the damning inferences that may be drawn by members of the criminal justice system if they believe that the patient shows no remorse, considerable caution is required. The situation must be very rare indeed where a psychiatrist can reasonably and confidently assert that the defendant experiences no remorse.

CHAPTER 2

The Agenbite of Inwit, or, The Varieties of Moral Experience

James Gilligan

Everyone talks about remorse, but almost no one does anything about it. That is, it is amazing how little effort has been devoted to studying this moral emotion, either clinically, theoretically, or empirically, given the importance we attribute to it. Whenever someone commits a violent crime, or even a more trivial, non-criminal offence, the first characteristic of the offender that is often looked for is the presence or absence of remorse. And it is easy to see why this would be so. When any of us are attempting to decide what to do in response to someone's violation of another person's rights, one of the most practically important questions we need to answer concerns the likelihood of the individual's repeating such behaviour. And remorse has almost universally been considered to be an index as to whether the person truly repents of his or her actions, and is fully committed to changing, or whether he or she feels fully justified in committing such behaviour and is therefore likely to repeat it in the future.

So it is not surprising that judges, juries, priests, forensic psychiatrists, journalists, and the general public often speak of it as though it were among the most centrally important indices of a person's moral character and the state of his or her soul. What is surprising is the relative paucity of investigations into such a significant human attribute. How much do we actually know, for example, about whether offenders really are more likely to commit further violations of others' rights if they express no remorse? We seem to feel that we do know, for we use the word 'remorseless' as a synonym for people and acts that are cruel, pitiless and conscienceless – hardly characteristics likely to inspire confidence in the likelihood that a person will treat others considerately in the future. Nevertheless, lack of confidence is not the same thing as knowledge; do we *know* that the recidivism rate is higher among the remorseless? Just as important, if it is true, are the related questions: *why* is it true? what exactly does the mental state of 'remorselessness' consist of, and how can we understand it? and most important of all, what can we do about it, so as to decrease the likelihood that children born today will grow into adults who are remorseless about even the cruellest behaviour? Or to put all this the other way around, how sure can we be that people will *not* harm others in the future, if they *do* express remorse? And how much do we understand about the psychological dynamics of the relationship between thoughts and feelings of remorse, and the proclivity to engage in antisocial or violent behaviour?

The present chapter is intended as a small first step in the direction of rectifying that imbalance between the importance of the subject and the degree of neglect it has received. But how can we best begin such a daunting task? It would be difficult to exaggerate how central the issue of remorse has been in our attempts to regulate and rectify our relationships with each other, and even with ourselves – and yet it still remains one of the central relatively unexplored and unilluminated mysteries of the human soul.

The Christian tradition regarded remorse as so important that it elevated the main ritual for dealing with it – the performance of acts of penance – to the status of a sacrament. Another ritual that is part of the process of enabling people to express and resolve their feelings of remorse – confession – is regarded as so important in both religious and legal contexts that elaborate rules (or 'sub-rituals') have been developed in both of those contexts to safeguard the performance of it, and to ascertain that it will be performed properly and legitimately.[1]

---

1   *Why* this is regarded as so important – that is, *why* everyone is so uncomfortable with unacknowledged, unresolved or undischarged remorse – or in other words, *why* it is that 'chronic remorse, as all the moralists are agreed, is a most undesirable sentiment', as Aldous Huxley observed [quoted in *Webster's* 1986, p.1670, in article on 'penitence'] – is a question that I will take up later in this discussion. It is enough for now to notice that both to those experiencing it and those witnessing it, remorse is a most uncomfortable, distressing, 'disequilibrating' mental and emotional state that people simply cannot tolerate or leave alone, any more than they can avoid wanting to scratch an itch. Our whole culture devotes enormous amounts of time, energy and expense to the effort to expel this uncomfortable, undesirable and intolerable feeling from our midst, whether by means of: (1) magical religious rituals to expiate sin, such as the self-punishments of penance and the self-humiliations of confession; (2) legal rituals and exorcisms, called punishments, to discharge the guilt incurred by the commission of a crime; which originated in the superstitious belief that unless a crime was exorcised from the community by means of an adequate punishment ritual, it would pollute the whole community – the innocent as well as the guilty – and bring down the wrath of God on everyone, as in the story of Sodom and Gomorrah; as though moral and legal guilt were a concrete ontological or deontological substance, a real presence that would go on existing until it was eliminated by means of punishment, so that failure to exorcise guilt by punishing it amounted to condoning or endorsing it and allowing it to continue to exist; (3) neurotic symptoms or symptomatic acts to undo feelings of unconscious guilt over equally unconscious, but never enacted, wishes and fantasies; or (4) psychotherapeutic rituals designed to relieve the symptoms caused by the psychic pressure of unexpressed, unacknowledged or unconscious remorse.

So it is hardly surprising that the secular version or adaptation of these rituals for coping with remorse – called psychotherapy and psychoanalysis – has also been surrounded with barely less elaborate 'sub-rituals' in order to safeguard the integrity of the whole process. In place of the confessional or the witness stand, there is a couch. Instead of being required to perform acts of penance, or pay court-ordered fines or other penalties, the individual is required to pay a monthly bill. And just as in the religious and legal contexts, the patient in analysis is expected and instructed to tell 'the truth, the whole truth, and nothing but the truth' – except that here it is called the 'primary rule' of free association.

My point is not to caricature either the clinical work that my colleagues and I do, or the functions that priests and judges perform. My point is simply to remind you of what a central place the issue of remorse has in our whole culture – in our moral, religious, legal and psychological lives, and in the functioning of many of our most central institutions, from religious to legal to medical. Assessing the depth and sincerity of remorse is one of the central tasks performed by priests, judges and psychotherapists, as they go about the task of assessing the past, present and future behaviour of the individuals before them; as indeed it is for all human beings, as they attempt to understand, influence, and forecast the behaviour of their neighbours and themselves.

So how can we improve our understanding of remorse in a way that will facilitate our ability to perform these tasks? Freud commented once that the 'royal road' to understanding the unconscious mind of an individual was through the analysis and interpretation of his or her dreams. Joseph Campbell summarized that and other psychoanalytic insights in the formula that dreams are individual or personal myths, just as myths are collective dreams – so that the analysis and interpretation of myths can throw light on our collective cultural unconscious. I would add that there is another 'royal road' to understanding our collective cultural unconscious, namely, through the study of etymology – examining the history and development of language, and the interrelationships among the words in the various languages of which we have knowledge. And I would also add another method – namely, the examination and interpretation of the symbolism of behavioural acts (or 'acting out') as a non-verbal form of communication, whether the acts involved take the form of rituals (be they religious, legal, psychotherapeutic, or neurotic, as in the compulsions of obsessional neurosis), of sexual perversions, of eating disorders (since many people today are 'hunger artists,' as Kafka called them, and art, as everyone knows, is a symbolic form of communication), or of the violent, highly ritualized and horribly meaningful mutilations of the body and violations of the soul that all too many individuals inflict on others (in the course of committing violent crimes) and/or themselves (in the form of self-mutilations, or even suicide).

Let me begin first, however, with the dictionary definitions of remorse, as the word is used in contemporary English. According to my Unabridged Webster's, the first and most central meaning of remorse is 'a gnawing distress arising from a *sense of guilt* for past wrongs (as *injuries done to others*): *SELF*-REPROACH' (emphases added). The first contemporary (that is, not obsolete or archaic) meaning listed in the *Oxford English Dictionary* is: 'A feeling of compunction, or of deep regret and repentance, for a *sin* or wrong committed'; and 'remorseful' is defined as 'impressed with a sense of, and penitent for, *guilt*'. So there seems to be a consensus that the sense of *sin* and the feeling of *guilt* over past wrongs or *injuries* committed *against others* are central to the experience of remorse.

Is there any difference, then, between the feelings of guilt and of remorse, or are they merely synonyms? The definitions just quoted imply an answer, in that they define remorse as the painful feeling of self-reproach that occurs *after* one has harmed another. Freud concurs with that assessment, and concludes that:

> when one has a *sense of guilt after* having committed a misdeed, and because of it, the feeling should more properly be called remorse. It relates only to a deed that *has been done*, and, of course, it presupposes that a conscience – the readiness to feel guilty – was already in existence before the deed took place. (Freud 1961a, p.131)

Later, Freud distinguishes between five closely related concepts: 'super-ego,' 'conscience,' 'sense of guilt,' 'need for punishment,' and 'remorse,' of which he says,

> They all relate to the same state of affairs, but denote different aspects of it … Remorse is a general term for the ego's reaction in a case of sense of guilt … it is itself a punishment and can include the need for punishment … the term 'remorse' should be reserved for the reaction after an act of aggression has actually been carried out. (Ibid.,p.136–7)

The distinction Freud is making here is similar to the distinction he makes elsewhere between 'signal anxiety,' in which the feeling of fear is a warning signal, alerting the person who experiences it to an impending danger (specifically, a danger that threatens from within, i.e., the welling up of an impulse or wish that is threatening or unacceptable to the self, but before the danger has overwhelmed or overpowered the ego, and against which the ego can therefore still defend itself), and 'anxiety as such,' for example, the flooding of the ego with overwhelming anxiety, as occurs in panic reactions and phobias, when the ego has not been successful in warding off or defending itself against the threatening impulses. Thus, the existence of a fully developed conscience or super-ego means that an individual always has the capacity and potential to feel guilty whenever he begins to experience hostile impulses and wishes toward others. These are what stimulate guilt feelings, and it is against such wishes that the guilt feelings motivate the individual to defend himself (such as by being exaggeratedly kind and loving and considerate toward others, and correspondingly hostile and punitive toward the self). Remorse, then, is the form in which guilt feelings occur *after* one has already acted out the hostile impulses toward others which guilt as signal anxiety was unsuccessful in motivating sufficiently strong defenses against (so that the hostile or violent behaviour could be avoided).

Freud's distinction between premonitory guilt feelings (guilt as a form of signal anxiety, warning oneself not to give in to the temptation to hurt others) and guilt feelings after the fact of having hurt them (remorse) is clear enough. But if we adopted it too literally or mechanically, it would disable us from dealing with the actual fluidity and plasticity of mental life. For example, in *Richard III*, Shakespeare depicts a dialogue between the two murderers who have been hired to assassinate Clarence. Before they do so, one of them is reminded that their victim will wake on Judgement Day, at which point he comments that 'The urging of that word "judgement" hath bred a kind of remorse in me' which leads him to hesitate about committing the murder.[2]

Clearly, Shakespeare is here describing a kind of 'premonitory remorse,' that is, the anticipation, because of the power of the mind to imagine a future situation before it has actually occurred, of the remorse he will feel at a later date if he goes ahead and commits the murder that he is currently hesitating to do – which seems to me a perfectly legitimate use of the term, and one that not only can be

---

2   *Richard III*, I.iv.108. He is quite right that it is only 'a kind of' remorse, rather than the thing itself, because his fear is of being punished for the crime he is about to commit (by being damned), not of being morally guilty because of it; that is, his fear is of an external punisher (God), not of his own moral self-condemnation and self-punishment, i.e., his own conscience, which it would have to be in order to be remorse or guilt *per se*. In that sense, what he is feeling here is the exact opposite of remorse.

In other words, this murderer exemplifies the theological distinction between true remorse, also called contrition, and another type (incomplete, imperfect – 'a kind of' remorse, rather than the real thing), called attrition. The latter is fear of being punished for one's sin, whereas true contrition would consist of feelings of horror, self-blame and self-condemnation, because of having committed the sin *per se*; the feeling that one deserves punishment (penance) and therefore desires it; and that only actively submitting to or even seeking out one's punishment will wipe out or undo the state of sin in which one has placed oneself. The primary fear in contrition, in other words, is the fear of remaining in a state of sin and guilt, not fear of punishment; indeed, punishment is *desired* rather than feared, as the only thing that can undo the sin. For the truly conscientious, guilt-ridden, remorseful person, as one Bishop Hall put it in 1656, 'there is no hell but remorse' (quoted in OED, article on remorse 1971); no additional hell or punishment is needed, possible, feared, or even conceivable.

These remarks may also clarify the difference between remorse and regret. Remorse is one species of regret – it is regret, accompanied by feelings of repentance and an urge to do penance, over being guilty of having inflicted an injury on someone else. But other forms of regret are possible, which are the opposite of remorse, such as regret that one behaved in such a way that one was injured, or rendered oneself vulnerable to being punished, by someone else. That would appear to be the kind of regret that Shakespeare's murderer is anticipating he would feel if he committed a murder that would result in his damnation.

accommodated within Freud's overall explanatory scheme, but is actually entailed by it. For as Freud repeatedly emphasized, people who have a strong and well-internalized conscience and a ready capacity to feel guilty over any hostile wishes they may experience toward others are very vulnerable to feeling guilty over the wishes themselves, even though (and, in fact, precisely because) they have not acted out those wishes by actually harming the people with whom they are angry.

That is to say, the unconscious makes no distinction between feelings of guilt (before the fact) and remorse (after the fact); on the contrary, the unconscious mind equates, or makes no distinction between, wishes and deeds, or between the past, present and future. Thus, 'remorse' and 'guilt' are simply different names for the same feeling, the same subjective emotional and cognitive state, as well as the same moral self-assessment and self-condemnation, even if their chronological relationship to the condemned impulses and wishes is different in objective reality. For purposes of logical and theoretical analysis of these words and concepts, and the psychological processes they refer to, we can differentiate between 'guilt' and 'remorse', and insist that the latter term refers exclusively to feelings over past behaviour; but for purposes of clinical psychoanalysis and therapeutic practice, we cannot, in the sense that our patients, in their unconscious minds, make no such distinction.

That is why people not only feel guilty *prior* to harming others, they feel guilty *instead* of harming others. That is the adaptive function and purpose, or benefit, of guilt feelings – to prevent us from acting out our wishes to inflict pain or injury or punishment on others. Their maladaptive side-effect, or cost, is that they accomplish that goal by stimulating wishes to inflict pain or injury or punishment on ourselves instead; and that not only can result in self-harm, it can even result in harm to others – for example, when they are dependent on us, and can only be injured by any harm we do to ourselves or that others do to us.

So far, we have drawn a distinction between two types of guilt: (1) premonitory guilt feelings, or guilt as signal anxiety, guilt before the fact, guilt over wishes and fantasies alone; and (2) remorse, or guilt after the fact, guilt over deeds actually committed. This distinction is important and relevant for a number of reasons. First of all, it helps to explain two observations about people, to which I will turn in a moment, which are of the utmost clinical and historical importance. Second, while everyday observation of oneself and others confirms that feelings of remorse do exist, accounting for them theoretically so as to understand their psychology is by no means self-evident. That is, the existence of remorse poses some major obstacles to the creation of a consistent theory of the psychology of conscience, guilt feelings, and moral development, which I will discuss shortly. Third, this distinction highlights one of the shortcomings of remorse as a moral emotion or moral force, together with corresponding shortcomings in such related phenomena as confession and penance.

I will deal with the latter point first. In his essay on Dostoevsky, Freud points out that:

A moral man is one who reacts to temptation as soon as he feels it in his heart, without yielding to it. A man who alternately sins and then in his remorse erects high moral standards lays himself open to the reproach that he has made things too easy for himself. He has not achieved the essence of morality, renunciation, for the moral conduct of life is a practical human interest. He reminds one of the barbarians of the great migrations, who murdered and did penance for it, till penance became an actual technique for enabling murder to be done. (Freud 1961b, p.177)

In other words, what good is remorse (or guilt feelings) after the fact – after the fact, that is, of having harmed or killed others? Moral emotions such as guilt and remorse are not ends in themselves; they have no value when they are limited to being ends in themselves. They serve an adaptive purpose – in Freud's phrase, they serve 'a practical human interest' – only if they motivate us to avoid harming others. And it is all too apparent that self-punishment (whether we call it penance or masochism) and confession (which can easily alleviate the painful feeling of guilt by serving as a form of self-humiliation) can serve as a means of bribing one's conscience to permit one to go on sinning, and thus defeat the whole rational, practical, healthy purpose of morality. For example, even if a criminal has a strongly developed capacity for feeling remorse for crimes he has committed in the past, we are not likely to want to release him into the community unless he will restrain himself from committing them in the first place, in the future.

But that brings me to the second difficulty that is created by the existence of remorse, and the differentiation between feelings of premonitory guilt and of remorse: namely, if a person's conscience and his capacity to identify with another person and feel empathy, sympathy and love for that person, and therefore to feel guilty about his desire to hurt that person, are sufficiently well developed for him to feel remorse afterwards, then how can he bring himself to hurt the person in the first place? One obvious explanation for this apparent paradox is the existence of conflict between mixed and antagonistic feelings – between the feelings of love, sympathy and guilt that serve to inhibit hostile feelings and behaviour, and the hostile feelings themselves that stimulate hostile behaviour. In other words, might not someone feel sufficient anger toward someone to hurt him, and at the same time feel enough love or sympathy toward that person and enough guilt over one's anger at him to feel remorse after having hurt him?

One problem with that explanation, however, is to explain where the capacity (the emotional energy) for guilt feelings comes from. In the *Genealogy of Morals*, Nietzsche made a very convincing case that the source of one's guilt feelings is none other than one's anger toward others turned against oneself (a theory that almost exactly anticipated Freud's virtually identical theory of the dynamics of guilt feelings). If this theory is correct – and there is a great deal of evidence that it is – it leaves the origin of remorse unexplained, or at least difficult to explain. For if injuring others discharges whatever anger one feels toward them, then what is the source of the anger that fuels the guilt feelings that remorse consists of?

There are several possibilities. One is that sometimes even killing someone else is not capable of discharging all of one's anger at that person, so that there is plenty left over with which to fuel the guilty feeling of remorse. I have talked to some murderers, for example, whose hate for the person they killed or attempted to kill was so bottomless and insatiable that they only regretted they could not kill him (or her) over and over again, or more slowly, or with more pain, or even that they could not keep the person alive and torture them until they begged to be killed.

However, those do not tend to be the fantasies and wishes expressed by people who express remorse after committing a murder. More typical of the latter was a man whom I will call Mr Dominick. He was the middle-aged publisher of a small-town newspaper who killed his wife a few years ago after having spent twenty years in a marriage that was, apparently, miserable for both of them. He described her as having repeatedly gone out of her way to damage his business by deliberately alienating his advertisers, employees and others. She also, according to him, said more than once that she was so miserable she 'would be better off dead'. On their twentieth wedding anniversary she said to him, 'Twenty years – what a waste!' and gave him a greeting card on which she had altered the repeated phrase 'Love Is …' to 'Love Was …' He went to bed that night feeling that 'I was drowning in an ocean of hate' – both his hate for his wife, and hers for him. He woke when it was still dark, and before he was even fully awake, dazed with rage, he took the leash of her pet dog and strangled his wife with it. As soon as he realized what he had done he was overwhelmed with horror, and ran out of the house to his car, which he drove into a nearby reservoir with the intent of drowning himself – that is, replacing the metaphorical ocean in which he had been drowning with a real one. The car sank with him inside it, and as the cold water rushed in it seemed to wake him out of his lethal stupor. He forced his way out of the car, came to the surface, and swam to the shore, where he lay collapsed until the police found him. When he arrived at the prison mental hospital I directed, 24 hours later, he was in a state of extreme anguish, an intense agitated depression, and paced the floor while saying repeatedly that he was the worst sinner who had ever lived and that all he deserved was death. He appeared to be a serious enough suicide risk for most of the following two years that he was repeatedly on suicide precautions of one degree or another.

How can we understand the behaviour of this man, who was by most demographic criteria (other than his sex) an unlikely candidate for committing murder? Murderers in America are more likely than the general population to be young, poor, uneducated, unemployed, people of colour, with a history of unstable and/or promiscuous sexual relationships, and of alcohol or other substance abuse. They are generally unsuccessful and without any prominence professionally and economically, and are alienated and without close ties to their communities or community groups, such as social, religious or professional organizations. To the extent that they belong to any group it is most likely to be what has been described as a delinquent sub-culture, or a sub-culture of violence. They have a sociopathic personality structure characterized by lack of the capacity to feel guilt and to respect the rights of others, together with a history of one or more prior criminal offences, including violence. Instead, he was middle-aged, middle-class, college-educated, self-employed, white, with no history of crime, violence or substance abuse, married to the same woman for twenty years, marginally successful and prominent in his community but certainly not an outcast, where he belonged to numerous organizations including a religious group with unusually low rates of criminal violence – the opposite of a sub-culture of violence. He bore about as little resemblance to the usual stereotype of the antisocial, sociopathic or 'criminal' personality as possible. Instead, he had a rather rigid, tense, somewhat obsessional personality structure characterized by low self-esteem, chronic guilt feelings, little capacity for intimacy or emotional spontaneity, and a tendency to be the passive-aggressive and masochistic partner in a sado-masochistic relationship with his wife, as well as by chronic tension, anxiety and depression which had deteriorated by the time of the murder into a psychotic, agitated depression which rendered him unable to work, and left him in a state of constant suicidal rumination.

In asking how this man could have killed his wife, and in asking how someone whose conscience was insufficiently intact to restrain him from committing murder could also have the capacity for remorse afterwards, I am of course not attempting either to excuse the perpetrator nor to blame anyone else, least of all the victim (his wife). I am attempting to understand, in the first place, what long-term trends made this human tragedy possible and, second, what immediate situational precipitants made it actual.

Among the major issues that came up in his psychotherapy, in addition to (and partly contributing to) his chronic depression, was the fact that his mother had died at the time of his birth, so that he had gone through life feeling that he was, in both his father's eyes and his own, the murderer of his mother. In fact, this belief on his part was so strong it was virtually a delusion of guilt – or should we call it a delusion of remorse? – that he had lived with for most of his life. The combination of his psychiatric history and his psychological testing led to the conclusion that he suffered from a chronic borderline psychotic depression that at times of stress crossed the border into a frankly psychotic state.

Thus, Mr Dominick was an unusually extreme example of the damaging effects of what Erik Erikson (1956, p.131) called the development of a 'negative' identity. He felt rejected, condemned, guilty, unloved and deprived from the time of his birth, neither expected nor felt he deserved to be loved, and entered into and stayed in a marital relationship which left him continuing to feel that way. Killing his wife, from that perspective, seemed less totally 'ego-dystonic' and more in character than it might otherwise have: after all, he was already a wife-murderer. Also, he felt that he had spent his whole life already being accused of and punished for a crime that in his saner moments he realized he had not actually committed, which apparently contributed to his feeling entitled to act on his rage when he finally did so. His attitude, to paraphrase it, varied between 'if you're going to call me a murderer and treat me like one, I might as well be one', and 'since I've committed an ambiguous murder and been punished informally, I might as well commit an unambiguous one and be formally punished'; or 'since I've already committed one murder, what difference will one more make?'

The murder could also be seen as the behavioural expression of what Freud called the repetition compulsion, that is, the compulsion to repeat or reconstruct an event that constituted precisely the worst trauma of one's life (possibly in the effort to see if this time one can master the trauma, instead of being overwhelmed and destroyed by it).

He seems also to have heard his wife's repeated statement that she would be better off dead as a virtual request on her part that he kill her. Marvin Wolfgang (1966, pp. 252–4) speaks of 'victim-precipitated' homicide to describe a situation in which one victim (usually a spouse, but usually the husband) provokes the perpetrator to kill him or her in ways that are often quite blatant. This can be seen as a form of vicarious suicide, or 'spouse-assisted suicide,' in some of the cases Wolfgang describes, and while I never knew Mr Dominick's wife (though I did see the wedding anniversary card that she had altered as described), it is clear that he responded as if she were behaving in this way. Given his descriptions of her, one would have to at least raise the question of whether she was not also chronically depressed and suicidal, and was provoking him to commit her suicide for her; though one could only raise such a question, not answer it, given the degree to which he may well have distorted or misunderstood what she was actually like. Again, this of course neither excuses nor accuses either of them; I am attempting, rather, to unravel the chain of causation of a process that resulted in one person losing her life and the other losing his freedom and, potentially, his future, by examining what the meaning of his behaviour was to him.

In order to understand more clearly the relation between Mr Dominick's feelings of guilt and remorse, and his homicidal behaviour, it will be helpful to analyze the difference between shame and guilt. I mentioned that he had become psychotically depressed by the time of the murder; and the close connection between his remorse and his deep depression is shown by the similarity between the etymology of the word 'remorse' and the psychoanalytic investigation of depression. Remorse comes from the Latin *remordere*, to bite back or bite again (from *re-*, again, and *mordere*, to bite). And that summarizes exactly what guilt motivates – namely, self-punishment, in which the punishment should fit the crime. If the crime has been one of biting, then the appropriate punishment would be to be bitten back. And those fantasies and associations have been found to be characteristic generally of people with severe depressions.[3] For example, the associations of people who are psychotically depressed have often been found to include references to biting, especially biting the nipples – so-called 'oral-sadistic cannibalistic' impulses, which give rise to what some analysts have called 'oral guilt'. The latter motivates people to do to their own nipples what they themselves had wanted to do to others' – usually their mother's.[4]

Also, the Indo-European root from which remorse derives, *mer-*, is also the root of 'murder'. So both etymologically and psychologically, there is a close connection between remorse (guilt feelings), *re-mordere* (biting back, i.e. self-punishment for one's oral sadistic biting cannibalistic wishes), self-murder (suicide, as punishment for one's homicidal impulses), and psychotic depression.[5]

But if Mr Dominick's suicidality and also his depression are related to his feelings of remorse, then how can we understand his homicidality? There we see the influence not of guilt, but of shame. For nothing stimulates homicidal rage more powerfully than the experience of being shamed and humiliated, and nothing is more shameful and humiliating than to be rejected, especially by someone to whom you have made yourself vulnerable. His wife's reaction to their twentieth anniversary was clearly the immediate precipitant or trigger of his murdering her, though his rage had been building up for many years.

The same dynamic relationships between shame, guilt and violence (shame leading to anger at others, and guilt to self-punishment) that we can see in Mr

---

3   I should emphasize here that these remarks are intended as part of an investigation of the psychology and phemomenology of depression, including the parts of the body that serve as symbols and metaphors of the mental state of depressed people. They are not intended as explanations of the etiology of this complex psycho-physiological illness.

4   For example, one woman who was psychotically depressed was a sexual masochist who could only attain sexual gratification by poking her nipples with pins, causing pain and bleeding, while she imagined that a starving, sadistic Nazi general was getting milk from them by biting them. In other words, she punished herself by doing to her own nipples what she wanted to do to her mother's, and only then could she allow herself to experience pleasure.

5   Interestingly, the Old English synonyms for 'remorse of conscience' that James Joyce quoted in a famous phrase in *Ulysses* (Joyce 1986, p.14) – 'the agenbite of inwit' – are exact parallels to the roots of our words 'remorse of conscience'. For example, 'agen-bite'/'again-bite' = *re-mordere*, and 'in-wit' = con-science.

Dominick are dramatized even more clearly by Shakespeare in the tragedy of Othello, who murdered Desdemona after Iago exposed him to shame by deceiving him into believing she had dishonoured him by making him into an object of scorn and ridicule – a cuckold; and who then committed suicide, after praying to be punished in hell ('Whip me, ye devils, ... roast me in sulphur! Wash me in steep-down gulfs of liquid fire!' V. ii. 277–80), when he discovered he had been guilty of killing an innocent person.

But perhaps the most important and relevant aspect of Mr Dominick's psychology, for purposes of this essay, is the light that this tragic story throws on the ways in which guilt, conscience, and remorse can in some circumstances not only fail to inhibit or prevent violence, but can actually stimulate it. Megargee (1966) distinguishes between 'over-controlled' and 'under-controlled' murderers, the latter being the typical bar-room brawler or neighbourhood tough who is constantly getting into fights, until he finally kills someone. Mr Dominick was clearly at the opposite extreme. He had a lifelong history of failing to respond even to rather extreme provocation and verbal assaults (not only from his wife) without expressing anger, or even letting himself consciously feel angry, let alone defend himself. It is not clear that he had ever learned to set limits on the degree to which he would allow people to attack or exploit him.

To say that he had a rigid and punitive conscience or super-ego that would not allow him to defend himself describes only part of the picture, for of course there is more to a person than his conscience. He also was becoming angrier and angrier (indeed, that had been true ever since his birth), but the rigidity of his moral code allowed him no way to express those feelings constructively, by putting them to work on his own behalf – such as by defending himself non-violently and preventing people from treating him in ways that could only make him more and more furious. Instead, he submitted to what he perceived as attacks and assaults, and turned his anger inward, against himself, with feelings of depression and worthlessness and thoughts and impulses of suicide – until he finally snapped, lost his temper, and committed a murder which he immediately followed with a serious and almost successful suicide attempt.

One can only surmise that if he had been able to be more aggressive (in defending and protecting himself) earlier, he would not have been so aggressive later; or in other words, that his overly rigid attempt to control his anger and prevent himself from hurting anyone again (following the death of his mother) was self-defeating and counter-productive. His over-control ultimately made him even more vulnerable to a disastrous and total loss of control than he would have been if he had been less conscientious and moralistic and had permitted himself a little more normal anger and aggression in the first place. It is as if too much morality – more than he could afford, emotionally – culminated in too little morality.

But the kind of picture Mr Dominick presented was extremely atypical of the vast majority of murderers and other violent criminals whom I met in the American prison system, of most of whom the most surprising characteristic is their total lack of remorse or guilt feelings after even (or especially) the most brutal and vicious crimes. But should that actually be so surprising? Shouldn't the statistical exceptions, such as Mr Dominick, be even more surprising? In other words, perhaps the lack of remorse that one observes after most violent crimes is exactly what one should expect, for if they had the capacity to feel guilty beforehand about impulses to hurt others, or to feel remorse after hurting them, how could they bring themselves to hurt them in the first place? The capacity for guilt feelings, together with feelings of love and empathy toward others, and of normal fear (the virtue called 'prudence') for the risks one would expose oneself to, are among the emotional capacities that inhibit normal people from committing a violent crime. So of course it would be reasonable to expect these feelings to be absent or deficient in those who do commit violent crimes; and that is in fact what one observes.

How can we understand why guilt-ridden, remorseful criminals are so rare, and criminals who feel completely innocent are so common? The more that guilt-ridden people inhibit and frustrate their hostile and violent wishes and impulses toward others, the stronger those wishes become. That is, wishes that have not been satisfied do not simply disappear of their own accord; rather, they increase in intensity (just as is true of unsatisfied thirst and hunger). But if they are not satisfied, where do they go? There is only one place they can go; since guilt feelings forbid their being directed at others, they become directed against the self, and thus become the feeling of self-hate. But that is simply another way of saying that they further intensify the feelings of guilt — for that is what guilt feelings are, namely, feelings of self-hate (i.e. self-condemnation, and the wish for self-punishment, up to and including capital punishment, i.e. suicide). And the stronger guilt feelings become, the stronger the inhibitions against aggression become; for guilt is the emotion that motivates us to defend against impulses to hurt others (i.e. motivates us to inhibit those impulses, by introjecting them, or directing them toward ourselves).

Freud once expressed the paradoxical truth that no one feels more sinful than the saint — and this analysis explains why that is so. The more saintly peoples' behaviour, the guiltier they feel; and the guiltier they feel, the more saintly their behaviour. So it is no wonder that one does not find many guilt-ridden (or remorseful) people in prison, and that the capacity for feelings of guilt and remorse will in general tend to inhibit violent behaviour.

But there is a counterpart to Freud's formula regarding the saint: namely, *no one feels more innocent than the criminal.* That is, it is precisely those whom others call most guilty who themselves feel most innocent. This phenomenon, which I have seen repeatedly, is so clear and so extreme that my colleagues and I used to say that *you never meet a guilty man in prison* (well, hardly ever – Mr Dominick was one of the rare exceptions to that rule).

This characteristic of most violent criminals is often so extreme that one might almost be tempted to coin the term 'delusion of innocence' to describe it, in analogy to the 'delusions of guilt' that we see in some psychotically depressed individuals, such as Mr Dominick, who accuse themselves of crimes and sins they did not commit. What I am referring to here is the capacity most criminals show to consider themselves completely innocent, blameless and justified in whatever they did, no matter how horrendous it may appear to others – indeed, the more horrendous, the greater the innocence.

But of course what else could we possibly expect? It is precisely their lack of capacity for guilt feelings that permitted them to commit their crimes to begin with. I am not speaking here of men who deny their guilt as part of an attempt to overturn their conviction in court, nor of those who deny it in order to avoid being beaten, raped or killed by other inmates, most of whom believe they have a moral obligation to punish many of the crimes for which men are sent to prison (especially those against women and children, as opposed to those committed against men). I am speaking rather of those who do not deny they committed the acts of which they were convicted, but who simply fail to feel that there was anything wrong about doing so. They are, in other words, remorseless.

I have mentioned one respect in which Mr Dominick's guilt feelings did not serve the purpose of inhibiting his violent impulses, and even stimulated them. Now I would like to mention another context in which guilt feelings, rather than inhibiting violence, actually stimulate it. Although guilt ordinarily motivates the direction of aggression toward the self and not toward others, there is a small group of people who, when psychotically depressed, will decide that the only means by which to spare their loved ones (usually their children) from the suffering that they, in their guilt, have caused them is to kill those whom they have irreparably harmed (which they rationalize as 'mercy-killing'), and then expiate their guilt by committing suicide. (One could suggest that these homicides also represent the return of the repressed aggression that underlies guilt in the first place, and which is simply being rationalized here as 'altruistic homicide' or euthanasia.)

Despite these (fortunately rare) guilt-motivated, or guilt-rationalized, homicides, the clinical and epidemiological data are consistent with the statistical generalization that, other things being equal (i.e. in situations that are perceived as allowing the possibility of voluntary choice between the two forms of violence – and in most situations that choice is possible), guilt motivates suicide rather than homicide. Because of that very fact, of course, guilt is hardly a panacea in our effort to reduce the toll of violence, for a person is just as dead if he has killed himself as if someone else killed him. On the other hand, a person can only commit suicide once, whereas he can commit homicide repeatedly; so the development of the capacity for feelings of guilt and remorse may, within limits, prevent more violence than it causes.

That the feelings of guilt and remorse normally stimulate compunctions and inhibit aggression toward others was an aspect of the psychology of those feelings that Shakespeare illustrated in *Macbeth*, as when he has Lady Macbeth pray to the evil spirits of murder:

> Come, you spirits ...
> Fill me from the crown to the toe topful
> Of direst cruelty! Make thick my blood,
> Stop up th' access and passage to remorse,
> That no compunctious visitings of nature
> Shake my fell purpose ...' (I. v. 40–47)

And the fact that some people who are so shame-driven as to commit the most terrible crimes can still be capable of some residual capacity for guilt feelings, and thus be tormented by the conflict between shame and guilt, is illustrated repeatedly throughout the play by both Macbeth and his self-indicted co-conspirator, whose peace and happiness, and even sanity and will to live, are consumed and destroyed internally by this conflict long before the two are defeated by their external enemies. Given how closely the real human tragedy recounted in this chapter conforms to the psychological principles illustrated in Shakespeare's tragedy, one can only conclude: thus does life (and death) imitate art.

CHAPTER 3

Necessary but not Sufficient

The Personal View of a Psychiatric Member of the Parole Board

David Tidmarsh

The author of this chapter worked for many years as a consultant forensic psychiatrist at Broadmoor Special Hospital and subsequently as a member of the Parole Board of England and Wales. It is essential to point out therefore that the views expressed are his alone and must not be taken to be the official views of either organization nor, of course, of any other individual. It is also necessary to say that psychiatrists on the Parole Board deal with a biased sample of cases which may distort their views about the far greater number of non-psychiatric cases considered by the Board. Although there has been research into the way the Parole Board works, this has only incidentally touched on questions of guilt and remorse. The reader will therefore look in vain for figures or conclusions based on surveys specifically designed to address these issues and will have to be content with a basic and idiosyncratic outline of some of the issues which may be important.

GUILT AND REMORSE

The author will leave it to others to discuss in detail the various definitions of remorse and reparation but a few observations may be in order if only to show how he uses these terms. Allied to remorse, and perhaps always preceding it, there is guilt. Guilt has two meanings, the first, the abstract legal one, being the state of having broken the law and the concomitant liability to a penalty. The second is a state of mind, the painful or uncomfortable emotion caused by the awareness or feeling of having done wrong. As we will see later, recent High Court judgements appear to have confused these concepts and caused the Board some problems. By 'wrong' is meant the contravention of moral or social standards. At the simplest level these standards are based on empathy and are learned in early childhood. A normal child exercising what we must now call a normal theory of mind will in due course understand that a tearful sibling is feeling what he feels in similar circumstances and his own feeling of distress will modify his behaviour. In some, as in those with Asperger's syndrome, this process is impaired or, as in some cases of schizophrenia, blunted in later life or bypassed by the process of projection.

At another level is guilt as fear of punishment. Failure to behave empathetically may be reinforced by punishment but it is perhaps where the connection between action and the distress of other people is less direct that punishment, in the psychological rather than the physical sense, becomes more important. Here of course there are various possibilities. Exposure to straight-forward rules of social and ethical conduct and role models who obey these rules is likely to lead to a clear sense of right and wrong with a corresponding ability to experience guilt appropriately. Conversely, experience of the conflicting behaviour and erratic rewards and punishments of a dysfunctional family may lead to a confused and ineffective conscience and an impaired capacity to experience guilt. Experiencing guilt and being able to act upon it are separate abilities. Thus although those with psychopathic personalities classically neither experience the emotion nor act upon it, there are those whose feelings of guilt stand no chance against their antisocial impulses or the imperatives of addiction. It is from this population that a high proportion of those dealt with by the Parole Board come. Guilt resulting from wrong done to family and the immediate social circle is easy to understand and is expected. Less common, is guilt related to offences against society as a whole or the common good and one looks for it in vain in those who commit certain types of fraud. A more complicated issue arises with those from other cultures. Conviction for behaviour acceptable in one culture may lead to a sense of injustice rather than the expected feeling of guilt in another. The global village is by no means a reality when it comes to the definition of antisocial behaviour.

The question of cultural difference leads on to the issue of cultural change. Again I leave it to others to document these changes but it is impossible to be unaware of the growth and influence of the concept of the fault-free society. According to this concept behaviour is due to social and economic forces so blame can only be attributed to others. As Whitehead (1993) commented in the context of changes in family structure: 'The dominant view appears to be that social criticism, like criticism of individuals, is psychologically damaging. The worst thing you can do is make people feel guilty or bad about themselves (p.80).' According to this concept nobody should feel guilty about their offences and guilt is an unhelpful emotion. I believe that Parole Board members are fully aware of the social antecedents of crime but, faced with individuals and the actual harm they have done, do not find these concepts helpful and go along with the policy of the prison system, based on persuading offenders to accept responsibility for their offences and to take control of their own lives.

THE FUNCTIONS OF THE PAROLE BOARD

The history and organization of the Parole Board were described in the report of the Committee set up to review parole chaired by Lord Carlisle (1988), by Tennent (1990) and in greater detail by Creighton and King (1996). It was originally set up in 1967, the first prisoners being released on parole licence in April the following year. Since then it has grown considerably both in terms of its workload and the number of its members and its responsibilities and procedures have changed. Its current terms of reference, derived from the Criminal Justice Act 1991, are to:

> advise the Home Secretary on the release on licence of both determinate and life sentence prisoners, on the recall to prison of anyone so released coming to adverse notice while on licence and on any other matters referred to it. In addition, the Board may give a direction for the release of a discretionary life sentence prisoner and has responsibility, delegated from the Home Secretary, for the decision to grant parole to a discretionary conditional release prisoner sentenced on or after 1 October 1992 to a determinate sentence of from four years to less than seven years. (Parole Board 1997, p.6)

All those sentenced after that date to sentences of one year and over are subject to a period of statutory supervision which may be preceded by a period on parole. In other words the Board is responsible for the release of all those serving sentences of between four and seven years and those serving life sentences for offences other than murder. It advises the Home Secretary about those serving seven years and over and those serving life sentences for murder. The Act empowered the Secretary of State to give the Board directions as to the matters to be taken into account in discharging any of its functions. The directions for the release of determinate sentence inmates are as follows:

> In deciding whether or not to recommend release on licence, the Parole Board shall consider *primarily* the risk to the public of a further offence being committed at a time when the prisoner would otherwise be in prison and whether any such risk is acceptable. This must be balanced against the benefit, both to the public and the offender, of early release back into the community under a degree of supervision which might help rehabilitation and so lessen the risk of re-offending in the future. The Board shall take into account that safeguarding the public may often outweigh the benefits to the offender of early release. Before recommending early release on licence, the Parole Board shall consider whether:
>
> (1) The safety of the public will be placed unacceptably at risk. In assessing such risk, the Board shall take into account:
>
> (a) the nature and circumstances of the original offence

(b) whether the prisoner has shown by his attitude and behaviour in custody that he is willing to address his offending behaviour by understanding its causes and its consequences for the victims concerned, and has made positive effort and progress in doing so

(c) in the case of a violent or sexual offender, whether the prisoner has committed other offences of sex or violence, in which case the risk to the public of release on licence may be unacceptable

(d) that a risk of violent or sexual offending is more serious than a risk of other types of offending.

(2) The longer period of supervision that parole would provide is likely to reduce the risk of further offences being committed.

(3) The prisoner is likely to comply with the conditions of his licence.

(4) If the prisoner has failed to meet the requirements of licensed supervision, temporary release or bail on any previous occasion whether this makes the risk of releasing him unacceptable.

(5) The resettlement plan will help secure the offenders rehabilitation.

(6) The supervising officer has prepared a programme of supervision and has recommended specific licence conditions.' (Parole Board 1997, pp.41–42)

In addition to the above, the Board has before it under the heading 'Training Guidance' a list of twelve factors which should generally be taken into account when coming to its decisions. One of these is relevant in the present context:

Remorse, insight into offending behaviour, attitude to the victim and steps taken, within available resources, to achieve any treatment or training objectives set out in a sentence plan. (Parole Board 1997, p.18)

There is a similar list for life sentence prisoners. What emerges is *how little the concepts of guilt, remorse or reparation figure in these directions*. Risk is virtually all that matters. Neither excellent behaviour nor the reverse count for anything on their own: what matters is the effect they have on the risk, or perhaps more accurately, the perceived risk of reoffending and this is as true for guilt and remorse as it is for the acquisition of trade skills in prison, a good response to an alcohol programme or the presence of a supportive family. Guilt, remorse and reparation are not mentioned in any of the Board's annual reports nor in the Carlisle report, suggesting that they have not been the subject of any official or political discussion.

PRACTICE

The Parole Board deals with the cases presented to it in two ways. For discretionary lifers, that is those who are serving life sentences for offences other than murder, there are hearings by a panel of three members chaired by a judge at which the lifer and his legal adviser put his case calling on witnesses if they choose. The Home Secretary is also represented. Panel members are able to question both the prisoner and the witnesses. All other cases are dealt with from dossiers, those serving life sentences for murder by a panel of four, the others by a panel of three members. These dossiers contain reports starting with the police account of the offence and pre-sentence reports, comments by the trial judge, reports written during the sentence and reports by prison staff and probation officers focused on the question of release. The reports are nowadays in a fixed format under the prearranged headings of the sentence planning process. The 'Initial Profile' completed by prison officers at the beginning of sentence has the questions 'Does the prisoner admit the current offence/s?' and 'Does the prisoner accept the sentence received?' to be answered yes or no, and the open-ended question 'what is the prisoner's attitude to the victim/s of his/her offence?' The 'Initial Sentence Plan' asks 'Has the prisoner's attitude to his/her offence/s and victims (if any) changed since the Initial Profile?' and asks for comments. This question is repeated in subsequent 'Sentence Plan Reviews' and the 'Prison Assessment for the Parole Board'. These questions allow, but certainly do not demand, any consideration of guilt or remorse and one has the impression that prison officers are asked to put far less emphasis on this subject than before.

Probation officers, who are given headings to address rather than forms to fill in, are able to say rather more. However the report that confronts this issue most directly is, not surprisingly, the one provided by the prison chaplain which has the heading 'Sense of guilt concerning offence (e.g. penitent, remorseful, justifying, denying guilt)'. In addition to these standard reports are those written as a result of attendance at the various courses designed to address some of the factors thought to cause the offending. Alcohol and drug awareness, anger management and the Sex Offender Treatment Programme are examples. Some of these refer to guilt explicitly but the concepts of victim awareness or victim empathy are more usual. In the case of the Sex Offender Treatment Programme there has to be an acceptance of guilt, if only in the legal sense, before the prisoner is accepted for the course. Thereafter the course instils or reinforces feelings of guilt by forcing the participant to confront the harm done to the victim, perhaps a tacit acknowledgement of the importance of this emotion. The last report in the dossier is written by a member of the Board who has interviewed the prisoner and this report often has the great merit of filling in gaps and clarifying the rest of the dossier. This member does not sit on the panel which considers the case. The prisoner sees his dossier and is able to comment on it in addition to making his own representations.

It is very probable that guilt, like any other emotion, is normally at its strongest soon after full awareness of the implications of the event which precipitated it has occurred and that it then gradually fades. At first it may preoccupy consciousness for long periods, then intermittently and perhaps eventually only when there are reminders of the event and its consequences. It may therefore be unrealistic to expect guilt to be shown and reported late in a long sentence although no doubt the pangs of guilt, like flash-backs in post traumatic stress disorder, are a reality. It is also a moot point whether punishment or the retributive aspects of a sentence either should, or in fact do, abolish the unpleasant feelings of guilt leaving only its intellectual awareness. Should parole panels therefore be looking for it after the tariff has expired?

It is the experience of this author that Parole Board panels are very reluctant to recommend release for someone who does not accept that he has committed the crime for which the court has convicted him. They are only slightly less reluctant when the inmate shows no evidence of remorse. But *however necessary these expressions of remorse are, they are not sufficient.* Remorse no doubt begets reform but evidence of this is needed. Prison staff are more impressed by a willingness to attend offence related courses or the effort needed to acquire, perhaps for the first time, educational qualifications or vocational skills than they are by expressions of remorse on their own, however convincing. Probation officers, more in touch with families, are happier with evidence of the rebuilding of relationships or the abandonment of a malign peer group. Chaplains, who have a long experience in this area, ask inmates how they are trying to show their remorse and expect evidence such as letters they would like to send apologizing for what they did. They are also well aware of the propensity of sex offenders to attend chapel and become enthusiastic about bible classes but fully understand how it is that these offenders often have nowhere else to hide or find acceptance. Experience therefore leads them to a very cautious belief in the preventive powers of religion or long-lasting effects of religious conversion without any other manifestations of change. All, however, seem to be agreed that if remorse leads to a change in life-style this will reduce the risk of reoffending and conversely, to quote the first annual report, that 'the so called 'good prisoner' is often the worst of citizens'. The problem is to know which is which.

RESEARCH

The parole process has been studied in detail by Hood and Shute (1993 and 1995). Their interviews with prison officers in 1992 showed that they attached great importance to an inmate's expressions of remorse and regret, 30 per cent rating this factor very relevant. Out of fifteen factors only 'efforts to maintain family contact' and 'efforts to make use of facilities to improve himself in prison' rated higher. Surprisingly only 13 per cent considered addiction to be very relevant and one wonders whether the routine random testing for drugs in prison introduced since then will alter the perception of the relative importance of these two factors. The prison officers readily acknowledged how difficult it was to recognize genuine remorse. 'With murder', said one, 'you get remorse: robbery, you get regret' – meaning regret at being caught. Certainly at that time reports coming before panels had a lot to say about the genuineness or otherwise of this remorse. Not surprisingly the researchers did not find a consensus about the weight that should be attached to demonstrations of remorse in judging a prisoner's suitability for release and panels had particular difficulties when a failure to express remorse was linked to an unwillingness to admit the offence.

In their second study, from August 1993 to May 1994, the authors considered the question of denial in more detail. They found that out of their sample of 545 cases, 78 (or 14%) denied their offences but denial was not distributed evenly over the various offences. Thus of 126 sex offenders, 44 (or 35%) denied compared with 34 (or 8%) of non sex offenders. How much this is due to fear of persecution by other prisoners and how much to less obvious psychological mechanisms is anybody's guess. One cannot say for sure that what is most socially unacceptable creates the most guilt or the most repression of that guilt. Denial considerably reduced the chances of panels releasing inmates before the last review although this was not the case when the last review was reached. This research was done before prisoners sentenced under the present system had served long enough to be eligible for parole or statutory supervision. It was also before the present system of documentation was introduced and before the Sex Offender Treatment Programme was generally available.

In a wider context Kennedy and Grubin (1992) explored the phenomenology of denial in sex offenders in fascinating detail but have not as yet linked this to outcome. There are in fact very few studies in which this has been done (Hanson *et al* 1991, Marshall 1990) and in one the results were counter-intuitive. Thus Marshall and Barbaree (1990) found that a group who were treated did best but deniers did no worse than those who, for administrative reasons, could not have treatment. Clearly a lot needs to be done before we will know the prognostic relevance of guilt in this or any other category of offender.

LEGAL PROBLEMS

The question of denial of guilt has always been a problem for the parole system with high profile cases receiving publicity from time to time. Thus in 1991 Anthony Alexandrovicz had served twenty years for aggravated burglary. He had always protested his innocence and the Parole Board had recommended release but he was turned down by the Home Secretary (Utting 1991). Roger Payne served twenty-four years of a life sentence for murder he throughout denied committing. The Parole Board eventually recommended release but his case was also turned down by the Home Secretary and he absconded, being on the run for six months. Home Office Ministers were reported as saying that denials of guilt were not always grounds for refusing release but a senior judge and former Parole Board member was quoted as saying: 'It is standard practice, and it has always appalled me. The system takes no account of the possibility that these people may actually be innocent. It requires them to grovel, supposedly to come to terms with their offence, before it will consider setting them free' (Rose 1991).

Some of the opprobrium previously directed at the Home Secretary may now be directed at the Parole Board. This is because as a result of the decision of the European Court of Human Rights in the case of Thynne, Wilson and Gunnell (1990) responsibility for the release of discretionary lifers now rests with the Parole Board. Experience leads one to the view that there is a great deal of difference between giving advice to the Home Secretary and actually being responsible for releasing these serious offenders.

The case of Zulfikar, decided at Judicial Review (1995), was the first to deal with denial in the context of parole and made it clear that a prisoner should not normally be refused parole solely because he did not admit that he was guilty of the crimes for which he had been jailed. Zulfikar had been convicted of arson and was serving eight years. The basis of the panel's reasons to refuse parole was that as a result of his denial he had not engaged in any offence-related work in prison and his release plan contained no intention to undertake such work on release. Lord Justice Stuart-Smith said that the relevance of a prisoner's refusal to admit his guilt depended on the circumstances of each case and went on to give three reasons why a prisoner would not accept his guilt. (1) He might genuinely have been wrongly convicted. (2) He might be unwilling to accept that he had lied in the past or be unwilling to confront loss of face in accepting what he had hitherto denied. (3) He might have genuinely persuaded himself that he did not have the necessary intent. The Parole Board therefore had to reconsider the case but again refused parole. Zulfikar again went to Judicial Review. However this time the Board had bypassed the question of denial relying instead on the fact that the risk, as indicated by the seriousness of the index offence, had not been reduced by treatment in prison and this argument won the day.

Denial of guilt is thus a very live issue but particularly so with sex offenders, a third of whom deny their offences. Others stop short of denial but rationalize, seeing themselves as pawns of circumstance or victims of the system which has imprisoned them. Those running the sex offender treatment programme do not accept on it anybody who does not admit that he has committed the offence for which he has been convicted and indeed it is difficult to see how it could be otherwise. The hope is that such people can be induced to change their minds and sign on later but many do not. Instinctively one feels that deniers and rationalizers present a higher risk than those who do admit what they have done and are willing to do something about it but in the absence of adequate research data one wonders whether instinct, common sense and folk criminology are in fact sufficient guides. It is probable, therefore, in line with the research described above, that at present those who deny are more likely not to be paroled and only released at the end of the custodial part of their sentences for the period of statutory supervision. One also feels that there is a moral issue. Should those who deny, or at least those who deny consciously, be rewarded by not having to undergo the emotionally harrowing experience of the sex offender treatment programme and run the risk of disclosing information on the programme which might add to the perception of their dangerousness by those writing reports about them, never mind the added risk from their fellow prisoners?

The case of Powell (1996) also dealt with denial. Powell was serving an eight-year sentence following conviction for five sexual offences committed over a four-year period all of which he denied. At Judicial Review it was held that, where the pattern of offending behaviour was such that there was a significant risk of further offences of a violent or sexual nature, the Parole Board was entitled to take into account the prisoner's continued denial of guilt in determining the extent to which he had examined his offending behaviour and had thus reduced the risk of reoffending. What was not permissible was for the Board to refuse to recommend release merely because he denied his guilt without further consideration of the circumstances, as the reasons given for the decision had made it seem they had done in this case. In practice this means that panels must come to a decision about risk based on evidence about the circumstances of the offence, the likelihood of their being repeated and on any available statistical predictors of risk, always bearing in mind that predictors for sexual offences are not the same as those for other crimes. The arguments for there being a high risk must then be spelled out in the reasons, otherwise the recommendation or decision not to release may be unlawful. Only then does one turn to what has been done or, more likely, what needs to be done to reduce this high risk. Conversely, if there are no reasons to suspect a high risk, denial has to be ignored. This may be the case when sexual abuse in a family has been disclosed long after it has come to an end followed by a substantial period when no further offences have occurred and there is no evidence of risk factors such as personality disorder, criminality or alcoholism. In these cases, therefore, one may feel that denunciation, deterrence, incapacitation, and retribution as objectives of sentencing have all been satisfied leaving only what, in these circumstances, are the doubtful benefits of rehabilitation and reparation.

REPARATION

The author cannot recall sitting on any panel when the issue of reparation has been raised. Again he will leave it to others to chart the history of the concept from the Anglo-Saxon ideas of restitution by the offender up to modern times and the relief of the victim by the State by means of the Criminal Injuries Compensation Board. It is also becoming obvious that there is some loss of confidence in the remedies provided by the criminal law with its high standard of proof and a growing recourse to the civil courts to litigate against people who have committed crimes for which the State has been unable or unwilling to convict. These issues are, however, no longer relevant by the time that a prisoner is eligible for parole.

There is a feeling that one can atone for bad behaviour by behaving well and that somehow one can actively pay back one's debt to society or that it is somehow repaid if one is punished enough; but these are abstract and, in the present context, unhelpful concepts. Perhaps the nearest one gets to the concept of reparation is in the regime of open prisons for prisoners coming to the end of long sentences. The aim is to provide opportunities for testing their reliability in the community by allowing them to work. For a variety of reasons jobs with voluntary bodies are the easiest to come by and one therefore often reads about the most dedicated work for handicapped children or the elderly in their homes. This may not be reparation by an individual offender to his victim but the emotions may not be displaced all that far and there is certainly an element of the repayment of the debt to society. Panels will however, inevitably, attach more importance to this as evidence of social competence and trustworthiness than of penitence.

CONCLUSION

This brief survey of guilt, remorse and reparation as they affect the Parole Board does not lead to any dramatic conclusions. Expressions of guilt are important and, though probably necessary for a confident recommendation for release, are not sufficient. Remorse is far more convincing when translated into action and the more relevant this action is to the offence the more convincing it is. Guilt may or may not motivate those who attend vocational courses or religious activities and some of the energy devoted to them may derive from the suppression of guilt but when it comes to the sex offender treatment programme and other courses involving victim empathy, it is difficult to see how prisoners, other than the truly psychopathic, can complete these courses without an acceptance of responsibility for the offence and a sense of guilt to motivate them.

Conversely, panels are reluctant to release in the presence of persistent denial being influenced both by the moral issue and believing, from experience and common sense rather than from a solid basis of research, that denial is an indicator of a bad prognosis. It is a pity that recent judicial decisions have undermined the psychological as well as the legal importance of this denial, but it is likely that they will influence the wording of the reasons given to the prisoner more than the underlying thinking. At present the reoffending prediction scores available to panels are based almost entirely on criminological variables as they are at the time of sentence. It is for panel members to assess how far these predictions are altered by what happens in prison and there is little enough evidence about this from research in this country. It would be even more interesting to discover whether guilt in its various manifestations has any effect on prognosis and whether denial is as bad prognostically as it morally. As a concept it may not be acknowledged but may nevertheless underpin the thinking of those involved in releasing offenders to an increasingly intolerant community.

EXAMPLES

In the great majority of cases expressions of guilt and remorse are not an issue for panels and do not stand out from the rest of the dossier, although sometimes they seem to epitomize it:

Case 1

A 26-year-old man serving five years for wounding. Report by prison probation officer:

> Although he does not recall holding a knife or stabbing the injured party, he now fully admits the offence and shows considerable remorse. This is in contrast to Dr A's observations, pre-sentence, that he did not show a great deal of remorse and the seconded probation officer's opinion at the early sentence planning stage that he minimizes the injury.

Case 2

A 24-year-old man serving six years for rape and buggery. Sex Offender Treatment Programme report:

> Initially he saw the fact that his victim was a prostitute and that he felt cheated concerning the money as partially to blame for the offence but as the course progressed he realised his total personal responsibility.

There are times when remorse is extreme:

Case 3

A 36-year-old man serving four years for causing death by dangerous driving. The offence occurred in a setting of acute on chronic stress and heavy drinking.

He spent much of his sentence in a psychiatric hospital with clinical depression. Report of Interviewing Parole Board member:

> When I asked him about the offence he immediately broke down again in a torrent of weeping and when he recovered said that apart from his prison sentence he had been given a life sentence he could never escape, the fact that he had taken someone's life as a result of his stupidity.

Conversely there are times when it is quite clear that there are no feelings of guilt intellectual or otherwise:

Case 4

A 30-year-old man serving four years for supplying drugs. Report of the Interviewing Parole Board member:

> For starters I don't really regret this one too much. I don't feel anything for the people I was supplying to. It's down to their choice. If it wasn't me it would be someone else. It's different from a burglary or an assault.

Guilt may be denied but nevertheless appear to motivate behaviour:

Case 5

A 38-year-old man serving four-and-a-half years for deception on a large scale. He denied the offences but devoted his whole sentence to bible study. Report by the Interviewing Parole Board member:

> 'However, realistically I did not commit these offences if indeed any offences have been committed'. He went on to say that there was no prospect of his committing any further offences as he had been baptised as a Jehovah's Witness and it would be against his beliefs to break the law in any way.

There are times when a sex offender's denial almost beggars belief. Such denial will almost invariably be accompanied by an adamant refusal to attend a treatment programme:

Case 6

A 60-year-old man serving ten years for the rape of his step-daughter. He was a pillar of his church and married the victim's mother to gain access to her. Report by Consultant Psychiatrist:

> … he maintains that his child victim initiated attempts at sexual intercourse. He states that he would never have initiated this as he believes sexual intercourse outside marriage is a sin … he suggested that if he refused to have intercourse with her she may refuse to allow him to take photographs or videos of her.

Acknowledgements

The author is grateful for help and advice to Lord Belstead PC, Chairman of the Parole Board, to Mrs Ann Barker and Mr Mike Todd of the Parole Board, to Dr David Thornton, Head of Programme Development Section, HM Prison Service, to Rev Paul Newman, Chaplain, HMP Downview and to Rev Stuart Brace, Prison Service Training College.

CHAPTER 4

Freud and Remorse

Cleo Van Velsen

Freud returned to the theme of guilt consistently during his writing and the concept of an 'unconscious sense of guilt' was vital in his formulation of the Superego, the controlling, censoring judgmental structure in the mind. Teasing out the way in which guilt has been described by psychoanalysis is complex because as, Laplanche and Pontalis (1988) put it, it is a:

> term applied very broadly. It may designate emotional states (varying from the remorse of the criminal to apparently ridiculous self approaches) which follow acts which the subject deems reprehensible, though the reasons he gives for doing so may or may not be adequate ones. Or again, it may refer to a vague sense of personal unworthiness unconnected with any particular act for which the subject blames himself. A sense of guilt is also postulated by psychoanalysis as a system of unconscious motivations that accounts for 'failure syndromes' delinquent behaviour, self inflicted suffering, etc. The words 'feeling' and 'sense' should be employed with caution in this connection, since the subject may not feel guilty at the level of conscious experience.' (p.414)

In an early work Freud discussed guilt in terms of self reproach which may be transformed into other states of mind, for example hypochondria (fear of its bodily effects), and shame (fear of other people knowing about it) (Freud 1896a, p.224). Later in the same volume (1896b, p.226) he speculated on Hamlet's inability to avenge his father by killing Claudius. It suggests that conscience, in the line 'thus conscience does make cowards of us all', is actually Hamlet's unconscious sense of guilt about his Oedipal wish to murder his father. Ultimately he brings down punishment on himself by suffering the same fate as his father, namely being poisoned by the same rival.

In 1906 Freud delivered a lecture to lawyers, who were interested in psychoanalysis as a tool for investigating the guilt or innocence of an accused person. Freud was cautious as to the relevance of psychoanalysis to criminal investigation but did draw an analogy between the criminal and the hysteric, both of whom he saw as 'concerned with a secret'. With the criminal the secret is hidden and with the hysteric the secret is unknown; in other words a conscious versus an unconscious one. He described symptoms of hysteria as plaguing the patient in the same way as the guilty conscience does the criminal (Freud 1906, p.108).

Always central to Freud's theory is the Oedipus Complex which, at its simplest, is the struggle that occurs in the mind of a child and covers the unconscious wish for the death of the parent of the same sex, associated with rivalry and sexual desire for the parent of the opposite sex. This is balanced with jealousy and hatred for the opposite sex parent and identification with the same sex parent. As well as believing that this was fundamental to the organization of the personality Freud believed that it could also be traced anthropologically as he described in 'Totem and taboo' (Freud 1913) and in 'Civilization and its discontents' (Freud 1961a). He tells a story of the sons and brothers in a primitive cannibal tribe killing and eating the father who 'presented such a formidable obstacle to their craving for power and their sexual desires' (1913, p.143). However, as Freud continues:

> they loved and admired him too. After they got rid of him, had satisfied their hatred and put into effect their wish to identify themselves with him, the affection which had all this time been pushed under was allowed to make itself felt. It did so in the form of remorse. The sense of guilt made its appearance which in this instance coincided with the remorse felt by the whole group. (1913, p.143)

After remorse comes the tribe's rule, or taboo, against the killing of the totemic animal, except in special ceremonial occasions, and a giving up of any claim to the women now available due to the death of the father. Thus he argues that out of a sense of guilt arises the taboos fundamental to the functioning of primitive society, namely murder and incest. This, then, is the beginning of civilization with its rules and religions.

In such little space it is hard to do justice to the elegant unity and compelling nature of Freud's description of the origination of civilization as described in 'Totem and taboo', including an analysis of original sin in Christianity. Perhaps most important from a psychological point of view, at the end of the volume Freud links 'the creative sense of guilt in the neurotic' to the production of 'new moral precepts and persistent restrictions; there is an atonement for crimes that have been committed and a precaution against the committing of new ones'. He also emphasizes that 'behind the sense of guilt of neurotics are always psychical realities and never factual ones. Thus a wish, impulse or phantasy of killing and devouring the father is enough to produce a moral reaction' (1913, p.159).

In 'Mourning and melancholia' (1917) Freud attempts an elaboration of the concept of the sense of guilt when he compares the mourning of a real object, such as a loved one, with melancholia which is concerned with unconscious object loss. He comments on the way melancholic patients seem to have an insistent communicativeness with a need to constantly expose their guilt and badness. He approaches what he later developed as the concept of the superego by describing one part of the Ego as setting itself over and against the other, judging it critically and he comments that in melancholia 'dissatisfaction with the Ego on moral grounds is the most outstanding feature' (p.248). He details, in terms of what is now called the countertransference, the way that the complaints of patients about themselves actually sound like complaints about other people and that instead of arousing in the people around them an attitude of sympathy they can make the 'greatest nuisance themselves and always seem as though they felt slighted and had been treated with great injustice' (p.248).

'Criminals from the sense of guilt' (Freud 1916) suggests that adult criminals might be divided into those who commit crime without any sense of guilt from those for whom the criminal act can come as something of a relief, justifying as it does an unconscious sense of guilt for which there seems no cause. This proposition has more recently been tested and discussed by Gudjonsson and Roberts (1983, 1985) where, although descriptively, psychopaths seem to show lack of remorse and shame, when tested they actually demonstrate particularly high feelings of guilt. They argue that it is the poor self concept of the psychopaths (patients at the Henderson Hospital) that is reflected in the constant feeling of guilt whether or not they have been involved in antisocial behaviour. They contrasted it to normal subjects who seemed only to feel guilty when they did actually violate acceptable norms. They do make the point however that the results might not be applicable to primary psychopaths perhaps of the kind that one sees in prisons. Kernberg (1992) dissects in detail the difference between antisocial and narcissistic personalities and writes that:

> the crucial differentiation between both passive and aggressive antisocial behaviour as part of a narcissistic personality disorder, from an antisocial personality disorder proper depends on the absence in the latter of the capacity for feeling guilt or remorse. Thus, even after being confronted with the consequences of their antisocial behaviours and in spite of their profuse protestations of regret, there is no change in their behaviour to those they have attacked or exploited or any spontaneous concern over this failure to change this behaviour. (p.75)

In his view, the true antisocial personality disorder is characterized by the lack of the capacity to feel guilt and concern; and it can take sensitive and experienced interviewing skills in order to identify the antisocial patient who may confess his guilt, but only because he has been caught rather than out of genuine remorsefulnes.

In 'The Ego and the Id' (1923) Freud finally gives us the Superego, a development of the concept of the 'critical agency' that he had talked about previously. It had moved a long way indeed now from his original simple description of dream censorship. Freud's view, as summarized in 1933, is that children are amoral, possessing 'no internal inhibitions against their impulses in striving for pleasure' (p.62) and that the function of the Superego initially is represented by parental authority. He saw parental influences operating either by offering proofs of love or by punishments which symbolized, or represented threats of loss of love – an important concept in the moral notion of guilt.

The Superego is seen as the internalization of the parental authority, although Freud remarks on the way that the Superego seems to concentrate on the parents' strictness and severity rather than the love. He describes people who have a relentless Superego, even if their actual upbringing was mild and gentle. In his chronology it is at the resolution of the Oedipus Complex that the Superego is formed. Taking the Superego into account, he hypothesized, would give a much greater understanding to social behaviour, in particular delinquency:

> mankind never lives entirely in the present. The past, the tradition of the race and the people lives on the ideology of the Superego, and yields only slowly to the influences of the present and to new changes; and so long as it operates through the Superego it plays a powerful part in human life independently of economic conditions. (Freud 1933, p.67)

Large parts of the Ego and the Superego are conscious, in contrast to the Id which is totally unconscious i.e. 'dark, inaccessible part of our personality' (p.73). The Ego tries to mediate in a world with 'three tyrannical masters' (p.77) namely the external world, the Superego and the Id:

> observed by the strict Superego, which looks for definite standards for its conduct, without taking any account of the difficulties of the Id and the external world, and which, if those standards are not obeyed, punishes it with intense feelings of inferiority and of guilt. Thus the Ego, driven by the Id, confined by the Superego, repulsed by reality, struggles to master its economic task of bringing about harmony among the forces and influences working in and upon it; and we can understand how it is that so often we cannot suppress the cry: 'life is not easy! (p.78)

Once Freud had delineated the existence of the structural model it helped him to understand clinical findings he had encountered in his work, for example the negative therapeutic reaction. This is when some sense is made in the room with a patient and such discovery, rather than being followed by relief and abeyance of symptoms can be followed by exacerbation. Freud equates an unconscious sense of guilt with the need for punishment, so that punishment, which is being ill, is what is needed to justify the internal strong sense of guilt.

What I have attempted to do here is summarize briefly the way in which understanding guilt and responsibility is woven in a steady thread throughout

Freud's work. Although remorse is mentioned at times in his writings it is usually in conjunction with the sense of guilt and it wasn't until Melanie Klein began her investigations especially through child analysis that the importance of remorse and its fellow reparation became clear.

CHAPTER 5

A Defective Capacity to Feel Sorrow

Interferences to the Development of Remorse and Reparation

Leslie Sohn

The previous chapter has given a broad survey of the way in which the psychoanalyst conceptualizes the dynamic substrate of *Remorse and Reparation*. Attention is now focused upon those factors which may interfere with their development.

In the opening of an address on 'Love, Guilt and Reparation,' forming the second part of the book *Love, Hate and Reparation*, Melanie Klein states that she attempts to give a picture of the powerful forces of love and the drive to reparation, which are complementary to the forces of hate, greed and aggression, described in the first part of the book. This division, she says, cannot clearly convey the constant interaction of love and hate – but in the emphasis in their descriptions she tried to show the ways in which feelings of love, and tendencies towards reparation, develop in connection with aggressive impulses, and in spite of them. This statement, and that of Joan Riviere's (quoted in Klein 1975) make it quite clear that they are concerned with stressing two factors. First, unconscious experience – in the growing infant and later the adult. Second, normal mental processes, taking place where the loving relationship between the mother and the growing infant mitigates, alters, and encourages the development of the drive towards reparation leading to a relatively 'normal' adult.

This chapter is concerned with interference to such normal developmental processes so that hate and greed, no matter whether it be psychotic, or non-psychotic, is predominant and continuous and where the fantasies of the infant/growing child/adult, are translated into destructive actions. And where reparation or restitution in the remaining non-psychotic parts of the mind must be felt to be impossible to undertake in the first place, or to complete if ever attempted.

Within the same elements of the mind such reparative drives may be contained in a high degree of conflict with aggressive impulses. This exploration will attempt to show what happens under such circumstances and the changes that are produced. One of the cases to be described had a long-term psychotherapeutic experience (under the author's supervision). Another has had numerous unsuccessful eclectic attempts at producing intrapsychic changes. Yet another will exemplify the difficulties in embarking upon a therapeutic alliance while the aggressive elements are so prominent.

In law courts one hears frequently that an individual has achieved a state of remorse concerning the crime which has been committed. On the basis of that assessment, mitigating circumstances will enter into the judgment. The converse is equally true. Where there is no manifest remorse, the judgment will reflect such a lack.

If one believes in alternating states of mind in the perpetrator, all that has been recognized in such a transaction is that the less hateful, or even loving aspects of the criminal, are now evident. In the case of bipolar swings in depressive patients such a state is a genuine possibility, although such reasoning would simply be a situation of rewarding part A and punishing part B. In a non-psychotic individual, such claims to remorse need to be sceptically considered. If the normality and strength of being sorry, with full recognition of remorse and reparative possibilities is being claimed, only a fully truly depressive illness would fit such a credence. The normal mind would be totally overwhelmed by reparative awareness so shortly after a major crime, such as homicide.

The life histories and mental patterns of the patients I will be describing, and their responses to such deprivations and deficits, have a peculiar similarity. In each of them an omnipotent strand is present throughout to a greater or lesser degree. They exhibit lost opportunities, careless disregard for their safety and future, and an omnipotent disregard for other issues of significance. They have all been in possession of 'satisfactory' alternatives such as alcohol, drugs/lies/fantasy worlds, belief in weird relationships, or promiscuity, all of which made them feel well insured against any awareness of such deficits, so that their self-esteem regulation was satisfactorily maintained.

CLINICAL VIGNETTES
Mr A

Mr A told me that he found himself where he was 'because of the bloody dog'. (He was in a medium secure unit, having been sent there by the courts charged with a serious assault on another man.) He felt this was nonsense and that he had done nothing wrong at all. And even if he had, the other man deserved it. The victim was a young white man whom our patient had known slightly. He enlarged on his ideas about the dog. The bloody black and white dog had crossed the road, leading the police directly to him … if it hadn't crossed, they would never have thought that they should direct their attention to him and later arrest him… (he had committed the assault in full view of many onlookers). Our patient stuck firmly to his belief about the dog's culpability – and he soon elucidated the significance of the black and whiteness. He was the son of a white woman of European descent and a black father who had abandoned the family. He hated his mother for not maintaining her purity (these were his words) by marrying a white man; he equally castigated his father, for spoiling his purity by marrying his white mother – his life had been 'dogged' by this complexity for years – he loathed his own black and whiteness. The young white victim of his attack was envied for his attractive purity (he hated for similar reasons a white youth on the ward) and had a complicated system of belief that this youth mocked and derided him.

Sympathy, remorse, and any reparative development, were totally obscured by his predominant beliefs. I have outlined what I believe was the skeletal structure of his illness – superimposed upon which were both the psychotic and non-psychotic parts of his personality. I have simplified the story. For him the different parts of his narrative were kept separate from each other, so that his mind could not gather the coherent parts together. He could not say 'I hate this – I hate that – I hate the result called me – and the white youth has what I would wish to have'. Were he sane, he might have put it together in that way. He could not get it right. He only knew that in relation to the allegations of the offence the bloody black and white dog had implicated him. It was as if he made a coherent, yet mad statement, derived from a psychotic conjunction of discrete split-off parts of his mind. He then made this repetitious sentence which encompassed his black and whiteness, his aggressive hatreds and his response to his feeling of lifelong deprivations.

Behind all this still existed his pathological envy and jealousy. It involved giving up so many natural rights, ending up in this dreadful result called himself. All of this protected him from any awareness of the sadness of his and his victim's plight. His legal and clinical future remains questionable. One wonders whether he will ever be in a state to re-integrate these varied and disparate parts of his mind.

Mr B

Mr B has been seen quite a few times, strangely enough never for any direct therapeutic reasons. When I first saw him, despite his relative youth he had been in long-term maximum security care for a considerable time. Many years previously he had been considered unfit to plead in court, being charged with murder, and had immediately been sent to a long-stay hospital.

Prior to this offence he had a very chequered life, which he discussed quite openly with me. There were no signs of overt psychosis throughout the interviews

I had with him. He openly felt that he could say whatever he liked to me and he was convinced that he was soon due for discharge into the community. As I had no legal significance in his life, and could not interfere with his hoped for discharge, my views were therefore irrelevant. He had been put up for adoption at birth. He was quite sure his biological mother was of aristocratic origin, although this was untrue. There was a strong suggestion in the notes that she was suffering from a psychotic illness at his birth.

He described in lurid detail the behaviour of his adopted mother. She sexually teased him, and stimulated him, and later withdrew any loving care.

In late adolescence he joined the Army, having failed at school. He was frequently in trouble with the authorities for repeated minor offences. The Army had not been a success; he was discharged as being mentally unfit. He felt this was a punishment for having reported an NCO for making homosexual advances towards him. A series of short-term employments followed. He met a young woman with whom he claims to have had a successful love affair which was terminated when her family interfered, because they didn't like him. It was her father who particularly distrusted him. She decided that she was going to go to a university and successfully began to prepare herself by further study, and formed new friendships. She was due to leave the small town in which they lived. He stalked her, and watched her every movement, becoming more and more wildly jealous of her relationship to others and envious of the capacity to work successfully. He also clearly envied the strength of her attachment to her family, in that she had agreed with them that she should leave him. He imaginatively rehearsed murdering her, going through a murder pantomime with another young woman who lived in the same house as he did. Finally he met up with the young woman, forced her into his house, and raped her repeatedly. He said to me 'I can never forgive her, I asked her to cover her face with a handkerchief and not look at me'. She refused. So he stabbed her violently and frequently, until she was dead, and this was followed by post-mortem coitus. The essence of what I want to describe is the difficulty he had in forgiving this innocent girl for what he felt was the crime of provoking him: she didn't cover her face! Remorse and reparation were absent. There was just cold self-justification and projection of responsibility onto this poor girl. *The onus of responsibility for the event lay totally in her dead hands and mind*, despite the long hours of jealous preoccupation, preparation and rehearsal that had taken place.

In the midst of his jealous and envious feelings this man felt totally humiliated, which must have accentuated the humiliation about his own origins which he falsified. He had boasted that he had done important surgical operations and that he was being sent for postgraduate surgical tuition. There was so little authenticity in this man's life, in marked contrast to that of his victim, who lived in such an integrated world. The destructive capacity of such symptoms was shown in his total unawareness of the cause for concern, remorse or the need for reparation. He was immunized against such possibilities. It was no accident that the jealousies remained so fresh in his mind. The projection of such feelings into others confirmed my beliefs as to what was going on. 'They' were felt to envy and admire him. 'They' were nursing staff, fellow patients and medical staff. Unfortunately he has never been offered psychotherapy and is therefore constantly exposed to the vagaries of the death instinct within himself as evidenced by hate, destructiveness and negativistic trends. These are all the modes of behaviour which are antagonistic towards making or maintaining interpersonal or intra-psychic connections as described by Melanie Klein (1957).

Freud (1925, p.164; 1937, p.238) suggested that the main technique available to the life instinct, in its fight against the death instinct, is the outward deflection of the death instinct. He regarded this mechanism as the origin of the process of projection. These last two ideas, to a large degree describe the fate of the mind of Mr B. Unfortunately, there is a further complication in the vicissitudes of his life. When he is totally in the grip of death instinctually derived feelings without projection he is then even more dangerous. Were he to be in the outside world, particularly if he imagined himself to be in love, and exposed thereby to the possibilities of real or imagined jealousy, others would be at risk. Without the prospect of long-term psychotherapy and regular monitoring, his outlook is bleak.

Mr C

I now wish to talk about two other men. Mr C is aware of the possibilities of seeing things in a new way. He is beginning tentatively to consider his victims and his offence seriously. He committed a multiple murder; he knew the victims well and the offence appeared to be without meaning, occurring during the course of a psychotic illness. His changes in perception are distinctly related to developments in his psychotherapy.

A few years ago, during the course of a psychotic illness, he killed some members of a family which had befriended him. Both Mr C's parents had been born abroad and came to England after the war, the mother having been more scarred by wartime events than the father. She was hospitalized, due to mental illness, and Mr C and his siblings were committed into care.

In his early teens he was informed that both parents had given up their traditional religious beliefs into which they had been born, and which they had practised extremely seriously. They now adopted a new system of belief which carried certain definitive prohibitions against a variety of activities, such as sexual activity outside of marriage, smoking, drinking. Both parents, who had been heavy drinkers and smokers, stopped both of these habits and changed completely.

Mr C's psychotherapy is undertaken by a female psychologist who discusses his progress in a supervision seminar. Gradually she has been able to establish her patient's developing awareness of his mental state and its relation to his history. Conversion has been a central theme; frequently of a psychotic nature. This is to say that if a magical alteration, in which everything could be seen positively, could take place, all would be well. He would leave and live happily outside of the hospital. In contrast to this omnipotent denial of his true mental state, there has been a slow appreciation of an alternative, firmly grounded reality.

He announced recently that he would like his therapist to arrange a change of ward and that she should recognize a new state of affairs in him. This would be based upon the fact that he merited promotion. It was really no different from previous wild statements and would mean that he was engaged in one of his processes of conversion in his own mind which he hoped could be echoed in his therapist's mind. He confirmed this by pointing out that he had been thinking about Mr X, a particularly wild and disturbed patient, who had similarly demanded such promotion recently. When she indicated that once again they were hearing about the unopposed quality of some of his thought, where one part of his mind was totally dominated and therefore 'converting' other parts of his mind into absolute belief, he began seriously to talk about himself and his past and of the events leading up to his offence. He said he had really liked the daughter of the family, whom he had killed; but he had liked her 'from afar' and that quite against the rules of the church he would masturbate with thoughts of her in his mind. One of the family members had tricked him into admitting that he masturbated and reported him to a senior pastor who publicly attacked him and derided him for his relation to the Devil and to the Devil's practices.

He still masturbated, but no longer with thoughts of that particular girl, and could not even remember her name. The patient related this in connection with thoughts about having his medication either considerably reduced, or totally stopped. The truth was that he was having his medication changed because he had complained to the ward doctor that the medication affected his capacity to ejaculate. The therapist alluded to the way in which one part of his mind was dominated by magical conversion powers, and the other wished it could get back at least to the young man he felt he had been, with a potential for loving and caring.

Unfortunately, there was a mad dominant part of his mind, represented by the memory of the totally disapproving pastor, that made him feel that such positive thoughts were amoral and devilish. Mr C confirmed that his idea of thinking only 'positive' thoughts was like murdering contradictory truth in his mind and he felt that he had been in the grip of a devilish feeling when he had murdered.

I report this piece of therapy to indicate the attempts being made by a patient, to become something that needed to be recognized by himself as undevilish, thoughtful and loving, despite the contradictory propaganda which had developed in his mind. He maintained a view that such a proposition was a promotion. In the same session he confirmed this mental 'posture'. I call it a posture because at this stage these propositions can only be viewed as postures, time and testing will confirm their permanency and stabilizing qualities. The confirmatory quality came from a story about a conversation on a working course, which centred upon the possibilities of escaping from the hospital. He felt this was an invitation to permanent persecutory fear – how could one live outside, with the constant fear of being recaptured and returned. We considered this to be an insightful beginning to further healthy development, which negated the value of maniacally derived quick solutions.

Thus far I have only described some factors which interfere with the development of remorse and reparation and therefore the maintenance of unconcerned detached and truly careless 'mental states'.

Mr D

I now want to discuss Mr D, a patient who came into treatment after a very long stay in a maximum secure hospital. I treated him myself over a three-year period, after he was transferred to a medium secure unit. His treatment took the form of psychoanalytic sessions four times per week.

The group of patients (nine in all) from which this patient comes, were all seen at the Denis Hill Unit at the Bethlem Hospital, which is part of the joint Maudsley-Bethlem Hospital. I will concentrate on one representative of this small group. My original approach to these patients was to further an enquiry into their suitability for psychotherapy on the inpatient unit.

The initial presentation was a keen wish to speak and to be 'spoken to' not necessarily 'about'. Gradually a life-long mental-illness-dominated defence manifested itself, and induced truancy, lack of interest and unwillingness to attend sessions. There was a uniform lack of interest in the sane self. The initial enthusiasm was a vain hope to fully regain delusional objects, felt to be possibly lost *via* this new treatment system.

From the outset the very nature of Mr D's referral to the unit allowed for a long-term view of his treatment. There were no limitations of time. His future was intimately related to long-term treatment, and I was conscious throughout of the fact that, should there be any untoward developments in his illness and therefore in the therapy, I could rely on a full back-up system for further inpatient care on the unit. Another factor was his capacity to be interested in and to maintain, to the best of his ability, his interest in being my patient. We met regularly over a three-year period. A minor version of his tendency to act out was physical illness, clearly exacerbated by his excessive smoking. On a few occasions this necessitated treatment in bed. His sessions were thus interfered with on two occasions, once for a period of a fortnight. But he dealt with this with a cheerful, manic carefree smile.

Far more serious were episodes of excessive drinking. I am sure that on a few occasions he smoked cannabis; although when his urine was tested, it proved negative.

The further complication was that by the very nature of their treatment in a medium secure unit, all the patients were legally detained. They were clearly told at the onset that they could expect confidentiality, unless a breach of security was involved. Our contractual relationship would allow me to notify the unit authorities if such a breach occurred. Fortunately, this never took place.

By the time I saw Mr D he was a sixty-year-old, worn out man. He had been an inpatient in a secure special hospital for fifteen years, having been admitted under section in the late 1970s. He was emphysematous, and he smoked. Until he got used to the fact that he could speak to me in an ordinary fashion, he spoke in an ordered, sycophantic, apologetic way, as if I was a pompous superior officer who not only demanded this but could punish him for its absence. He would agree with everything said to him, as if disagreement was dangerous. He had waited a very long time to come to the Denis Hill Unit, and this was the only means available to him to ensure his stay there and balance his unbalanced mind. He would punctuate his ideas, occasionally at the outset but more frequently later, with statements from literary and dramatic sources, and was clearly well read and informed. He claimed an attachment to racist political thoughts, and to Roman Catholicism. He certainly had a history of racist attitudes, and was occasionally overtly racist and superior.

He had grown up in the North of England, the fourth and youngest child in a coalmining family. His father, a heavy drinking man, was described by our patient as having no status in the mining community. The patient had himself worked underground for a year, failed to stay, and ran away from home at sixteen to join a circus. Later, he went into the Guards, following one of his older brothers. His good record in the Guards was periodically spoiled by drinking episodes, but he finished his service despite a long period in detention. Various occupations and interests and wanderings followed. There are constant reports in the various notes that he was felt to be rather a good journalist or a good actor, but invariably something interfered and spoiled the situation. The first admission took place in his late twenties followed by a series of admissions, terminated by apparent cures, promises to stop drinking, and promises of refusal to take drugs. He was frequently discharged because of aggressive destructive behaviour and some violence toward the staff.

Throughout all this, he was always given the diagnosis of schizophrenia. But there were phases where he read, worked well, and published short stories, literary criticism, and some poems. But he never seemed able to attach himself to anybody or anything. He was married twice; both wives left him. He was promiscuous, and there was a history of homosexual prostitution.

His story about the index offence varied in two essential details, firstly about the preface. He originally told me that his welfare benefits were a day late in arriving, which worried him. Later he corrected this. He had arrived at the DHSS office a day late because of heavy drinking, and had expected that the 'nice lady' at the office would be helpful, because she had always been nice to him. She was unable to help, and asked him to return later, but expressed doubts as to whether it would be available. The doubt transmitted itself to him reaching its climax on the platform of the tube station when he was on his way home. He stuck to this version throughout his time with me. Somebody who had been so helpful and kind was giving up on him, and it was his own fault. He was angry, excited, miserable and penniless. He grabbed a man, a stranger, and pushed him forcibly toward the line. Fortunately, though the man's legs were over the edge, he was saved from major injury. This is where the second change in the story occurred. Mr D behaved as if he were convinced that the man was trying to commit suicide. He remembered this in his session with me, and admitted that he had great difficulty in giving up his belief. He added in this context that his own behaviour was simply intended to frighten the man out of such behaviour. In a later version, the man had insulted him by calling him a Jew, and this upset him.

Actually the two stories, though in a physical sense so far from each other, are not so dissimilar. In the first instance, he clearly projects his murderously suicidal ideas into the man. By trying to frighten him, it tells us how he split the conflict existing in the psychotic part of his mind. And we know, in the second instance, about our patient's racist attitudes. 'Jews' were not very much higher in his social scale than 'niggers'. Here, once again, in his picture of himself at the time of the offence, is a depressing disparity of his mind's idealized view of himself.

After the attack, his behaviour was described as grandiose. He claimed to have won the VC, and seems to have justified himself by racist comments about Jews and black people.

My formulation of the psychopathology is as follows. We are looking at the events as perceived by the psychotic part of Mr D's mind; so that he feels himself to be inferior to the person he was before the traumatic disappointment in the welfare office. In him, such a feeling is furnished not only by the characterological defects of a racist, but with all the exaggerations of maniacal superiority that a psychotic mind can produce. Projections are split off violently and suddenly. They carry the need for delusional certainty. His good object, exemplified externally by the lady in the office, is but a protective veneer to his concept of delusional objects. She could be considered a possible symbol of his delusional objects with which he communes and ruminates. Thus the total imagery of his psychotic mind, at that moment, is unaffected by any mitigating sanity, so that the feeling of murderousness towards the 'nice lady' has to be got rid of very quickly, if only to protect his own mental hoard. So that when he feels inferior, he does feel as if he is an inferior Jew or black man, or a combination of both. He successfully rids himself of such identifications, confirmed by the material when he said he is accused of being a Jew or the man is suicidal, or he is only trying to frighten the man. This is clearly related to the projection of psychotic anxieties engendered by the events. But the question does arise, however, once he has achieved such a relatively bland, hypocritical position *vis-à-vis* the victim, why isn't it enough that he should walk away smugly, feeling all is right with his mental world? This must have happened to him many times before, and could be seen, when he continues to smoke despite his crippling emphysema, over which he triumphs. Not only by denying it, but treating it as a statement of inferiority in somebody else. He spent much time persecuting his emphysema. But this time it is different. His mind is due to lose its feeling of having good, albeit delusional, objects within itself. This means that he cannot project that feeling as he did the others without the physical enactment to reassure him. I will explore and explain these dynamics.

In Mr D a sense of grandeur takes place following these events. Loss, and the various responses and results of it, feature in his sessions with me. In an indirect fashion he would talk about what was, what had been, what could have been, what so-and-so said or wrote, and said or wrote no more. He was always protected from the actual experiences of loss by a veneer of superiority, which in his everyday dealings on the unit irritated others. He read and he discussed what he read, and wrote quite readable material for the hospital magazine. Gradually, his childhood entered in the sessions. He could not really understand why everybody made such a fuss of the failure of the family to be in touch with him, and he with them. It was simply a continuation of his childhood experience. He felt he was by now inured to such deprivation, albeit incorrectly. For him and his own egocentric world, what counted was what 'they' thought of him. I never really got to the full constitution of 'they', but he admitted that he daydreamed all the time about him and them, and he fantasized conversing and smoking with them all, and they drank together. He once joked, and he said that if he published his thoughts, there would be a large market because of their pornographic quality. Clearly, his dream world kept him well thought of and warmly welcomed by his private circle. Despite his being exposed by his drinking at that time, I began to feel optimistic about Mr D's future.

Where his analysis was so different from a conventional analytic situation, was in the strangely restrictive world in which he had lived for over four decades. I refer in the first instance to the real interferences and inroads his illness had made upon his mind, no matter whether we refer here to what were genuinely believed to be the psychotic illnesses, or to the long alcoholic episodes and the interferences with ordinary life. There was also the fact that he'd been enclosed for nearly two decades in a maximum security hospital. For him, the unusual situation of an analysis taking place in a medium secure unit was quite acceptable and easy to tolerate. The sessions themselves had a peculiarly enclosed and enclosing character, almost a claustrophobic quality, which I felt were a reflection of his mind's penumbrated quality. But behind this, he was having a long-term relationship of total privacy and primacy. He was the subject of interest, though sometimes unfortunately only to myself, which in the perverse areas of his mind served its own purpose. He could be as delinquently careless, even as mad, as he liked to be. There was always a figure listening and caring about him, a situation he had never previously known.

I was perturbed by what seemed to be the perverse quality of such behaviour, which would vary from sleepiness and inattentiveness to paroxysmal episodes of sleepiness of almost narcoleptic intensity. On the other side were periods of manic chatting and gossiping. These patterns were gradually linked to his identification with his heavy drinking father and his own feeling of himself as like his father, a man of poor status and little respect, which he was so busy denying by his behaviour patterns. Later, the perverse character of his behaviour was linked with his periods of homosexual prostitution, when he enjoyed not the physical, but what he called the social lives of these relationships; some casual, other repetitious. Gradually a more thoughtful person emerged; unfortunately, even this had a quality of ambiguity and cynical 'jokiness'.

One day he had decided on his way to the session that he would like to, or perhaps that he would, smoke. He had given up smoking during sessions. He felt that we were beginning to recognize his capacity to be provocatively aggressive because he knew that I disliked his smoking, and he became silent for a while. I was suddenly extremely doubtful about the sincerity of his presentation, as if I was being invited to believe something that I would later feel foolish about having believed. I shared my doubt with him, and added that he didn't know if he was being sensible or trying to please or trick me. He replied that he was having difficulty in keeping me out of the pornographic conversations that he had with himself. I said that he felt relieved that I had openly questioned his sincerity, that he was afraid of corrupting me as he did his own mind, sometimes consciously, with his fairy stories, or that he felt his mind to be corrupted more seriously as had happened in his index offence. This time he had not kept his promise to himself not to smoke in the session. He then spoke about his anxieties about the future, as to where he was going to live and work when we ended. He said he looked so much like that comedian on the TV who could distort his face so completely and become as if he was somebody so unlike himself, but also become the person his face was alluding to. He clearly was talking about his weird identification again, and its distorting effect upon his mind and behaviour, and how easily he lost his sense of self.

This session was typical of the last few months of his stay on the unit, which gave the opportunity to reflect the kind of work his illness required. His serious problem in this session was that a joke can rebound; and he could be left feeling empty of future and purpose. The joke is however a 'serious', in which his mind is distorted into a belief that it can't work properly and he feels freakish. In later sessions, the metaphor of the comedian with the distorting face was replaced by the various psychiatrists he'd known over the years, who had avoided knowing about his mind and its vagaries by being very friendly and talking in advisory generalizations. As he said, 'Fancy advising me'. All this was a graphic re-presentation of his own previous thoughtless and somewhat condescending attitude to himself. This of course was at the centre of the problem of tricking, being tricked and of trickery itself. He felt that he had either tricked the doctors into stupidly believing in a potential in him which he couldn't maintain, or that they now contained his own trickery and condescension. That was why he felt so relieved in the session described when I queried his sincerity. At the same time, life had tricked him by giving him so many real talents and not the equipment to use them. This carried the unhappy identification with his father who drank and had no status, which was relieved by drinking.

He ended treatment and left with an awareness of his aggressive behaviour and potential, and its role in the index offence. He asked, 'Was I born insane, or did something make me insane?' I suppose the answer to both is 'Yes', even though I didn't know enough about his earlier years. He also knew that there were times when the only thing that interested him was drinking. Maybe it would have been more profitable if we had met thirty years ago. He had become interested in himself and the sessions; not only in a narcissistic fashion, which was his usual mode, but *also introspectively and seriously in the actual himself.* He was fully aware of the extravagant loss to himself, to the chances he had had and the parents and family he had so badly let down.

In the normal development of the individual, remorse and reparation are part of the ongoing process of life. In the mentally and or characterologically disturbed, the process is very different and far less predictable. I believe, the capacity to feel sorrow and the wish to restore and repair, both internally and externally, is central to the core of change. I take a pessimistic view of claims made by and for such patients of developing such capacities either spontaneously or through medication. It is true that the sedative qualities of major tranquillizer can reduce unconscious anxieties. If there is a diminution of persecutory anxiety un- consciously, there is a lessening of the potential or need for enactment. The patient's awareness, via self knowledge, and not through behaviouristic recital of what should or should not be done is not enough. Awareness as a mantra to be used against internal bedevilment is a very chancy affair! I prefer Mr D's albeit periodically cynical, self-awareness. We both felt safer for it.

The capacity for reparation and remorse is in the intrinsic developing healthy mind. Unfortunately, where it is most needed – and most lacking – is in the violent, the aggressive, and the dishonest. In the tortuous turns of the psychotic mind, preoccupied with avoidance of self-involvement, it is singularly absent. It is a necessary part of the corrective process, but no amount of behaviouristic persuasion or reassurance will produce the slightest intrapsychic change. And when one hears judicial opinions saying seriously 'At least the defendant showed profound remorse' after committing a violent offence against the person, this must be responded to with a sceptical, 'How did that come about?'

CHAPTER 6

Feelings of Guilt and Reparation for Criminal Acts

Gisli H. Gudjonsson

INTRODUCTION

Research into the ways offenders attribute blame for their criminal acts was very much neglected until the 1980s (Gudjonsson 1984; Gudjonsson and Singh 1988, 1989). During the past decade there have been a number of studies which have looked at the attribution of blame by offenders and these have furthered our understanding of the ways in which they view their crime. There is also increased recognition that offenders' perception of their offence in terms of blame is related to personality and guilt proneness (Gudjonsson 1997).

In this paper the author reviews some of the work on offenders' reporting of feelings of guilt after transgression and shows how this relates to their perception of their crime, type of crime committed, personality, and the eagerness with which they confess to the police.

ATTRIBUTION OF BLAME

Attribution is concerned with the processes by which individuals attempt to construct causal explanations for their behaviour and the behaviour of others. Heider (1958) presented the first conceptual framework for formulating attributions. He recognized two types of attribution, referred to as 'internal' and 'external' attributions. Internal attribution located the causal explanation for the behaviour within the individual's personal qualities. In contrast, external attribution locates the cause for the behaviour in social and environmental factors.

Another type of attribution is the perceived freedom to act (Snyder 1976). This relates to the extent to which the behaviour is seen to be amenable to or beyond self-control. Distorted perceptions, impaired judgement, and sudden loss of self-control, are all mental factors which may impair criminal responsibility.

The internal–external and responsibility dimensions are both relevant to the ways in which offenders attribute blame for their criminal acts. Gudjonsson

(1984) suggested that attributions of blame may function to reduce anxiety and feelings of guilt for the criminal act. This is particularly true of external attribution, which is likely to be negatively associated with the reporting of feelings of guilt. Since attribution of blame with regard to mental responsibility has an internal locus (i.e. it is associated with factors located within the offender's character and temperament, it is unlikely, in contrast to external attribution, to be negatively associated with feelings of guilt. Indeed, in view of its internal locus it may well be associated positively with feelings of guilt.

BLAME ATTRIBUTION INVENTORIES

Two scales have been constructed to measure offenders' attributions for their criminal acts. These are known as the Gudjonsson Blame Attribution Inventory or BAI (Gudjonsson 1984; Gudjonsson and Singh 1989) and Attribution of Blame Scale or ABS (Loza and Clements 1991), respectively. These scales were developed independently and differ in some major ways. Both rely on self-report by the offender. They aim to measure the offender's perceptions and under-standing of his or her crime rather than actual causes.

Gudjonsson (1984) devised the Blame Attribution Inventory in order to measure two types of attribution relevant to how offenders attribute blame for their criminal acts. First, 'external attribution', which measures the extent to which offenders report external justification for their crime (e.g. blaming the offence on provocation, social and environmental factors). Second, 'mental element attribution', which measures the extent to which offenders blame their crime on mental factors, such as low mood and a temporary loss of self-control. Here the offender views the criminal act as being 'out of character'. The BAI also measured the amount of guilt or remorse that offenders reported feeling about the offence they had committed.

The BAI was revised in 1989, retaining the three factors, 'external attribution' (EA), 'mental element attribution' (MEA), and 'guilt feeling' (Guilt). The reason for revising the inventory was to overcome two problems with the original inventory (Gudjonsson and Singh 1989). First, the items making up the inventory measured both a general attitude towards crime and attitude to a specific crime or crimes. The kind of general items were: 'Victims of crimes nearly always deserve what they get' – EA; 'Criminal behaviour is often caused by mental illness' – MEA; 'I feel ashamed of my past'– Guilt.

The second problem with the original inventory was that the items loading on external attribution and guilt were all scored in the positive, which raised the possibility of an acquiescence bias. The revised inventory corrected those difficulties. It consists of 42 items: 15 measuring external attribution, 9 measuring mental element attribution, and 18 measuring feelings of guilt.

Examples of items measuring external attribution are: 'Society is to blame for the crime(s) I committed'; 'I had good reasons for committing the crime(s) I did'; 'In my case the victim was largely to blame for my crime(s)'; 'I am entirely to blame for my crime(s)'; 'I did not deserve to get caught for the crime(s) I committed'.

Examples of mental element attribution items are as follows: 'At the time of the crime(s) I was fully aware of what I was doing'; 'I was very depressed when I committed the crime(s)'; 'I was in full control over my actions'; 'I was feeling no different to usual at the time of the crime(s)'.

Items measuring feelings of guilt are as follows: 'I hate myself for the crime(s) I committed'; 'I feel no remorse or guilt for the crime(s) I committed'; 'I feel very ashamed of the crime(s) I committed'; 'I will never forgive myself for the crime(s) I committed'; 'I deserve to be severely punished for the crime(s) I committed'.

The Attribution of Blame Scale (ABS) of Loza and Clements (1991) is designed to measure the offender's general criminal attributions rather than attributions in relation to a specific crime. It contains 24 items, which are rated on a six-point Likert scale. Three of the items ('Criminal behaviour is often caused by mental illness', 'Victims of crime nearly always deserve what they get', and 'There is no such thing as an innocent victim') are identical to those constructed by Gudjonsson (1984). The first two of these items had the highest loading on Gudjonsson's external and mental element attributions, respectively.

The ABS contains four subscales, focusing on four types of blame, 'Victim Blame', 'Offender Blame', 'Societal Blame', and 'Alcohol Blame'. The focus of the scale is therefore on specific domains, such as alcohol, victims, offender, and society. The advantage of this is that it directly reflects the offender's general attitudes within specific domains, irrespective of the nature of a specific crime. The disadvantage is that the ABS cannot be used to measure the attitude of the offender to a specific crime he or she had committed. Also, in some ways the ABS is more narrowly focused conceptually than the BAI. For example, many of the items focus specifically on the crime of rape and are only applicable to males. In using the ABS Loza and Clements (1991) found alcoholics more commonly blame their crimes on alcohol than non-alcoholic offenders. Recently Fazio, Kroner and Forth (1997), using the ABS, found on the basis of factor analysis that two factors emerged, labelled external and internal attributions, respectively. These two factors resemble the external and mental element attributions measured by the BAI and support the view of Gudjonsson and Singh (1989) that mental element attribution is conceptually different to an internal attribution as an inverse continuum of external attribution. That is, internal–external attribution is probably best construed as two types of attributions rather than one attribution on a continuous dimension.

ATTRIBUTIONS AND TYPE OF OFFENCE

It is reasonable to assume that the more serious the offence the more offenders will report feelings of guilt after transgression. Irving (1980) noted, during his observational study at Brighton Police Station, that sex offenders appeared to express more guilt for their offence than other offenders. In order to test this hypothesis, Gudjonsson and Singh (1988) analyzed the attributions and guilt scores among 171 offenders according to type of offence on the revised Gudjonsson Blame Attribution Inventory. Sex offenders were found to have higher guilt scores than did other offenders, followed by violent offenders. Gudjonsson and Petursson (1991a) and Gudjonsson and Bownes (1991) obtained the same results among 98 Icelandic and 80 Northern Ireland offenders, respectively.

The results from these studies suggest that crimes against the person are associated with more reporting of guilt feelings than, for example, property offences. It is likely that the more socially – disapproved the crime, the stronger the feelings of guilt after transgression. For example, taking sex offenders as a group, one would expect those who offend against children to report more guilt feelings than those who offend against adults (i.e. paedophiles versus rapists). Surprisingly perhaps, Gudjonsson and Bownes (1991) did not find this to be the case, although it is noteworthy that the number of rapists in their sample was very small. Future research should continue to separate different types of sex offenders in terms of their attribution and guilt scores. A factor that needs to be taken into account when studying sex offenders and their blame attribution is that paedophiles tend to be older than rapists (Gudjonsson and Bownes 1991).

Differences between types of offenders and attributions have been noted in a number of studies. Violent offenders consistently have the highest external attribution score (Gudjonsson and Singh 1988; Gudjonsson and Bownes 1991; Gudjonsson and Petursson 1991a). For mental attribution, violent offenders had the highest scores in two studies (Gudjonsson and Singh 1988; Gudjonsson and Petursson 1991a) and sex offenders in the Northern Ireland study (Gudjonsson and Bownes 1991). The main conclusion that can be drawn is that external and mental element attributions are typically most associated with violent offending. The association of violence with mental element attribution is not surprising since violence is commonly accompanied by mental disorder and drunkenness (Gudjonsson and Petursson 1990). The consistent and marked relationship between violence and external attribution is more difficult to interpret. Why should external attribution be most associated with violent crime? One of the explanations could lie in the relationship between perceived provocation and violence. Violence is an interpersonal crime where the victim may be seen by the perpetrator as contributing to the incident. In cases of theft, for example, there is normally less direct contact with a victim. Another explanation is that in cases of violence the offender has greatest need to place some of the blame on the victim, which functions to reduce the anxiety and guilt associated with the crime. In cases of property and sexual offences, where external attribution is typically much lower, it would be more difficult for the offender to attribute blame in terms of victim provocation, although other factors may help them justify their crime (e.g. that they are providing a helpful sexual experience in cases of paedophilia, and that stealing from the rich is justified). In some cases of rape, offenders may claim sexual provocation, for example in the way the woman allegedly dressed or behaved.

Gudjonsson and Bownes (1991) point out that certain cultural and historical factors may influence the way offenders attribute blame for their criminal acts. For example, significant differences in mean scores have been found for similar crimes in different cultural settings. For example, violent offenders in Northern Ireland obtained significantly higher external attribution scores than violent offenders in England (Gudjonsson and Bownes 1991). Such differences may be related to the longstanding political violence in Northern Ireland, which is used by violent offenders to partly justify their crimes. Another interesting finding is that property offenders in Northern Ireland obtained significantly lower guilt scores than English property offenders. Future research should investigate the reasons for such cultural differences.

REMORSE AND ATTRIBUTIONS

Gudjonsson (1984) suggested that offenders' attributions of blame may reduce their feelings of anxiety and guilt. However, there is now considerable evidence that the reporting of remorse is negatively associated with external attribution but positively with mental element attribution. In the original study into blame attribution, Gudjonsson (1984) found that mental element attribution correlated positively with the guilt score. Subsequently, four separate studies, using the revised Gudjonsson Blame Attribution Inventory, have found the positive correlation between mental element attribution and the guilt score. The size of the correlations are given in Table 6.1.

Table 6.1 also gives the correlations between external attribution and the guilt score. Two of the studies, Gudjonsson (1984) and Dolan (1995) do not give the correlations for external attributions. The three remaining studies found a significant negative correlations between external attribution and guilt scores. All the correlations are very low (between -0.22 and -0.33).

Table 6.1 The correlations of remorse with external
and mental element attributions

Remorse	Mental element	External	N
Gudjonsson (1984)	0.18*	–	224
Gudjonsson & Singh (1989)	0.45***	-0.29***	176
Gudjonsson & Bownes (1990)	0.57***	-0.33**	80
Gudjonsson & Petursson (1991a)	0.51***	-0.22*	98
Dolan (1995)	0.41**	–	52

* $P < 0.05$
** $P < 0.01$
*** $P < 0.001$

The positive correlation of the guilt and mental attribution scores raises an interesting theoretical point. It suggests that blaming the offence on mental factors does not reduce guilt feelings about the crime, whereas the reverse is true for external attribution. Why should a person who denies responsibility for his offence due to mental factors experience enhanced feelings of guilt? One possible explanation is that mental element attribution is a type of internal attribution, where such offenders still partly blame themselves for the offence. For example, persons who commit serious crime when mentally disturbed, which may be very much out of character, could be preoccupied with the thought that if they had been mentally well at the time of the offence, it probably would not have happened. Another possibility, which will be discussed below, is that those offenders who score high on mental element attribution are of a certain personality type that makes them more prone to guilt feelings after transgression.

ATTRIBUTIONS AND PERSONALITY

A number of studies have been conducted into the relationship between personality and how offenders attribute blame for their criminal acts. In one study involving 40 forensic patients, Gudjonsson (1984) found that external attribution of blame correlated significantly with the psychoticism score on the Eysenck Personality Questionnaire (EPQ), using the original BAI. In another study of 169 English prisoners, Gudjonsson and Singh (1989) found that external attribution correlated significantly with psychoticism, using the revised version of the BAI. Introversion and neuroticism were significantly associated with how much remorse the criminal reported feeling about the offence. In the third study, conducted on 68 prison inmates in Iceland, Gudjonsson *et al.* (1991) found that psychoticism correlated significantly with external attribution on the revised BAI. Again, remorse was significantly correlated with introversion and neuroticism. As far as mental element attribution is concerned, there were positive correlations with neuroticism in two of the studies (Gudjonsson 1984; Gudjonsson *et al.* 1991).

Dolan (1995) studied the relationship of BAI scores with personality disorder and mood among 57 offenders referred for assessment for an intensive probation programme. In addition to the revised BAI, the participants completed the Personality Diagnostic Questionnaire-Revised (PDQ-R; Hyler *et al.* 1987) and Irritability, Depression and Anxiety Scale (Snaith, Constantopoulos and McHuffin 1978).

External attribution of blame was found to correlate significantly with the following six personality disorder categories: schizoid, avoidant, obsessive-compulsive, passive-aggressive, narcissistic, and borderline. External attribution did not correlate significantly with the depression, anxiety or irritability scores. Dolan suggested that the findings were consistent with external attribution correlating most strongly with those personality characteristics associated with criminality. It is perhaps surprising in view of this that antisocial personality disorder did not correlate with external attribution of blame.

In the Gudjonsson (1984) and Gudjonsson *et al.* (1991) studies the Gough Socialisation Scale (Gough 1960) was also administered to the offenders, but no significant relationship was found with external attribution of blame in either study. This is perhaps surprising in view of the fact that the Gough Scale is a valid measure of anti-social personality disorder and criminality (Schalling 1978; Gudjonsson and Roberts 1985). This raises some interesting issues about the nature of EPQ psychoticism and external attribution. It indicates that it is the toughminded and unempathetic criminal who has the greatest tendency to blame other people or circumstances for his or her crime. Emotional coldness and lack of empathy are perhaps the most important causes of external attribution of blame. These personality characteristics are probably more directly measured by psychoticism than by the Gough Socialisation Scale. This conclusion is consistent with the work of Schalling (1978) into the validity of the Gough Socialisation Scale among Swedish criminals and is to a certain extent corroborated by the findings of Dolan discussed above.

Guilt feeling scores for the crime committed were significantly correlated with schizotypal, avoidant and dependent personality disorder and with irritability directed inwards. Dolan interprets this as an indication that high scorers on the BAI are of anxious and fearful personality types in accordance Cluster C on the PDQ.

The findings that remorse was positively correlated with introversion and neuroticism and negatively with psychoticism support Eysenck's theory of the development of conscience as a conditioned response. Eysenck's initial ideas on crime and conscience were developed in a commissioned article for the *British Journal of Educational Psychology* (Eysenck 1960). He suggested that 'conscience is a conditioned anxiety response to certain types of situations and actions' (p.13). According to this theory, the development of moral or prosocial behaviour is produced by undesirable behaviour being punished by significant others (e.g. parents, teachers). The punishment implemented produces emotional pain, and fear and autonomic disturbances, which become associated, by means of Pavlovian conditioning, with certain situations and actions. A conditioned emotional reaction is then experienced whenever the person encounters a similar *situation* and *action* in the future. This emotional response *conscience*, is according to Eysenck, precisely what prevents people from offending.

REMORSE AND CONFESSIONS

Gudjonsson (1992) put forward the argument that there is a fundamental difference between feelings of shame and guilt in relation to confessions made during police interrogation. A feeling of shame for the crime committed inhibits people from admitting to the crime, whereas a feeling of guilt facilitates the making of a confession. In this context, shame is best construed as a fear of negative evaluation. This is comprised of a self-focused attention, a comparison between self and others, and feelings of self-consciousness, inferiority and humiliation, all of which motivate concealment. In contrast, guilt is concerned with reparation, the need to 'get it off one's chest', and the desire to make amends, all of which facilitate openness and the willingness or need to make a confession. Support for this distinction between shame and guilt is provided by Lewis (1971) and Gilbert, Pehl and Allan (1994).

Sigurdsson and Gudjonsson (1994) found that among prison inmates the feeling of shame concerning a criminal act was significantly correlated with the reluctance to confess, whereas a feeling of guilt was associated with an internal need to confess. Sex offenders have been shown to be most ambivalent about confessing to their criminal act, because of their being reluctant to confess due to a feeling of shame, while at the same time experiencing a strong internal need to confess (Gudjonsson and Bownes 1991, 1992; Gudjonsson and Petursson 1991b; Sigurdsson and Gudjonsson 1994). For this reason American interrogators have recommended subtle psychological manipulation to overcome the shame experienced by sex offenders (Inbau, Reid and Buckley 1986). Such manipulations raise serious ethical concerns (Gudjonsson 1992, 1994).

ATTRIBUTIONS AND COGNITIVE DISTORTIONS

One study (Gudjonsson 1990a) investigated the relationship between the Abel and Becker Cognitive Distortion Scale (Abel *et al.* 1984; Salter 1988) and the scores obtained on the BAI. The two tests were administered to 25 prison inmates convicted of paedophile offences against a family member or a relative. The Abel and Becker Cognitive Distortion Scale measures the cognitive distortions and self-justification common seen among child molesters concerning their offence, such as their claim that having sex with children does the child no harm and provides good sex education. The correlation between BAI external attribution and cognitive distortions was 0.62 (P < 0.001). The mental element and guilt scores did not correlate significantly with cognitive distortions. The findings suggest that cognitive distortions regarding child molestation are significantly associated with the tendency of sex offenders to externalise blame for their acts. Both are probably associated with faulty socialization in childhood.

AGE AND ATTRIBUTIONS

The age of offenders has been found to be significantly correlated with the reporting of guilt as measured by the BAI (Gudjonsson and Singh 1989; Gudjonsson and Bownes 1991; Gudjonsson and Petursson 1991a). That is, older criminals obtain higher guilt scores than the younger ones. Part of the explanation may be due to the finding that both social desirability and introversion increase with age (Eysenck and Eysenck 1991). It is likely that the guilt score on the BAI predominantly measures feelings of guilt, although it is possible that a feeling of shame may also load on the guilt factor (indeed, one of the items on the BAI specifically asks about feelings of shame and that item had the highest loading on the guilt factor). Interesting theoretical questions include the extent to which a feeling of guilt is exacerbated by people being apprehended for the crime they committed, and the extent to which feelings of shame interact with feelings of guilt, and perhaps exacerbate it.

REMORSE AND PSYCHOPATHY

Psychopaths are generally seen as lacking the capacity for remorse (Hare 1975), although the studies of Foulds, Caine and Creasy (1960), Marks (1965), and Gudjonsson and Roberts (1983) indicate that psychopaths report experiencing strong feelings of remorse after transgression. An important distinction here is the primary–secondary categorization of psychopathy. In contrast to primary psychopaths, secondary psychopaths exhibit strong symptoms of anxiety and autonomic arousal (Lykken 1957).

Mealy (1995) discusses some important differences between primary and secondary psychopaths, which are relevant to feelings of guilt. The main difference is that secondary psychopaths are primarily antisocial due to exposure to environmental risk factors, whereas the antisocial behaviour in primary psychopaths is primarily determined by their genotype (i.e. have a substantial genetic component). Another difference between the two types of psychopaths is that secondary psychopaths, in contrast to primary psychopaths, are capable of experiencing some sincere social emotions (e.g. guilt, shame, sympathy, empathy).

The work of Gudjonsson and Roberts (1983) into feelings of guilt and self-concept in secondary psychopaths raises some important questions about the nature of guilt. Twenty-five male and 25 female psychopaths, who were being treated in a therapeutic community in England, were compared with normal subjects with regard to Morality-Conscience Guilt as measured by the Mosher True–False Guilt Inventory (Mosher 1966). The psychopaths scored significantly higher on the guilt inventory than the normal subjects, which contradicts the common view that psychopaths experience little guilt after transgression. The Semantic Differential technique (Osgood, Suci and Tannebaum 1957) was administered to the patients in order to measure their self-concept, including feelings of guilt and shame when transgressing. The patients rated themselves on the ten bipolar dimensions with regard to the following concepts: 'Myself as I am', 'Myself as I would like to be', 'Myself when I lie', 'Myself if I were to steal', 'People who lie', and 'People who steal'. Factor analysis of the ten bipolar dimensions revealed three factors, referred to as an 'evaluative' (good–bad), 'potency' (strong–weak), and 'guilt' (remorseful–unremorseful, and ashamed–unashamed) factors, respectively.

The psychopaths had significantly greater semantic distance between their self and ideal self than the normal subjects on all three factors, which reflects their poorer self-evaluation. As far as the guilt factor was concerned, the normal subjects had very little discrepancy between their self and ideal self, whereas the psychopaths wished to feel less guilt and shame. The normal subjects reported a marked increase in their feelings of guilt and shame when they were transgressing (i.e. lying or stealing), whereas in the case of the psychopaths there was no change in their degree of guilty feeling when transgressing.

The findings suggest that some psychopaths have poor self-concept which is reflected in internal distress and negative preoccupations, which they label as 'guilt' or 'shame', regardless of whether or not they are engaged in antisocial behaviour. Normal subjects, in contrast, only experience feelings of guilt when they perceive violation of some norms. If some psychopaths do experience strong feelings of guilt, which are unrelated to specific situational transgression, then this may explain why their feelings of guilt fail to inhibit antisocial behaviour. That is, engaging in antisocial acts does not make them feel any worse than they already feel.

If the guilt reported by some psychopaths represents genuine feelings of guilt, rather than mislabelling, how does one interpret their apparently high degree of guilt? One possible explanation may relate to these psychopaths being punished indiscriminately in childhood for both prosocial and antisocial behaviour. Irrespective of the moral value of their behaviour, they are punished. They can never do anything right in the eyes of significant persons in their lives. They consequently develop a conditioned response to their own behaviour which becomes generalized rather than being situation specific to legitimate trans-gression. Placing this finding within the framework of Solomon and his colleagues into the differences between the development of feelings of guilt and resistance to temptation (Solomon, Turner and Lessac 1968), the psychopaths in the Gudjonsson and Roberts (1983) study never learned to resist temptation due to the timing of the punishment implemented in childhood, which resulted in strong indiscriminate emotional responses to perceived punishment.

The psychopaths in the Gudjonsson and Roberts study are best described as secondary psychopaths in view of their high level of trait anxiety and physiological reactivity (Gudjonsson and Roberts 1985). It would be interesting to repeat the Gudjonsson and Roberts (1983) study on primary psychopaths in order to see if differences in guilt response can be documented experimentally between primary and secondary psychopaths.

An interesting question is whether under certain circumstances guilt may actually be a precipitating factor in the commission of a crime. In other words, rather than guilt preventing a crime can it actually increase the likelihood of its occurrence? The empirical evidence for this proposition is lacking, but this does not mean it could not be true. Freud (1957) put forward the proposition that this can happen and referred to such cases as 'criminals from a sense of guilt'. According to Freud, here guilt-ridden individuals are preoccupied by their free-floating guilt, like the secondary psychopaths in the Gudjonsson and Roberts (1983) study, and by committing a crime the guilt is attached to something tangible and this is accompanied by a sense of mental relief. Another possibility is that a strong feeling of free-floating guilt is associated with emotional instability and strong autonomic arousal, which can lead to impulsive and antisocial behaviour by virtue of its drive propensities such as Eysenck originally proposed for neuroticism (Gudjonsson 1997). Feelings of guilt can be pathological, either because they are not attached to a specific act of transgression (free-floating) or because they interfere with the effective prosocial functioning of the individual.

TREATMENT IMPLICATIONS

The mental element and external attributions may have a bearing on the legal outcome in criminal cases. The mental element attribution is relevant theoretically to issues surrounding 'mens rea' (legally guilty intent). External attribution, accompanied by a lack of remorse, is likely to indicate a lack of insight into the crime, denial of responsibility for the offence, and lack of empathy. This has important treatment implications. It suggests that psychological interventions of external attributors should focus on modifying their attributional style and lack of empathy by the use of cognitive behavioural methods and empathy skills training.

Gudjonsson (1990b) found that psychotherapy techniques appear to reduce external attribution and increase guilt scores on the BAI. However, the lack of insight of external attributors into their offending and poor propensity for guilt responses are likely to make them poorly motivated to change their attitudes and behaviour. Their lack of lack of motivation will need to be addressed and overcome before therapeutic techniques can be effectively applied to their faulty attributional style.

CONCLUSIONS

The present chapter has raised some interesting questions about feelings of guilt. For example, what is it that determines the degree of guilt reported by offenders? How is the feeling of guilt associated with the ways in which offenders attribute blame regarding their criminal acts? How do feelings of guilt differ from feelings of shame? Do feelings of guilt after a criminal act reduce the likelihood of further offending? Why do secondary psychopaths score higher on guilt inventories than normal individuals? Can feelings of guilt in certain circumstances increase the likelihood of criminal acts? Can psychological treatment change the ways in which offenders attribute blame for their crime?

I have tried to answer some of these questions, but more empirical research is needed. Feelings of guilt after a criminal act are an important subject matter to be investigated. The ways offenders attribute blame for their criminal act and the role of guilt in this process helps with the formulation of treatment programmes with offenders.

CHAPTER 7

Remorse for Being

Through the Lens of Learning Disability

Sheila Hollins

INTRODUCTION

As I began to explore whether remorse could have meaning for those with a developmental intellectual learning disability (of such a degree that they need special help to lead a normal life), I found myself focusing on factors inherent in the individual.

In the chapter which follows I will argue that regret, remorse and the need to make amends all occur in a social context and within relationships which are shaped by widely held ethical norms, complicated when severe learning disability is present. Does remorse (that sense of deep regret and guilt for some act or omission) always require the presence of intent, and actual responsibility for harm to someone else? Is the lack of understanding in people with learning disabilities so widespread that intent and/or responsibility are impossible, or do many simply lack the means of expression? Recognizing that there are always at least two people involved in a relationship, I have had to develop my thesis to show how severe disability is 'blame making' for both those with learning disabilities, and for the society into which they emerge as a disabled person. The experience of remorse by both people with learning disabilities and their parents will be considered. The capacity of someone who has learning disabilities to make everyday choices which balance personal rights with responsibilities to others will be explored. Finally, clinical illustrations focussing on sexual issues will be shared to allow consideration of similarities and differences with other groups of people.[1]

---

[1] The clinical vignettes bring together aspects of different people's experiences, thus preserving anonymity.

REMORSE FOR 'BEING'

So what do those with learning disabilities have to take responsibility for? What in their everyday lives do they have cause to regret or feel guilty about? The first answer has to be their disability. To consider this adequately requires attention to the developing meaning of disability in their own lives and the lives of their parents, relatives and carers.

The birth of a child with severe intellectual disabilities, often associated with other disabilities or the later realization of such disability, typically provokes a bereavement response in parents, particularly mothers (Bicknell 1983; Damrosch and Perry 1989; Hollins 1985; Olshansky 1962). Although this is not universal and is contested by some, it is widely recognized and extensively described. To some extent we all differ in some way from the 'perfect' baby expected by our parents, thus banishing any narcissistic fantasy of creating another human being in their own likeness. When this difference is more significant than hair colour, gender or aptitude, and threatens the likelihood of an independent adult existence, the adjustment required by parents may be a major challenge akin to grief but complicated by shame. Typical grief for someone who has died is a dynamic process characterized ultimately by resolution of the grief with hope in the possibility of a new life without the lost 'object' (Parkes 1972). Reminders of the loss, and reworking of the feelings of grief usually become less frequent with the passage of time. But the daily presence of a child with intellectual learning disabilities is a constant reminder of parental grief. With each new failed milestone or the realization of the real extent of disability, parents may revisit their initial feelings of shock, panic, denial or anger. Anger may be expressed as blame against oneself or others, but the accuracy of the location of blame may have no rational source. For example, a father might blame himself for doing too little to help his wife during pregnancy, or the midwife for failing to request a caesarean section during a difficult labour, or he might blame the child herself. Unresolved feelings such as these are likely to interfere with developing parent–infant relationships. The validity or otherwise of actual responsibility may have little relationship to the extent of the feelings of remorse experienced. Remorse may be part of the process of dealing with ambivalence towards another person (Juni 1991). For example, one father was too ashamed to admit to work colleagues that his only child had an intellectual disability, even when she had reached adulthood. He immersed himself in his work and refused to consider having another child after a 'friend' commented on his inability to produce a normal child.

The experience of being a disappointment to one's parents, and of coming face to face with the reality of one's own disability is a painful one commonly leading to a defence, so clearly described by Sinason in her classic paper 'Secondary Mental Handicap and its Relationship against Trauma' (1986). The secondary or exaggerated handicap may show itself, for example, as a handicapped voice, or an insincere smile. The real pain of being different – even if not that different – is obscured by the distorted representation which the onlooker receives. Such a defence does nothing to repair the narcissistic damage already done to parents who may blame themselves, or think the child blames them. Both may be true. Schneiderman (1988) suggested that narcissistically-based remorse derives from feelings of shame because of the belief in one's unfulfilled potential. In this situation maybe parental and child inadequacies are both experienced as unfulfilled potential. Blame experienced by the disabled person may serve to emphasize both the shame and the remorse experienced by the parent(s). With one party blaming the other and one feeling ashamed, it takes little imagination to see scope for development of a no-go area. Only when an honest dialogue is begun in which both parties share their hopes and fears, will knowledge about disability and its experience be truly shared. Psychotherapy may have a role to play here. The benefit of sharing and its contribution to improving each person's quality of life derives new significance as the possibility of reparation, begins to emerge. Reparation or cure of the primary impairment is however, not possible. A 'restitution' or cure narrative may helpfully be replaced by a 'guest' narrative (Frank 1995) in which full acceptance of those with learning disabilities as people first, can be followed by reparation and healing.

Who Told You You Were Naked?

Traditionally people with learning disabilities have been seen as 'eternal children': forever innocent and thus free from guilt and judgement. In 1988 I wrote about three secrets in the lives of people with learning disabilities. One of these secrets is that of their disability and dependency.

It is rare for parents and teachers to explain to someone why and how they are different, with many professionals believing it is wrong to give insight to those with learning disabilities about their intellectual limitations.

One delightful exception was a young woman born with Down syndrome[2] who explained to a scientific audience about her chromosomal make up and went on to describe what it had been like to grow up with Down syndrome. In one humorous aside, she said she had often wondered why it had been called Down syndrome – she thought Up syndrome would have been more positive!

To be aware of one's own difference but to know that the subject is 'taboo' can lead to fantastic fears and false explanations for the real cause, or to an unnecessarily exaggerated sense of being different. Scientific advances in recent generations have transformed medical and general knowledge about many causes

2   Down syndrome in the USA, Down's syndrome in the UK.

of intellectual disability. But fears about disability being 'catching' or being a punishment from God are still widespread, as are irrational feelings of inadequacy in not being able to parent a 'normal' child.

Many people with learning disabilities feel responsible for their own limitations and failure to achieve autonomy, and expect little for themselves. Perhaps if people feel it is their fault that they are different, then they feel responsible for making amends. But since they can never make adequate reparation, then they must expect to be punished for the rest of their lives by those who are so burdened by their presence. Of course I am not suggesting that this train of thought actually or necessarily takes place in this form. It may, however, explain the way in which many of those with learning disabilities behave towards their parents and/or carers, and it may explain the high risk of depression. To interpret their attitude and behaviour within the context of a psychotherapeutic relationship, and to see a behavioural change consequent on such an inter-pretation in their relationships, is further evidence for the sense of responsibility assumed for their very life. Sometimes one makes an interpretation within the psychotherapeutic relationship which changes the way someone behaves. For example one patient believed that if he was dead then all his parents' worries would cease to exist. In family therapy it was possible to explore his elderly parents' fears for his future and his wish to predecease them. By the end of the therapy his father had written a will including an agreed statement in which family members had been briefed on his future care. His weight – previously very low – had increased to a safe level.

How Can a Person with Learning Disabilities Begin to Make Amends?

One way is to be grateful for every deprivation or trauma, seeing each of them as a punishment. Another is to disguise the pain and present a contented and unquestioning face to the world. But if someone with learning disabilities is given the tools of understanding, perhaps she can disperse some of that anger by an acceptance of her difference and apportion blame only where blame is due.

Who One is or What One is?

Remorse and regret then become part of the dynamic, changing process of adjustment in which the experience of being accepted for who one is becomes more important than any assessment of ability, attribute or deficit, that is, what one is. In a subtle way the emphasis shifts away from factors inherent in the individual to factors within the culture.

Such reactions by disabled people, which portray them as more disabled than they really are, may have played their part in society's justifications for hiding disabled people from society's sight, and may be partly responsible for inhumane practices such as chaining people in back rooms, or despatching them to remote country asylums. Perhaps we feel a collective guilt for our past lack of acceptance of difference. In this last decade of the twentieth century, western society tries again to tolerate disability face to face, by developing care in the community, and supporting disability rights.

REMORSE AND MAKING CHOICES

People with learning disabilities may have difficulty making valid choices about many things due to lack of education or information, a reduced ability to reason, or a limited experience.

An adult man living in a shared, staffed home asked to change his bedroom for another which was less well appointed. The reasons for the request were not clear. Initially he said he wanted to look out over the road instead of the garden, but then he said he wanted a room where the lights turned on because his room was too dark at night. There had been a fuse in the electricity circuit which served his room and which nobody had noticed. His lack of knowledge about electricity and its role in providing light was truly disabling for him. However he showed an ability to reason in that he recognized that another room would provide him with light, but his lack of education and limited experience affected the validity of his choice.

The necessary requirements for the ability to make autonomous choices clearly depend on the complexity of the situation and previous experience. How far does the ability to have and express a thought affect the ability to act (Pinker 1994)? Can a lack of intellectual ability be compensated for by emotional intelligence? Does emotional intelligence exist as a separate entity and what role does life experience play in developing it (Goleman 1995)? The intellectual defences which most people use to obscure their emotional realities are insubstantial for people with learning disabilities and may be ruined by faulty reasoning. The absence of intellectual rationalizations leave people in touch with the only things which matter in life.

Intimacy – a Developmental Perspective

As children develop into adulthood they will have to face similar life changes and stages as other adults. A developmental perspective is essential to enable us to understand potential dilemmas such as how a young person's sexuality will be able to develop in reality. The difficult question of sexual intimacy and the possibility of lawful and informed consent for people with learning disability is one which challenges society's ideas about real autonomy for those with continuing dependency needs. The perspectives of many developmental psychologists and psychoanalysts inform our thinking here (Ainsworth 1982;

Erikson 1965; Robertson 1989; Winnicott 1964) with continuing work on attachment theory being particularly helpful.

Sex education is widely neglected in the special education curriculum, and awareness of sexual behaviour in others may be developed from media exposure, or from the personal experience of inappropriate sexual attention from a peer or carer. Being part of a family where intimacy has its proper place, but affection and appropriate touching have been enjoyed, may provide some preparation for the onset of sexual feelings at puberty.

Jenny is an attractive and lively 21-year-old who moved into a mixed hostel when she left school at 19. In addition to global intellectual impairment she also has disordered language with particular difficulty with comprehension. Her main interests are dancing and swimming. Despite attempts at sex education at school, her carers are unclear about the extent of her knowledge about the facts of life. Her unplanned pregnancy was not detected until three months before the birth of a healthy daughter. Her irate parents removed her from the hostel, and informed her social worker that they would care for Jenny and her baby themselves. Although Jenny named one of her peers as the putative father, he was not informed of this. Her parents did not enable her to attend antenatal appointments, nor parenting classes, as they saw them as pointless. They were excited at the prospect of a new baby, almost as if she would make up for their 'damaged' daughter. Her own autonomy was forgotten as some of the earlier dynamic responses to her disability were again played out.

Peter – the putative father – also has a learning disability but has held a regular job for more than a decade. If Jenny should convincingly identify him as the father of her child, he could be found guilty of unlawful sexual intercourse – regardless of whether Jenny says she consented to intercourse. Despite their disabilities they could be permitted by law to consent to marriage, and within marriage intercourse would not be unlawful. Peter has had previous steady girlfriends and his widowed mother would welcome her son's marriage, provided adequate support was available to the couple.

Jenny's parents still see her as a child and not as a sexual woman who might be able to form a relationship with a man. Adolescent trial and error which in all other areas of experience will be protracted for slow learners, instead becomes very public and limited insofar as sexual experience is concerned. Most young adults with learning disabilities live their lives in restricted social environments, largely isolated from the wider culture in which they live. They receive mixed messages about what is permissible, and what is expected of them in regard to sexuality and sexual behaviour through the media (especially television) in which socially unacceptable sexual behaviour is often presented as normative and therefore perceived as acceptable.

A Duty of Care?

Ethics is concerned with morality and with reasons for action or a failure to take action. When I act I should take responsibility for my actions. I can be blamed for my actions if I am capable of taking responsibility for them. I can regret my actions if I recognize that I made the wrong choice; or regret and feel guilty (in other words experience remorse) about them – if my choice was morally wrong and harms someone else. Such actions may be morally wrong but they could also be wrong for other reasons – for example due to ignorance, or carelessness. Usually ignorance of the law is no defence, but there are circumstances when people with learning disabilities are not held responsible for their actions. For example, the Sexual Offences Act (1956) states that it is unlawful for a man to have sexual intercourse with a woman who is 'mentally defective' (i.e. has intellectual learning disabilities), but the man is not held responsible if he could not be expected to know that she was a 'defective'. It might be assumed that a man with a severe learning disability would be ignorant in this matter. In other words such a man has no real choice or intent, cannot take responsibility and is assumed not to be capable of remorse. In practice, carers have a duty of care to ensure each person has consented to an intimate act.

Is the ability to distinguish 'right' from 'wrong' necessary in order to be able to experience remorse? We are reminded that such a distinction is difficult to make by the fact that philosophers from all world cultures have asked and tried to answer such basic ethical questions as 'What is good?' Whilst they continue the debate, most of us remain oblivious to the problem and make daily choices on matters affecting ourselves and others – either ignoring or accepting the rules of our own culture. Awareness of these rules develops through personal experience and the example of others; and thus people with learning disabilities will learn – albeit sometimes more slowly – in a similar way.

REMORSE FOR WRONGDOING

A minority of people with learning disabilities act in a manner which endangers themselves or others. One might expect that if remorse or even regret for wrong doing is to be found then it will be found in the experience of this latter small group whose behaviour falls so far outside social norms and expectations.

Two of the earliest words spoken or signed to small children are 'good' and 'bad'. For children who grow up with very limited language, these two concepts may be the most repeated in their daily lives, with 'good' meaning that an adult in authority is pleased with them, and 'bad' implying the opposite. Expressing their own displeasure or dissatisfaction by the use of 'bad' behaviour tends not to be encouraged. Feeling guilty (introjecting blame) rather than blaming others is thus developed from an early age.

This can be explored by asking simple questions such as – 'Do you feel you have done something bad?' Words such as 'guilty' or 'not guilty' may not be understood. Those with learning disabilities may assume responsibility for wrongdoing because of their lifelong experiences of being blamed and there is ample research evidence about the suggestibility of people with learning disabilities when accused (Gudjonsson1995). In other words, although good and bad are usually conceptualized as opposites, it does seem as if some people may experience a see-saw between these and other opposites such as guilt and blame, remorse and revenge. One expression of this may be through the transformation of the experience of being the victim of abuse by becoming the powerful abuser.

Brian is a man in his mid twenties, on probation for a sexual offence against a minor. He has an intellectual learning disability (mild according to ICD 10 with a formal IQ score of 60).

His early childhood memories are punctuated with disagreements between his parents which often involved drunkenness on his father's part, with physical violence towards his mother and/or whichever of the children were unfortunate enough to be in the way. These rows usually ended with lengthy periods during which his parents did not speak. His father died when Brian was only ten due to an accident which occurred during a bout of drunkenness. Brian is a man who physically resembles his father in appearance, although he is adamant that he himself has never hurt another human being.

After his father's death the family moved to London. Brian felt very lonely and missed playing football with him, or even experiencing some sense of companionship during his father's long periods of estrangement from his mother. He blames his father although he could not admit any anger.

His neighbours' son, many years younger and an only child, was a source of solace for him. His mental age was similar to his own but the younger boy looked up to Brian and was flattered by the time he spent with him. They were as close as brothers and encouraged in this by their mothers.

Their childhood intimacy continued into adolescence and became overtly sexual when Brian was chronologically – if not developmentally – an adult. The younger boy apparently continued to enjoy the relationship until his late teens when he started dating a girl seriously and confided in her about his involvement with Brian. Within no time Brian was under arrest and charged with indecent assault. For the purpose of this chapter, further comment needs to examine to what extent Brian recognized and understood the rights and wrongs involved, his own responsibility for the relationship, and the part of guilt, regret and remorse in his rehabilitation. The probation order included treatment recommendations. Brian still saw himself as a victim who had been mis- understood. He did not demonstrate remorse because he did not accept responsibility for any wrongdoing. He regretted the upset experienced by himself and his family because of the court case and associated publicity. He observed the terms of his probation order, and in his therapy sessions worked hard to present himself as a responsible and safe individual. It appeared to be unsafe for him to dwell on any sexual fantasy or feeling, and transference interpretations were routinely rejected. He saw moral issues in black or white terms, but always saw himself as right. He seemed unable to empathize with his victim or with other offenders.

For some people with learning disabilities I would explain this lack of empathy as being due to the lack of a theory of mind (Frith 1989).

In Brian's case the explanation could be found in developmental aspects of his own personality and his own abuse as a child. Later in therapy he described his offence as a 'slip up' which he would not allow to happen again. He talked about locking his memories of his childhood away so that they would not spoil his present and future life. He regretted his offence but did not own it as part of him. Later still he could accept the child he had been and was able to talk about his unhappy childhood. Around this time he also began to empathize with other people's experience in his social network. A breakthrough came when he described his offence to a new member of his therapeutic group, readily acknowledging it as wrong and something he regretted. Other group members were shocked by his admission and they recognized him as an offender rather than a victim for the first time. They confronted him with the times when they had been victims, and he was chastened by their confrontation.

There is no research data from work with people with learning disabilities to suggest that the expression of remorse is an essential part of successful rehabilitation. Clinically and intuitively I would remain concerned if a patient who had offended showed no empathy for the 'victim' or damaged part of others.

Brian was a man not dissimilar from many offenders without significant intellectual disability. His childhood was marked by violence, bereavement and social deprivation. He lacked education about right and wrong and in addition his childhood illnesses and learning difficulties left him frail, different and friendless. My surmise is that his friendship with a younger child was his attempt to repair his own 'wounded heart' (Vanier 1985) and put things right with his father. Although he had spoken of his offence previously, his admissions had been qualitatively different.

CONCLUSION

I have suggested that people with learning disabilities themselves do have the capacity to experience remorse, if they have the capacity to relate to another human being. The extent to which they can do this may depend on the extent to which they have achieved an adequate differentiation from their own mother: to know what is 'me' and 'not me', 'mine' and 'not mine'. This has implications for the understanding of personality and character development, and for the possibility that psychodynamic understanding could occur and achieve change, in an individual's self identity, even in the presence of severe learning disability.

I have hypothesized about the central place of blame, shame and remorse in the experience of parents, and later other carers, of people with severe learning disabilities – not just for their existence as disabled people, but for the additional traumas which they as carers may have had a part in inflicting. I hope I have shown that the emotional dependency between the cared for person with a learning disability and her carer is a two way phenomenon, and that a therapeutic intervention designed to free either the disabled person or the carer from the tyranny of continued dependence could take place with both together, or with either one of them. A focus on remorse and responsibility for reparation seems a good starting point.

Acknowledgements

The author appreciates the helpful comments of Jane Hubert, Kathryn Hollins and Martin Hollins on an earlier draft of this chapter, and the secretarial support provided by Freda Macey and Jenny Pearson.

PART II

Legal Perspectives

CHAPTER 8

Remorse and Rehabilitation

John Harding

In February 1997, the *Guardian* newspaper reported in its obituary column the death of a notorious armed robber and murderer, Pietro Cavallero, who terrorized Northern Italy in the mid 1960s. Cavallero was captured by the police in 1967 and served 25 years in a prison on the island of Elba. While in prison he fell under the influence of a prison chaplain, took up writing and painting and began to think about his violent career.

'The senseless things I have said and done', he once exclaimed to an interviewer. 'They are nightmares that have never left me. Now I want to put myself at the disposal of those who are suffering, so as not to lose hope' (Hooper 1997). Cavallero, after release, dedicated the remainder of his life to work in Turin for an after-care agency that focused on ex-convicts and drug misusers. Days before he died he wrote to his autobiographical collaborator from hospital, saying

> The evil things I have done come back to me, each time worse than before. I am suffering a lot. But I am glad to suffer, because I expiate, my faith grows stronger and my strength grows.

Cavallero's articulate testimony is an expression of both remorse – regret and self-blame for an act – and repentance, that is the renunciation of a way of living or thinking. His rejection of his homicidal ways is loosely paralleled by the experiences of two celebrated Scottish prisoners, Jimmy Boyle and Hugh Collins, both of whom, in separate decades, grew up in Glasgow's urban squalor, graduated to gangland violence and were ultimately responsible for the deaths of others. Their lives and thinking were transformed by time served in the special unit at Barlinnie Prison where, in a setting of trust and freedom of expression, they slowly began to take responsibility for who they were and what they had done.

> Parts of me had changed and for the first time in my life I was thinking not as a victim but as a person who has been responsible for doing things that I shouldn't have done. (Boyle 1977, p.251)

Boyle recalls that prior to his spell in Barlinnie Prison, the degradation and humiliation of other prison settings made him immune to his past and other people's suffering. Hugh Collins, released and practising as a sculptor in Scotland, is still haunted by the death by stabbing of his Glasgow victim.

I feel like a monster. I've never been the same person since. (Ferguson 1997)

These snapshots of high profile men of violence who finally took responsibility for their lives, following the experience of being valued and trusted by their captors and carers, raises profound questions about remorse and reparation and what part such thoughts and actions might play in the criminal justice process, which at least, in the western world, though not in Japan, is still dominated by retributive notions.

The retributive justice model which has dominated legal processes in Europe and the west for the past three centuries is one in which crime is defined as an act against the state. The offender is accountable to the State for the crime. As a result the state and the offender are in an adversarial relationship. The tremendous power of the state in this relationship makes it necessary to protect the offender through a system of rights such as the right to legal aid to defence counsel or to trial by jury. Accountability in this model is equated to suffering. If offenders have been punished, made to suffer, they have been held accountable. The outcomes of the system are measured by how much punishment was inflicted.

Victims are generally peripheral to the process of responding to and resolving the criminal incident apart from serving, on occasion, as a prosecution witness or being in receipt of a compensation award by the court. Under this retributive model, criminal justice is said to play a major part in controlling the level of crime. The reality, of course, can appear to be very different to those victims and offenders, the key participants in the crime incident before the apparatus of the legal system intervened in the shape of the police, the prosecution, the courts, the witnesses and other experts such as the probation service and psychiatrists. Let us run through the system once more and focus on the feelings, attitudes and behaviour of offenders and victims. Does the criminal justice process truly assist the offender to understand what he has done and make him accountable for his behaviour?

Take the example of a young man charged with several burglary offences appearing before a crown court. Following the court hearing, the prosecution statement and the police evidence and a finding of guilt, the judge may feel he has little alternative but to send the defendant to prison for a couple of years. While he has been punished for the offence, there is little likelihood that the criminal trial will help the offender make the connection between the act and the consequences for his victims. Indeed, it is not uncommon for the offender to construct a series of rationalizations to justify his behaviour once he is confined to a prison cell. He finds ways to divert the blame from himself to other people and situations. The victim may have deserved it. The victim was insured and thus will suffer no real financial loss. Indeed, the whole experience of the trial process, the remands in custody, the separation from his family, the suffocating nature of the prison regime may lead the offender to feel badly treated, to feel powerless, to feel worthless.

In consequence, the offender rarely sees the human costs of what he has done. What is it like to have one's private space invaded, one's personal possessions damaged or stolen? What impact did the burglary make on the quality of life of the victim and his or her children? How will they be compensated for loss if they lack the means to have adequate domestic insurance?

Howard Zehr, a leading American exponent of restorative justice suggests that the prison experience itself does little to help offenders confront the wrong that they have done and learn the interpersonal skills that could put matters right.

> He will have no way to deal with the guilt that such an offence causes. There is no place in the process where he can be forgiven. His alternatives are few. He can avoid the issue, rationalize his behaviour. He can turn his anger on himself and contemplate suicide. He can turn his anger on others. In any case, he will continue to be defined as an offender long after he has 'paid his debt' by taking punishment. The hatred and the violence bred in prison may come to replace any sorrow and grief he may have had. (Zehr 1990, p.44)

For victims this sense of powerlessness is paralleled. Despite the advances made in the past couple of decades in England and Wales and other western countries in compensation schemes for victims of violent crime, in the introduction of victim assistance schemes in crown courts, in the networked spread of victim support schemes that offer relief and information to crime victims close to the crime incident and, latterly, information supplied to victims of violence by the probation service about the prison discharge arrangements of their identified offenders, feelings of hurt, anger and unresolved tension still remain.

For many victims, the crime incident can be a highly traumatic process. Their sense of personal space, of autonomy of action has been violated, their trust in others questioned. This sense of powerlessness applies not only to those who have been the victims of violence but to those who have been the victims of burglary, car theft or vandalism. The loss in terms of worldly goods may be small but to the vulnerable, particularly those who are isolated or elderly, the quality of life is diminished, the sense of fear, anguish and anger raised. Self-doubt and self-blame can follow. Questions occur for which there are no clear answers. Why did this crime happen to me? How long has he been watching my house? What does he look like? Is he a neighbour or stranger? Could I have taken better steps to safeguard my house? Will he come back again? Dare I leave my house in future for a holiday or family visit? What kind of compensation or redress can I expect?

Even if the offender is apprehended, charged and convicted, in itself an uncommon event since the majority of crimes go undetected, the victim does not feel as if he or she is at the centre of the criminal justice process. Despite the publication of the first Victim's Charter in 1990 enjoining the police to keep a victim informed of the progress of a case as it passes through the legal process to the courts, many victims feel on the edge in terms of knowing what is happening to their case. They have little say in the charges that are brought, little say as to whether or how the case is prosecuted and, unless they are called as a prosecution witness to the crime, they will not necessarily know the date of the alleged offender's court appearance and the final disposition of the court.

In the light of this sequence of events, it is hardly surprising that many victims still have a lingering sense of suspicion, fear, anger and guilt. In the absence of a reconciling or clarifying experience, victims may well build on stereotypes, wanting a desire for vengeance. Their natural demand for some sense of justice has not been met, for some the case cannot be closed.

What happens to the offender who has been caught and convicted by the court under our current system? Reparation is sometimes voluntary and disinterested – a spontaneous attempt to make amends, or if that is not possible to express remorse. More often, as Walker (1991) reminds us, it is offered in the hope of dissuading the victim from complaining, or persuading the sentencer that remorse is genuine. More often still it is simply ordered by the sentencer himself.

The judge can order a compensation order but many offenders lack the means to compensate their victims adequately. In the case of crimes of violence and sexual molestation, the victim can make a separate call on State compensation. In acquisitive crimes, the victim, particularly the impecunious one, who cannot afford personal and domestic insurance, is often caught up in the court's sentencing dilemma. If the offender is relatively affluent and can pay compensation, all the sentencer has to do is to make a compensation order to make sure he does pay and then proceed to decide on the sentence. In the case of the poor defendant, the sentencer often has to balance the financial obligations of the offender to his family and his responsibilities to the victim; the outcome may well be a smaller award than the victim could have expected.

The situation is further exacerbated if the sentencer believes that prison is the appropriate penalty but the offender, who is the only possible source of compensation, can pay only if he retains his job. Imprisonment will lose him his job and make it unlikely that he will ever compensate his victim. To the retributive sentencer, a non-custodial sentence may constitute a position of less justice.

These dilemmas and questions naturally lead us to explore the possibility of reframing our current justice model so that is becomes more restorative, particularly taking into account the needs and expectations of the victim and less retributive, with a singular focus on the State's punishment of the offender.

The drive towards a more restorative system of justice is not new. Victim surveys have revealed that the public are not so punitive as had been expected and that many victims would welcome the opportunity to seek reparation or even reconciliation in place of traditional punishment (Hough and Moxon 1985). Over the past 20 years in Britain, the USA and Europe academics, criminal justice practitioners and policy makers have expressed discontent with the existing model of punishment and have advocated restorative justice more focused towards the aims of mediation and restitution (Harding 1982; Wright 1982, 1991; Marshall and Merry 1990; Galaway and Hudson 1996).

In simple terms, mediation offers a way of resolving disputes without recourse to the courts, allowing both the victim and the offender to explore the crime incident, ventilate feelings, acquire information under the guidance of a trained professional or an informed volunteer. The mediator can assist the parties in conflict reach a resolution but the final agreement whether it be an apology, an act of reparation or compensation must be owned by both sides. Mediation schemes as practised in the western world range across a continuum of the criminal justice process from diversionary projects which take place outside the court setting to court-based schemes taking referrals from sentencers prior to disposal to meetings of groups of victims and offenders where the latter are already serving a custodial sentence.

The first recorded victim offender mediation programme (VORP) was developed by the Mennonite community in 1974 in Kitchener, Ontario and later transplanted by the same movement to Elkhart, Indiana in 1978. As the title implies, the meeting was not solely concerned with reparation but also with the psychological impact of putting together both offender and victim and the opportunity it gave for both of them, through personal reconciliation, to be reunited with the wider community as well as becoming normal citizens again as opposed to remaining stereotypical 'victims' and 'offenders'. The Mennonites believed that they had a role in healing the wounds caused by crime rather than disclaiming responsibility and leaving it entirely in the hands of the legal system. In addition, their religious views stressed the need for the individual to be able to atone for misdeeds, which could be achieved by making reparation materially and symbolically.

Over the next decade many American towns and cities copied the VORP model, financed by local and State taxes. For the most part such schemes intervene at the court stage of legal proceedings, sometimes between conviction but more often post sentence in conjunction with a probation order.

The British experimentation in mediation and reparation began in the early 1980s following visits to the United States by practitioners and policy makers (Harding 1982; Wright 1982). They were also inspired by lecture tours given by leading American exponents including Howard Zehr and Burt Galaway (Harding

1989). The Home Office, in 1985, directly funded four, three-year experiments in Coventry, Leeds, Wolverhampton and Carlisle. The first two were essentially court-based schemes focused on mediation work with those offenders and their victims in a magistrates or crown court, the two others were diversionary schemes picking up referrals from the police at the point of caution (Marshall and Merry 1990).

Aside from the Home Office projects, practice has steadily grown in mediation and reparation as an added dimension of criminal justice procedures rather than an integral part. Critics suggest that while mediation has obvious attractions, can it really operate in the shadows of the court? The victim support movement has warned of the additional burdens it may place on the victim in terms of time, good will and energy (Reeves 1984). While mediation may have achieved some success in respect of crimes of low seriousness, it is doubtful whether it could really substitute for formal adjudication in the care of serious crime.

In essence, restorative justice rests on the recognition that crime is not only a wrong against society but not infrequently represents a private wrong by the offender to a specific victim. Christie, a Norwegian criminologist, argued in a persuasive paper that the State has 'stolen' the dispute from the hands of victim and the offender and, in consequence overturned the right of the victim to seek recompense for harms suffered (Christie 1977).

Restorative theories of argue that compensating and making amends to individual victims should be the primary aim of the criminal justice process. Such a process would reduce reliance on negative, purely punitive disposals and replace them with positive attempts to correct specific harm caused by crime.

The western paradigm of retributive justice stands by stark comparison to Japan, a highly developed industrialized society with falling crime rates. Why is their response to crime so different from their western counterparts? Typically, in Japan criminal justice is extraordinarily lenient. Haley reports that although many offenders are identified by the police, many are never reported to prosecutors. Although convictable, large numbers are released by prosecutors without prosecution. Although prosecution is tantamount to conviction, the over-whelming majority of those convicted receive no more than a minor fine, or have their sentence suspended (Haley 1996).

Leniency is considered an appropriate response by the authorities if the suspect shows a willingness to confess, demonstrates sincere repentance and seeks the pardon of the victim through atonement and compensation. Provided that the offender expresses shame for his conduct, the process of restoration can begin, he can be once more re-integrated back into the community and regain a sense of self-worth and self-respect by means of correction. It is not surprising to find this pattern of restorative justice so embedded in Japan where there is a high degree of mutual interdependence, a sense of collective identity and close-knit communities with little cultural diversity. Indeed, Japanese criminal justice agencies rely heavily on community participation in terms of an informal control on crime. In seeking to make amends for a crime the family of the offender (grandparents, parents and siblings) play a key role in not only negotiating terms of apology and compensation to the victim but of also ensuring that the offender keeps to the agreed settlement and is suitably scrutinized as to his future conduct.

The successful Japanese model in recent times has shown signs of implantation elsewhere, most notably in the concept and practice of family group conferencing in New Zealand and Australia (Braithwaite 1989; Braithwaite and Mugford 1994). In New Zealand, the 1989 Children and Young People and their Families Act introduced family group conferences as an option for dealing with young offenders. They are based on Maori methods of conflict resolution and can be used as an alternative to court, or as a disposal of the court. The key aims are to empower families to make decisions about their children and to exercise authority over them; and to mediate between the victim, or their representative, and the offender.

A professional co-ordinator arranges for the young offender, his family, the victim and supporters to attend a neutral venue at a time which suits the family and the victims. The family, as in Japan, should include the whole of the extended family and other individuals significant to the young person such as a local teacher. Both victims and offenders can bring an advocate or lawyer if they wish.

At the start of the meeting, the co-ordinator shares his knowledge, views and concerns with the family and answers any questions. Each participant, especially the victims, relates how he or she was affected by the crime. The offender is thus confronted with the fullest possible consequences of the act but is also given the opportunity to explain and express remorse. His family becomes an important source of disapproval as well as restoration. The offender is not left as an outcast but is enabled by the experience to begin to earn his way back into the community by accepting responsibility and making acceptable amends.

Any restorative plans need to be recorded and approved by the co-ordinator. Most plans involve some kind of reparation, with work, which a family member may arrange. Most take place over a three-month period. Since the focus is strictly on offending behaviour, welfare issues do not become part of the action plan.

In New Zealand, 50 per cent of victims say they are satisfied with the outcome. The satisfaction of the police, the family and the young offenders has been higher – 91, 85 and 84 per cent respectively. Little evidence is available yet on the impact of conferences on re-offending (Morris and Maxwell 1993).

What of other documented claims for effectiveness elsewhere? In an American study of the effectiveness of juvenile offender mediation programmes in the cities of Minneapolis, Oakland and Albuquerque, Umbriet found that offenders were far more likely to complete restitution payments to victims than a comparison group who were ordered to pay restitution without the benefit of mediation: 81 per cent as opposed to 58 per cent (Umbriet 1994). The same writer also analyzed reconviction data for the mediation and matched comparison groups of 160 cases each. Within a year of completion of the programmes, 27 per cent of the comparison group re-offended as opposed to 18 per cent of the group who went through mediation. The mediation group also tended to commit crimes that were less serious if subsequently reconvicted than the matched comparison group. The finding of a marginal but non-significant reduction of recidivism is consistent with the English study of victim–offender mediation in Coventry and Wolverhampton (Marshall and Merry 1990).

The Leeds mediation and reparation service, a part of the West Yorkshire Probation Service, one of the original Home Office pilot areas, also examined what happened to the 90 offenders who were involved in mediation in 1988. Eighty-seven per cent had a previous record; 25 per cent of these were persistent offenders who had five or more previous convictions. The research showed that 75 per cent had no further convictions after one year and 68 per cent no further convictions after two years (Wynne 1996).

Umbriet, in commenting on the American data, argues that the most important criteria in looking at reconviction material is whether offenders in victim–offender mediation recidivate at levels no higher than similar offenders in other programmes or court interventions. He maintains there are numerous other benefits of the victim–offender mediation process, for both parties. If these benefits occur, with no additional risk of higher rates of criminal behaviour, these programmes are quite effective. This is particularly seen in the significant impact of mediation upon successful completion of restitution, and upon reducing the fear and anxiety of crime victims (Umbriet 1996).

Seen in overall terms, the development of restorative justice, the opportunity for expressions of remorse, atonement and restitution, has made impressive strides over the past two decades in the various locations described in this chapter. However, there is little evidence that the movement has overthrown the paramount paradigm of retributive justice, save in countries such as Japan and Korea. Indeed, in most western style systems of justice restorative processes sit awkwardly alongside the existing punitive frameworks. If progress is to be maintained in the western block it is more likely to flourish in the field of juvenile justice, where the principles of welfare and punishment of the young person still co-exist and where public tolerance is stronger than with adult offenders.

The restorative movement does suffer from some further deficits. Some critics maintain that it may lack the deterrent or punitive impact necessary to control crime. It ignores the broader dimension of crime: that it is not only the victim but also society that has been wronged. If my house has been vandalized and the contents stolen then it is not only the householder who feels victimized but also the neighbours in the street who feel apprehensive and fearful. Restorative justice on its own cannot address these wider concerns.

Furthermore, in focusing on harm done, restorative justice ignores the issue of criminal intent. Criminal liability is as much about what an offender was trying to do or thought he was doing as what happened in a particular circumstance. There are many victimless crimes such as careless driving, a conspiracy to rob or defraud, or possessing an explosive, which we deem to be criminal although no 'actual' harm takes place.

Despite these inherent reservations, the reparative movement has succeeded in shifting the balance in criminal justice towards a more victim-orientated process without showing any signs of replacing the punishment model. The increased use of the compensation order by courts is a clear indication of this shift in balance. It is important, too, that criminal justice agencies are beginning to recognize that opportunities need to be provided at every phase of intervention with the offender from pre-trial work to post conviction for him to understand the significance of the victim's experience of crime and make appropriate gestures of remorse, atonement and, where possible, restitution.

CHAPTER 9

Remorse and Reparation

A Judicial Perspective

Henry Palmer

REMORSE IN THE CRIMINAL JUSTICE SYSTEM

Contrary to popular belief, judges do not have a completely free hand to impose whatever sentences they wish. The majority of sentences are decided within the framework of the standards laid down by the Court of Appeal, from which judges, should they see fit to depart, do so on the basis of factors which mitigate or aggravate the seriousness of the offence. For example, remorse may be a mitigating factor; and conversely, lack of remorse may be an aggravating factor. Judicial powers are also limited by the maximum sentences prescribed by Parliament at the time of creating statutory offences. Currently there are very few offences for which Parliament has laid down mandatory or minimum sentences. However, fundamental changes intended to curtail severely judges' sentencing powers in the case of certain repeat offenders by the introduction of a number of statutory mandatory and minimum sentences for certain crimes, have been included in the Crime (Sentences) Act 1997. Broadly speaking, the scheme of the Act is that, in the case of a second 'serious offence', the judge is required to impose a life sentence; and in the case of a third Class A drug trafficking offence or a third domestic burglary, to impose minimum sentences of seven years' and three years' imprisonment respectively. 'Serious offence' includes attempted murder, manslaughter, grievous bodily harm with intent, rape, sexual intercourse with a girl under 13 and robbery when in possession of a firearm or imitation firearm. However, the judge is not obliged to impose the prescribed sentences if he is of the opinion that, due to exceptional circumstances relating either to the offence or to the offender, the justice of the case would be met by the imposition of a lesser sentence.

At the time of writing, the provisions of the Crime (Sentences) Act 1997 have not been brought into effect and the present position is that the maximum sentence is often of little relevance, as, for example, in the case of theft by shoplifting where the maximum sentence is one of seven years' imprisonment; it would be difficult to think of circumstances in which a convicted shoplifter's sentence would begin to approach this maximum.

Nevertheless, there are situations where the statutory maximum sentence does prevent the judge from considering the imposition of a sentence which, apart from the statutory maximum, he might think appropriate. For example, in the case of R v Sharkey ((1994) 16 Cr. App. R. (S) 257), Bernard Sharkey, with another, took and drove a car without the consent of the owner; there was a high-speed chase through a residential area, during which the car struck a twelve-year-old boy, who sustained multiple fractures of both thighs and other injuries. Bernard Sharkey had had eight previous court appearances since the age of twelve, for offences including aggravated vehicle taking. He was 16 years of age (15 at the date of the offence). He pleaded guilty and was sentenced to 12 months' detention in a young offender institution, this being the maximum permissible sentence for an offender of his age. The judge said that the defendant had ruined the life of a twelve-year-old boy and it would be utterly wrong to pass any sentence other than the maximum. In view of these remarks, it seems likely that, had the defendant been over 21 years of age, and despite a pre-sentence report saying that he was 'genuinely remorseful' and 'shocked' by what had happened, the judge would have been seriously considering a longer sentence. The Court of Appeal disagreed with the trial judge and considered that the defendant was entitled to a discount for his plea of guilty and reduced the sentence to one of nine months' detention. The judgment of the Court of Appeal emphasized that the judge was required to pay due regard to the limits actually fixed by Parliament as the maximum and to the accepted principles of sentencing in relation to giving a discount for a plea of guilty. The judgment continued by repeating the well-settled principles that there are good reasons why pleas of guilty result in lower sentences than would have been appropriate after a trial; first, they are taken as an indication of remorse and, second, there is a public policy aspect in encouraging guilty pleas.

In recent years, the Court of Appeal (Criminal Division) has laid down guidelines for the courts to follow in a wide variety of offences including rape, drugs offences and robbery and there are numerous reported cases covering virtually all other types of offence. Where there is a precedent, the judge takes the guideline sentence or reported case as the tariff starting point and then exercises his discretion to vary the sentence upwards or downwards in the light of mitigating or aggravating factors. However, sentences which the Court of Appeal considers to have been too severe can be reduced and sentences which are considered to be too lenient can be referred to the Court of Appeal and increased. The tariff is intended to be based on the principle of 'just deserts', that is to say, a level of sentence which is commensurate with the seriousness of the offending behaviour. Accordingly, the gravity of the offence is the most significant factor in fixing the tariff. The reasons for imposing punishment on offenders have been variously justified as being required for the purposes of retribution, deterrence, the protection of the public, the reformation of the offender or a combination of such factors. More recently, the idea of compensating the victim or society as a whole has played an increasingly important part in the sentencing process.

As well as the nature of the offending behaviour, its consequences and any remorse expressed by the offender, some of the many other factors which the judge may have to take into account when deciding on the appropriate level of sentence are the offender's age, the extent of his or her participation, the relevance of any provocation, good character or any past history of criminal convictions, dangerousness, the effect of drink or drugs, domestic or emotional stress, financial difficulties, the effect on the offender's family, loss of career, poor health and whether there is any possibility that corrective treatment, rather than punishment as such, might be more effective in reducing the chance of future offending and to protect the public. Furthermore, judges are not unaware of the climate of public opinion.

If an offender expresses remorse, the judge has to decide if this is genuine. The question of remorse is usually irrelevant where the offender has to be sentenced after a contested trial, since a defendant who has just been telling the jury that he didn't do it can hardly hope to persuade the sentencing judge that he is sorry for what he has done! But where the offender has pleaded guilty, the judge has to make his assessment of the quality of the information presented to him in court from prosecuting and defence counsel and from witnesses such as friends, neighbours, relatives, employers, colleagues, churchmen and others prepared to speak of his character. The judge also has the benefit of a pre-sentence report, usually prepared by a probation officer, which gives an account of the offender's attitude to the offence and his probable response to various forms of disposal. In some cases there is also medical or psychiatric evidence dealing with the offender's physical or mental state. The judge is normally obliged to accept the version of events put forward by the defence but, where the defendant pleads guilty on a basis which is unacceptable to the prosecution, and the court is not prepared to accept his version, a procedure is available for holding an inquiry, known as a 'Newton hearing' (see R v Newton (1983) 77 Cr App R 13). This involves the judge hearing evidence on both sides, if tendered, and coming to his own decision on the facts. How does the judge decide if the defendant's expressed remorse is genuine? The received wisdom is that a plea of guilty is evidence of remorse but this may be open to question since realistically the main reason for the plea of guilty is as likely to be the expectation of a lenient sentence as it is to be an expression of genuine remorse. Nevertheless, there is a valid basis for the public policy aspect of encouraging pleas of guilty in that it saves court time and ends the need for prosecution witnesses to attend court to give evidence. Even so, there are rare cases where no discount is given, for example, where the prosecution case is so strong that the offender has no real alternative but to plead guilty. There is much stronger evidence of remorse in cases where the offender has surrendered himself voluntarily to the police; such a case was R v Hoult ((1990) 12 Cr App R (S) 180) where the offender, having committed a robbery at knifepoint in a public house, voluntarily went to the police three years later and admitted his part in the offence. The Court of Appeal said that the offender deserved greater credit for his plea of guilty than that due to a man who confessed to his crime only after he had been found out. The sentence was reduced from four years' imprisonment to two-and-a-half years' imprisonment on the ground that the defendant's conduct was evidence of genuine remorse.

Conversely, absence of remorse may be treated as an aggravating factor. For example, in the case of R v Wilson and Others ([1964] 3 All E R 269; better known as 'The Great Train Robbery'), one of the reasons for imposing very long sentences of imprisonment was said to be the defendants' lack of remorse and their failure to assist in restoring the proceeds of the robbery to the losers. The writer can recall a case (unreported) where the defendant pleaded guilty to serious offences and claimed to have decided to give up his criminal activities in the future; he was getting married, moving away from his old haunts and starting a new job on Monday (not an unfamiliar ingredient of a plea in mitigation, which is not always true!). Since his credibility was in doubt, he was given bail and told to return in a week's time with some evidence of his good intentions, and bring his fiancee with him to court. When the court re-convened a week later, he duly called a young woman as a witness, who said that she was engaged to be married to the defendant and, when asked, that she had become engaged the previous day. Perhaps the defendant was to be congratulated on being able to find a fiancee at such a short notice but, however that may be, the court was unable to accept the validity of his assurances of remorse and future good behaviour, with the result that, for a time, he was able to contemplate his future from a prison cell.

REPARATION IN THE CRIMINAL JUSTICE SYSTEM

The power of the court to order compensation is a useful sentencing tool. It enables the court, in a straightforward case, to order the defendant to compensate the victim for injury, loss or damage resulting from his criminal behaviour and to avoid the need for the victim to resort to civil litigation to recover damages. However, where a serious offence has been committed, the offender cannot escape the normal penal consequences of his criminal behaviour by the payment of compensation to his victim; in other words, he cannot buy himself out of a sentence of imprisonment (see R v Inwood (1974) 60 Cr App R 70).

Another useful sentencing power is the court's power to make a restitution order. This enables the court to order the return of property, usually stolen property, to the owner. The court is also able to make an order for restitution in respect of any other property representing the stolen property and for payment of money belonging to the offender and taken out of his possession on apprehension. Unless the offender himself has been instrumental in the recovery of stolen property (which would be evidence of remorse), the offender's sentence is unlikely to be influenced by the fact that a restitution order has been made in addition to some other form of disposal. In drug trafficking cases, there is a further power which enables the court, if it is satisfied that the offender has benefited from drug trafficking, to order the confiscation of his assets to an amount representing his proceeds from this trade.

A community service order can also be regarded as reparative in nature. This is an order which requires the offender to carry out unpaid work for the benefit of the community under the direction of the probation service. The offender has to attend for work as directed for the required number of hours and such a sentence enables the offender to continue living his normal life in the community, whilst at the same time involving him in a substantial deprivation of his liberty. Courts are able to deprive an offender of a significant part of his leisure time, coupled with a requirement to carry out useful unpaid work. In suitable cases this may be a disposal which meets the justice of the case. Reparation can also mean the making of amends by offenders to victims in the context of face-to-face private meetings between offenders and their victims. Experimental schemes have been set up with a view to investigating whether such reparation could be used as a form of mitigation. Research into the matter in 1989 concluded that neither offenders nor victims were in favour of using reparation in this way. Victims were at a loss to know what the meetings had achieved and, from the offenders' point of view, the hope of a more lenient sentence figured prominently in the decision to participate in the scheme; and neither victims nor offenders were in favour of a link with sentencing (see article 'Reparation as Mitigation' by Richard Young [1989] Crim L R 463).

REMORSE IN THE MENTAL HEALTH SYSTEM

By virtue of the provisions of the Mental Health Act 1983, Mental Health Review Tribunals have been given powers in relation to the discharge of mentally disordered patients who are being (or are liable to be) compulsorily detained in hospital for medical treatment. These powers apply to most patients who are being detained under the civil sections of the Act as well as to patients in respect of whom hospital orders under section 37 have been made by the courts, either with or without the special restrictions under section 41. 'Special restrictions' are applicable where the court, having heard the required psychiatric evidence, decides that they are necessary for the protection of the public from serious harm. An offender who has been made subject to such restrictions can only be discharged by warrant of the Secretary of State or by direction of a Mental Health Review Tribunal. Where there is a tribunal hearing which relates to a patient who is subject to these restrictions, the legal member of the tribunal must be a lawyer 'approved for that purpose by the Lord Chancellor' (see Rule 8(3) of the Mental Health Review Tribunal Rules 1983; 1983 S.I. No 942). In practice this means that the legal member of the tribunal must be a circuit judge or a senior barrister who is a recorder with experience of trying serious criminal cases.

It is not always appreciated that a Mental Health Review Tribunal is an independent judicial body which, in most respects, exercises the functions, and carries the responsibilities, of a court. The members of the tribunal must, therefore, assess the credibility of the witnesses and evaluate the evidence presented to them and, having decided the facts, must apply the relevant law to those facts. The criteria which have to be met before a patient who is subject to a restriction order is entitled to be discharged are set out in section 72(1)(b)(i) and (ii) of the Mental Health Act 1983; paragraph (i) sets out the 'appropriateness' criterion and paragraph (ii) sets out the 'necessity' criterion. Under paragraph (i) the patient must be discharged if the tribunal is satisfied that he is not now suffering from any form of mental disorder within the meaning of the Act of a nature or degree which makes it appropriate for him to be liable to be detained in a hospital for medical treatment; and under paragraph (ii) the patient must be discharged if the tribunal is satisfied that it is not necessary for the health or safety of the patient or for the protection of other persons that he should receive such treatment. If either of these criteria has been met, the tribunal is obliged to discharge the patient. In the case of a patient who is subject to a restriction order, the tribunal has no discretion (as it has in the case of an unrestricted patient) to discharge him irrespective of whether or not the statutory criteria have been met. Strangely, the need to protect the public from serious harm is not, *per se*, a reason for refusing to discharge the patient, nor is the fact that it is not in his best interests to discharge him.

The criteria for discharge are not identical to those for the original admission. In order for the discharge criteria to be met, the tribunal must be satisfied that something which was present is now absent and, if the discharge criteria (or one of them) have been satisfied, the patient must be discharged, without regard to how much of a nuisance, or even a danger, he may be in the community or how much better off he would be if he remained in hospital.

For the purpose of deciding whether either the 'appropriateness' test or the 'necessity' test has been satisfied, the patient's remorse is evidence of his awareness of his mental state and is one of the components of his 'insight'. Participation in therapeutic programmes may provide some indication of the genuineness of his remorse. A patient who expresses genuine remorse is more likely to satisfy the criteria for discharge than one who does not. However, lack of remorse is not, by itself, a reason for refusing to discharge a patient; the expression of remorse is not specifically part of either of the statutory criteria for discharge. The tribunal, like any other judicial body, has to assess the credibility of a patient who expresses remorse and has to weigh this in the light of other evidence presented to it. The tribunal may, for example, be advised by the Responsible Medical Officer that in his opinion the patient is not genuinely contrite and that he is only expressing feelings of remorse because he believes that, if he does so, he has a better chance of being discharged. The state of a person's mind is a question of fact and it is the tribunal's task to resolve such conflicts of fact. Many factors may be relevant in reaching a decision on this issue, for example, a patient who has behaved in an aggressive or a violent manner towards staff or other patients whilst in hospital is less likely to satisfy the tribunal that he is genuinely remorseful; and it is of great importance that violent incidents occurring before and during admission should be recorded fully and accurately. Sexual offenders present special problems since there can be little evidence to support the patient's expressions of remorse whilst he is being contained in conditions of high security and, in such cases, the supporting evidence has to comprise such matters as the patient's attitude and his sexual arousal pattern, together with any evidence of his behaviour whilst on community parole.

The medical member of the tribunal has a duty to examine the patient prior to the hearing so as to form an opinion of the patient's mental condition (see Rule 11 of the Mental Health Review Tribunal Rules) but he attends the hearing, not as a witness but as one of the members of a judicial body. The medical member is not entitled to substitute his opinion for that of the medical witnesses whose evidence is received by the tribunal. Dr Peay ('Tribunals on Trial' (1989) p.125) cites the case of a patient who was not discharged by the tribunal, despite the fact that he appeared to satisfy the criteria for discharge. He had shown no signs of mental illness for some years, was not a management problem, had no psychosexual problems, didn't lose his temper and socialized well. During the hearing he broke down, made an emotional appeal to the tribunal and showed convincing remorse. The tribunal supported the Responsible Medical Officer's plan for trial leave, although Dr Peay felt that the case was an example of caution seemingly overriding the potential impact of the statutory criteria. A tribunal is not bound by the same strict rules of evidence as a court. Rule 14(2) of the Mental Health Review Tribunal Rules states that the tribunal 'may receive in evidence any document or information notwithstanding that such document or information would be inadmissible in a court of law'. Nevertheless, the tribunal can only act on evidence received and failure to do so may lead to the tribunal's decision being over-turned by the Divisional Court on an application for judicial review. The evidence of a psychiatrist as to the patient's state of mind is opinion evidence given by an expert witness, which ought to be supported by evidence of the facts which enabled the witness to reach his conclusion, but the tribunal is not bound to accept the opinion of an expert witness and it is open to the tribunal to interpret the facts in another way so as to reach a different conclusion.

The potential flaw in all this is that a patient who has been wrongly convicted is in a 'Catch 22' situation; if he does not express remorse, he is regarded as devoid of insight, whereas he can confess and express remorse only by not telling the truth. Others are better qualified than the writer of this chapter to amplify the problems surrounding the issue of remorse and reparation in the mental health system.

PART III

Remorse and Reparation
from Other Perspectives

CHAPTER 10

Remorse and Reparation

A Philosophical Analysis

Alan Thomas

The aim of this chapter is to analyze the concept of remorse from the perspective of moral philosophy. In what ways does moral philosophy claim to be able to illuminate the nature of the concept of remorse? First, by presenting an account of this concept and its structure within a more general account of the nature of moral thought. Second, by drawing on the resources of the philosophy of mind.

Moral philosophy is continuous with the reflections serious people have always conducted on the sources of those actions we feel bound to perform, the nature of values and obligations, and the nature of moral ideals. It differs from ordinary moral thought only in drawing on a range of canonical historical texts bearing on these issues and by the thoroughness of its enquiry, born of its specialization. The philosophy of mind, however, seems to encroach on the territory of the established science of psychology in a way that moral philosophy does not, the latter being sole occupant of its particular domain. How can a philosophical analysis of remorse avoid competing with a psychological analysis?

The answer is that the philosophy of mind and moral philosophy between them treat of the concept of remorse at the level of conceptual analysis. This level offers truths which are relatively independent of experience – in philosophical terminology, truths which are 'a priori' – and proceeds at a level independent of neurophysiological or psychological realization of the concept under analysis. When this method works – and it does not always do so – philosophical enquiry can yield *insight* into a concept, which avoids either explaining it away, by suggesting that it can be replaced by simpler concepts from which it is constructed, or taking it entirely at face value. Since the analyzes philosophy offers are conceptual, not scientific, the relations it maps need have no actual realization. Different elements are mapped out in their full inter-relations in an activity which is prior to detailed empirical investigation in such disciplines as anthropology or psychology, or in the representative samples of moral consciousness offered by literary texts. This point should be borne in mind when assessing the following 'conceptual geography' for the location of the concept of remorse.

I will argue that to understand the concept of remorse we must place it in its conceptual relations to the concepts of shame and guilt. In this survey of the relevant recent literature on moral emotions I will attempt to place the concept of remorse in such a framework.[1] I take it to be revealing that several of these recent authors have been influenced by Nietzsche and by Freud.[2] The underlying reason for this is discussed by Bernard Williams in *Shame and Necessity*, namely the tendency of moral philosophers throughout the history of the subject to allow their psychological concepts and explanations to be shaped by their prior moral beliefs.[3] For impartial explanations of psychological categories in a moral context, it seems 'critics' of morality such as Nietzsche and Freud are more reliable sources than more orthodox moral philosophers such as Plato, Aristotle and Kant.

A central aim of the following enquiry will be to deflect a certain kind of scepticism; a scepticism which treats remorse as an obsolete concept only appreciable from a religious standpoint which has no secular counterpart. Following the pioneering work of Deigh, I will try and build up a case for the distinctive conceptual role of remorse, separable from the concepts of guilt and shame.[4] This will centrally involve casting light on Deigh's distinction between a moral system based on rules and an ethic of care, which has been the focus of much recent attention. An assumption of my argument that I will not be able to defend here is that a distinctive aspect of modern moral philosophy, particularly in the form it took in the work of Kant, is to offer a self-sufficient account of the nature of value that precisely dispenses with any religious, or in particular theistic, backing.

Conceptual analyses of moral concepts have recently been developed by philosophers most directly influenced by Nietzsche, as opposed to Freud; I will present a representative composite account of guilt, shame and remorse drawn from several different sources.[5] First, the concept of guilt, as analyzed centrally by

---

1   I will be drawing mainly on the following works: Gabrielle Taylor, *Pride, Shame and Guilt* (Oxford University Press, 1985); Bernard Williams, *Shame and Necessity* (California University Press, 1993); John Deigh, *The Sources of Moral Agency: Essays in Moral Psychology and Freudian Theory* (Cambridge University Press, 1996); Simon May, 'Overcoming morality: A study of Nietzsche's ethics' (PhD dissertation, University of London, 1997).

2   Williams and May have been influenced by Nietzsche, and Deigh by Freud.

3   Williams, *Shame and Necessity*, pp.161–2.

4   This is the central proposal of John Deigh, in 'Love, guilt and the sense of justice', in *The Sources of Moral Agency*, esp. pp.48–52. While I focus on this single paper, this entire collection is a rewarding study of moral psychology.

5   This analysis is a composite of the analysis presented by Williams, *Shame and Necessity*, pp.219–223, balanced by that of May which stays closer to the original source in Nietzsche, May's 'Overcoming morality', pp.88–91.

Williams. Guilt depends on an identification with a set of standards which one is conscious of having violated. This prior identification is crucial to the concept as it suggests that the agent is already oriented to moral standards and that he has internalized his authority. One experiences this failure to live up to these standards painfully, motivated by the thought of a victim of the failure, who may be oneself (one may have been one's own victim, so as to speak). The painful experience is precipitated by an 'enforcer' or 'judge', who is necessarily internal to the psychology of the agent.[6] The agent's reaction to this witness is one of fear, fear *at* the internalized judge's anger, which can be developed into the more sophisticated concept of fear *of* justified recrimination for the wrong done.[7] However, contingently, the necessary internal judge may be accompanied by a genuine 'external' observer. The experience of pain at the failure to live up to standards may be accompanied by a sense of one's impotence in living up to one's ethical obligations. However, this feeling of powerlessness is not central to the experience of guilt.

This analysis offers an illuminating contrast with the closely related emotion of shame. Shame, by contrast, begins with the experienced impotence of the agent which is only of marginal importance in the case of guilt. In the case of shame, any failure to live up to standards is merely an expression of one's impotence and that is the ethically significant feature of the situation for the agent. This does not, however, make shame an egocentric or narcissistic phenomenon, as the standards may themselves be ethical and non-egoistically focused.[8] The 'witness' in this case may be external or internal and must be of concern to the agent – the agent will only feel shame in the eyes of a witness whose opinion carries weight with the agent. However, the witness must necessarily be internal for guilt, but can be external for shame, and one need not be identified with the ethical standards of the witness. His or her mere presence is enough to precipitate the feeling of shame. Shame need not involve a victim and is focused on the agent's feelings of powerlessness or impotence.

Remorse stands at a greater conceptual distance from the pairing of shame and guilt as it is already more heavily moralized. To explain remorse we need a set of moral assumptions, broadly the distinction between a morality of standards and

---

6   Williams prefers the term 'enforcer' to May's more neutral 'witness'.

7   However, Williams argues that this more sophisticated development should not be further refined to the point where it loses a key virtue of the more primitive analysis, its focus on victims: 'If it is to be an inherent virtue of guilt, as opposed to shame, that it turns our attention to the victims of what we have wrongly done, then the victims and their feelings should remain figured in the construction of guilt, as they are in the primitive version of the model. When the conception of guilt is refined beyond a certain point and forgets its primitive materials of anger and fear, guilt comes to be represented simply as an attitude of respect for an abstract moral law and it then no longer has any special connection with victims'. *Shame and Necessity*, p.222.

8   A point well made by May, 'Overcoming morality', p.89.

an ethic of value.[9] Remorse, by contrast with either shame or guilt, seems to involve the destruction of value rather than the infringement of standards of right and wrong.[10] The infringement of standards involved in guilt involves the idea of righting the wrong caused by the violation of the standards; this is part and parcel of the standards being standards with which the agent is identified. The mutual recognition underpinning the idea of a social rule demands recompense from the guilty in the form of 'righting the wrong'. As Nietzsche originally suggested, the guiding metaphor here seems to be that of indebtedness to a creditor. Yet in the case of remorse, 'there are no set ways to remedy evil'.[11] One has destroyed an object of value and this destruction may be, precisely, irremediable. Whereas guilt is experienced as an incurred debt from which one seeks to be released, remorse does not have a natural outlet and can lead to a paralysis of the will. Comparable to grief, it is focused on the past and on the destruction of that which is now lost.[12] It has been proposed as a distinctive mark of the emotion that remorse is typically felt over irremediable evil, a destruction of value that cannot be remedied.[13] As a moral emotion, it shares guilt's primitive focus on the victim of the act: the value that was destroyed voluntarily.

Thus, the experience of remorse indicates a certain kind of wrong doing, which Deigh marks off with the term 'evildoing', and which is focused on value, not rules or standards. These values may paradigmatically be the value of other people, although not necessarily so. If, while out walking in the countryside, I wantonly destroy the last wildflower of an endangered species, not protected by any legal or moral sanction, I have voluntarily destroyed an object of value. Remorse for the irreparable destruction is appropriate. But the fact that other people are the paradigm locations of value is, I will suggest, part of the deep significance we attach to remorse.

---

9   This broad distinction has recently been focused by the work of Elizabeth Anscombe, Bernard Williams and others in such a way as to redress the balance in favour of an ethic of care and direct altruism, rather than a morality of rules. From a very large literature I cite as representative Lawrence Blum's *Friendship, Altruism and Morality* (Routledge and Kegan Paul, 1980). The vague distinction I draw here requires considerable sharpening: for scepticism about the distinction see, for example, Robert Louden's *Morality and Moral Theory* (Oxford University Press, 1992). For some counterbalancing considerations see my review of Louden, 'My duties – to myself', in *The Times Literary Supplement*, 13 August, (1993) p.22. Naturally, I cannot discuss this wider issue here in the detail it deserves.

10 Deigh, 'Love, guilt and the sense of justice', p.48.

11 Deigh, 'Love, guilt and the sense of justice', p.49.

12 Points made in the course of the debate between Robert Rosthal, 'Moral weakness and remorse', *Mind* 76 (1967), pp.576–579 and Irving Thalberg, 'Rosthal's notion of remorse and irrevocability', *Mind* 77 (1968), pp.288–289. They are endorsed by Deigh, 'Love, guilt and the sense of justice', p.50.

13 A claim advanced by C.D. Broad, *Five Types of Ethical Theory* (Routledge and Kegan Paul, 1930), p.203 and David A.J. Richards in *A Theory of Reasons for Action* (Oxford University Press, 1971), p.256.

The overall effect of remorse can be to inhibit action. Action seems to be merely symbolic or to be an actual evasion of the central problem, a failure to acknowledge that the situation cannot be put right. This certainly problematizes the link with reparation, a point to which I will return. The analogy with grief is revealing. It too focuses on irremediable loss and the variety of means with which agents 'cope' with the situation resists easy analysis. Suffice to say that a 'living through' or 'passing beyond' the situation can be the psychological mechanism via which an agent copes with grief, and the situation seems analogous in the case of remorse.[14]

These reflections suggest that Deigh is correct that remorse is aligned with an ethic of care and concern for that which we value, whereas guilt is aligned with an ethic of rules which we identify as governing social life. While this distinction is broadly useful, it may be reconcilable at a deeper level if one acknowledges that the existence of the social institution of rules is premised on a desire for mutual recognition to function as the basis of self-respect. The core idea here is that the 'rule like' set of prohibitions which constitute the cultural surface form of moral codes, teachable across generations, is not a self-standing phenomenon. An explanation of why we take such a list of prohibitions to be binding over our actions will not invoke further rules, but rather the ultimate values underpinning our commitment to morality. In this case, the relevant values will be the values of rational agents, who stand in reciprocal relations of mutual respect. The fundamental ethical relation between such agents will be that of direct altruism – an ethic of care, rather than a morality of respect for rules *per se*.

If this account is correct, it would suggest that to be able to feel remorse, one must be capable of empathetic identification with, for example, a specific person one values. As Deigh points out, a wrong done to that person without remorse is expressive of 'remorselessness', verging on cruelty if that person is a person one loves.[15] One expresses in one's conduct that one did not, in fact, identify with the victim; whereas guilt at the infraction of a rule is premised on continued identification with the validity of those social norms. Remorse, like guilt, necessarily involves an internal authority before whom one is judged. Like shame, it involves a sense of impotence; in this case, however, the impotence of having destroyed something valuable which cannot be repaired.

The question arises of why, in a context of moral or legal judgement, one demands remorse of a wrong-doer and its expression in acts of reparation. It seems on the face of it to be more rational to demand a sense of guilt. Guilt is premised on acceptance of the standards violated and offers both agent and judges socially accepted means of expiating guilt and relieving the burden of

14   A point made by Rosthal, 'Moral weakness and remorse', p.578.
15   John Deigh, in 'Love, guilt and the sense of justice', p.50.

'debt'. This line of argument grounds Hegel's suggestion that wrong-doers have a right to be punished. The demand that the wrong-doer experience remorse seems to have a different focus.

That an agent be capable of remorse seems to indicate a fundamental capacity to enter into ethical relations; to be capable of identifying with an object or person of value and hence to experience value. Even if a morality of rules is fundamentally premised on structures of mutual recognition, mere identification with rules does not seem, ethically, to go deep enough. It can seem as if the domain of guilt does not touch on the underlying ethical reactions of experiencing people as valuable and irreplaceable and as the loci of self-respect and hence of value. The demand for reparation seems to have a solely symbolic or expressive role if it is indeed true that remorse is properly felt in circumstances when the value one has destroyed cannot be repaired. Guilt is premised on a continued identification with a social order, whereas remorse is based on a fundamental ethical identification with the sources of value which underpin that order, centrally other agents.

There is, then, a natural relationship between the 'problematization' of reparation and conceptions of punishment. The experience of irremediable wrong paralyzes the will. Guilt's connections with endorsed social standards offers an obvious outlet for action by way of compensation for wrong, but there is no obvious outlet in action for the experience of remorse. The attitude of mind called for by the experience of remorse is focused not on action, but on reflection; on an attitude of contemplation of the damage done. This state of mind has been well expressed by a moral philosopher who is also a novelist, Iris Murdoch, in a number of novels, such as *The Good Apprentice* in which the protagonist Edward Baltram experiences a paralyzing combination of remorse and grief at having caused the death of his best friend.[16] Murdoch's fascination with remorse explains a recurrent structural device in her novels: the remorseful individual gains release from his or her emotion by living through a structurally analogous scene to that of the initial trauma. This is an artistic expression of the remorseful agent's fantasy of being able to reverse time and live the moment of the irreparable harm again, to avoid causing the damage.[17]

Outside the confines of literary art in the service of the moral imagination, time cannot be reversed. What role, then, is played by the demand for reparation? Its role seems purely expressive and symbolic, reflecting one aspect of our concept

16   Iris Murdoch, *The Good Apprentice* (Penguin Books, 1976). Murdoch also discusses remorse in her more reflective philosophical mode in *The Sovereignty of Good* (Routledge and Kegan Paul, 1970).

17   Rosthal, in 'Moral weakness and remorse', describes Kierkegaard's analysis of remorse so concisely I will quote it in full: 'remorse is associated with a desire to nullify a past actuality', p.578.

of legitimate punishment – as expressing and symbolizing our collective emotion as to the wrongful act and as demanding a similar acknowledgement on the part of the agent.

The word 'acknowledgement' plays an important role here; the problematic demand for reparation in the case of remorse seems to reflect our demand to the agent that he or she do more than recognize that he or she brought about the bad state of affairs through his or her agency. Rather, that the agent should acknowledge that he or she understands what he or she has done – some writers have spoken in this connection of a deepening sense of the 'moral meaning' of an agent's action.[18] The deep point, once again, is that such acknowledgement can be taken as indicative that the agent understands what it is to enter into ethical relations with other people, other locations of value and agency with whom the agent can stand in ethical relations of mutual respect. It is such a symbolic proof of a fundamental orientation to the ethical that we seek when we demand reparation from the remorseful.

In conclusion, then, the sceptical suggestion that the concept of remorse is historically obsolete for the purposes of moral philosophy can be resisted. Its continued usefulness becomes apparent in the context of a revival of value based, as opposed to rule based, accounts of moral thought. The distinctive conceptual role for remorse as opposed to guilt is, as Deigh suggest, connected to a fundamental difference of emphasis in our conceptions of morality. Remorse is part of an ethic of care for that which we value; it seems indicative of a fundamental form of ethical orientation and for that reason is central to the responses we expect from those who have destroyed value, in extreme cases destroying the irremediable value of another person. It intensifies guilt's salutary focus on the victim of the transgression and is problematically related to the phenomenon of reparation, which seems to have primarily an expressive or symbolic role. Serving all these ethical functions, 'remorse' does not seem a plausible candidate for replacement or revision in our ordinary moral thought.[19]

18   Raimond Gaita, *Good and Evil: An Absolute Conception* (Macmillan, 1991), especially 'Remorse and its lessons', pp.43–66. However, Gaita does not clearly distinguish guilt and remorse and on occasion the psychological concept seems to be shaped by a prior view of morality in the way Williams cautions against (see footnote 3).

19   Thanks to Kathryn Brown for her invaluable help in the preparation of this chapter.

CHAPTER 11

'The Most Dreadful Sentiment'

A Sociological Commentary

Michael Borgeaud and Caroline Cox

'Such is the nature of that sentiment, which is properly called remorse: of all the sentiments which can enter the human breast the most dreadful. (Adam Smith, *The Theory of Moral Sentiments,* 1759)

A skim through sociological literature reveals a paucity of references to the concept of 'remorse'. Such neglect raises questions about the preoccupations of, and tensions within, modern sociology. The task is to formulate the social character of an apparently intensely personal phenomenon and to examine the *social* factors which may engender, exacerbate or heal this 'most dreadful' sentiment.[1]

We begin by introducing, to readers unfamiliar with the discipline, some of the contrasting ways in which sociology can contribute to our understanding of the social dimensions of remorse and reparation.

SETTING THE SOCIOLOGICAL SCENE: A SCHEMATIC, SIMPLIFIED OVERVIEW

Sociology is not a unified discipline, but a cluster of perspectives, with different assumptions about the appropriate way to study inter-relationships between individual human experiences and the wider society.

These perspectives can be arranged on a continuum from 'microsociology' to 'macrosociology'. This is an oversimplification as, in our view, sociology at its best transcends such restrictive dichotomies. However, this continuum provides a

---

[1]   Whilst sociologists have recently turned attention to 'the sociology of emotions', they have yet to develop studies specifically on remorse and reparation. For recent discussions on the broader issues within this field, see for example Bendelow and Williams (1998); Shilling (1997), Wentworth and Ryan (1994).

framework for understanding the different starting points and assumptions of various sociological schools.

Macrosociological approaches begin by looking at ways in which the characteristics of a society shape individuals' cognition, experiences and behaviour. The orderliness of everyday life is seen as the effect of supra-individual, exterior forces. Consequently, these approaches treat emotion as a residual category. Sharing this level of analysis, which forms the mainstream of traditional sociology, are theorists such as Karl Marx, Emile Durkheim and Max Weber. However, there are radical differences between them. For example, Weber's famous thesis of the relationship between the emergence of the Christian Protestant Ethic and the rise of capitalism questions Marx's emphasis on the primacy of economic factors in shaping a society and the life chances of its inhabitants.

Macrosociology is necessarily comparative and historical, offering insights into how changes in one society, or differences between societies, explain individuals' life experiences and even their psychic structure. Cross-cultural studies have revealed considerable diversity in the content of 'normal' or 'deviant' behaviour. These observations fit well with the idea of 'social constructionism', whereby realities, previously taken to be anthropologically invariant, or otherwise embedded in the objective natural world, are seen as fabrications of particular social conditions. In relation to our topic, this view has contributed towards the development of theories attacking the concept of any universal moral values, sowing the seeds of extreme cultural and moral relativism, with far-reaching implications for the significance of what are called the 'moral emotions'.[2]

Microsociological approaches focus on individuals in interaction with each other, in the context of actual social settings. These approaches illuminate the processes by which people make sense of their own and others' actions and experiences. Ways in which interactants express and recognize feelings are clearly of interest. Insight into the phenomenon of remorse might then come from the analysis of those situations in which groups clarify the limits of acceptable conduct; how disapproval of those who behave 'unacceptably' is demonstrated; and the way specific types of emotional responses are induced in those who cause offence, including the use of the moral emotions such as guilt, shame and remorse.

Both micro and macro approaches attempt to explain the interconnection between individual experiences and the social context. Traditionally, macro-sociology simplified the problem by assuming the experiential level was largely determined by the social system. By contrast, microsociology pays close attention to the intricacies of the interpersonal processes which simultaneously express,

2   See Harre (1986).

create and embody cultural forms in the individual. The social order, or rather a localized sample of it, is called into play by individuals as and when relevant for their situated activity.

THE DEVELOPMENT OF A 'SELF' CAPABLE OF FEELING REMORSE, THROUGH THE PROCESSES OF 'SOCIALIZATION'

The concept of 'socialization' illuminates ways in which people, individually and collectively, develop the capacity for the moral emotions. This has been a particular concern for the 'Symbolic Interactionist' school, which studies the effects of personal relationships on the formation of selfhood – relationships which play a central role in regulating individual conduct in response to the expectations of a particular culture.

Socialization refers to the processes whereby human infants become social beings, initiated into the beliefs and behaviours of their communities and enabled to play their part in society. Through socialization individuals develop a sense of moral values and commitments which reflect the social definitions of 'good' or 'bad' behaviour, including that which is deemed so unacceptable that it would be expected to generate 'remorse' in the perpetrator.

The process of socialization involves the development of the concepts of 'self' and 'self-image'. G.H. Mead's (1934) classic account depicts the human infant as a 'tabula rasa' capable of transformation into a mature social being. He identified stages of differentiation between the 'I' and the 'me', when a child begins to see himself as 'object' as well as experiencing himself as 'subject'. At this stage, he 'steps out of himself' and sees himself from the perspective of other people who are close to him – his 'significant others'. In so doing, he is identifying with them and beginning to internalize their values and standards of behaviour. Later, he can see the 'me', not only in terms of a close relationship with particular 'significant others' but in terms of a 'generalized other' – the norms and values of the wider society.

This theme of the social derivation of selfhood, and of values by which to judge that self, is also found in Charles Cooley's (1922) concept of the 'looking glass self', whereby, particularly in childhood, we see ourselves as others see us.

It is through such processes that a sense of quintessential 'self' and self-esteem are socially given and continue to be shaped by experiences throughout life. Positive and negative evaluations by 'significant others' may also create self-fulfilling prophecies, whereby we may 'become' what others perceive us to be (see, for example, Blanck 1993). And, to the extent that we internalize the values and commitments of those close to us, of the wider society, and of more abstract religious, moral, or ideological value systems, so we will judge our own behaviour by them. Such judgement may strengthen or diminish our self-esteem and tarnish or enhance our self-image.

Thus it is through socialization that we become susceptible to the experience of the 'moral emotions'. For if we violate these socially derived values, we may stand condemned not only by society and those we care about, but also by ourselves. It is this self-condemnation which leads to a variety of emotional responses, including guilt, shame, remorse and the desire to make reparation.

THE 'MORAL' EMOTIONS: GUILT, SHAME AND REMORSE

In an overview of emotional states, Gabrielle Taylor (1996) provides a 'differential diagnosis' of guilt, shame, regret, embarrassment and remorse. There is clearly some overlap between the different emotional experiences, but they can be differentiated conceptually.

Guilt may be an objective and/or an emotional state. People are 'de facto' guilty if they transgress a law or other edicts of a given authority. However, they may only *feel* guilty if they accept the legitimacy of that authority. If they do not *respect* the authority, although they may be liable to punishment by the agents of social control, they may retain a clear conscience, as do many 'conscientious objectors' or 'dissenters' who oppose laws or edicts as a point of principle.

The behavioural responses to guilt vary accordingly. If one *feels* guilty, there may be a desire to try to put matters right. If the guilty action involved harm to another person, this may involve a wish to make reparation. Such responses vary from person to person: one person may feel guilty over stealing and seek to make reparation; another may justify theft, perhaps according to the 'Robin Hood' principle, feeling no guilt and having no urge whatever to return stolen property.

Shame is an emotion associated with damage to one's self-image and self-esteem. The characteristic response is to want to withdraw, to hide. Sometimes, shame may be associated with guilt and remorse. But shame does not necessarily have moral connotations. Some feelings of shame and damage to self-esteem may be caused by events over which one has no control and therefore no moral responsibility. An example would be stigma associated with physical disfigurement. This emotional state does not incur a desire to make reparation; rather, relief may be found in withdrawal.

By contrast, *remorse* is inherently linked with an action for which the agent was responsible and for which there were no exonerating factors. It may be associated with consequences about which he feels he should do something, although this may not always be the case.

> The person who feels remorse sees himself as a responsible moral agent, and so sees whatever wrong he has done as an action (or omission) of his about the consequences of which he ought, if possible, to do something. (Taylor 1996, p.72)

Taylor suggests that there are three options available for a person afflicted with remorse: to make repayment as best he can and to try to put the matter behind him; to continue to suffer unresolved tension; to adjust his self-image to reduce inconsistency with his guilty action.

The strategy of reducing psychic tension by trying to achieve consistency through 'growing' further into the 'deviant' role is reflected in sociological research into the development of 'deviant identities'.

For example, David Matza (1964) describes processes whereby, once embarked on a 'deviant career', it may be easier to live with oneself if one accepts a 'deviant identity' and commits yet more proscribed acts. In this way, the psychological discomfort of incongruity between self-image and actual behaviour is reduced and guilt is neutralized. Also, the 'deviant' person may find companionship in new peer groups, which provide both friendship and an alternative source of values which can affirm the new deviant identity. Matza's account of this kind of 'secondary' deviance suggests that this response may be less likely to evoke remorse, as the new value system may justify the deviant behaviour and generate less emotional need to make reparation.

By contrast, earlier theorists offered vivid accounts of the experience of remorse. For example Adam Smith (1759), in his *The Theory of Moral Sentiments*, graphically describes G.H. Mead's concept of 'the internalized generalized other' with his own concept of the 'impartial spectator'.

> By sympathising with the hatred and abhorrence which other men must entertain for him, (the murderer) becomes in some measure the object of his own hatred and abhorrence. (p.84)

Adam Smith views the processes whereby individuals experience negative emotions, such as remorse, as the most effective deterrent and the means whereby social order can be maintained in the interests of the most vulnerable members of society.

> Nature has implanted in the human breast that consciousness of ill-desert, those terrors of merited punishment which attend upon its violation, as the great safeguards of the association of mankind, to protect the weak, to curb the violent, and to chastise the guilty. (p.86)

THE SOCIAL 'FUNCTIONS' OF REMORSE

Sociologists argue that any society must have mechanisms of social control, if it is not to degenerate into a state of lawlessness. We can now consider the role of remorse in maintaining social order. We have already looked at ways in which social control may be facilitated through the mechanisms of socialization, whereby individuals may internalize a society's values and develop respect for its laws and rules. Once internalized, these values will serve as internal judges, generating guilt when rules are broken, and remorse when actions cause harm to others.

Now we consider the more macrosociological approaches, which focus on societal responses to deviance. Social theorists and historians have long been concerned to explain the changes which have occurred in penal philosophies and practices, including forms of punishment designed to inculcate different emotional responses to socially unacceptable behaviour.

One of the most influential recent books is Michel Foucault's *Discipline and Punish: The Birth of the Prison* (1977). This work, taken up enthusiastically by social constructionists, has been subject to both praise and criticism. It is also said to represent an ingenious, if flawed, attempt to traverse both macro and micro domains. The most pertinent feature of Foucault's argument, to which we wish to draw attention, is his detailed account of the many regulatory and organizational practices or 'moral technologies' deployed in the reformed prison, which contribute to the fabrication of the mind and soul of the offender, to render him penitent, docile, productive and ultimately self-disciplined. This disciplinary programme then forms a blueprint for the whole citizenry of modern society. Thus, the meticulously managed prison regime exemplifies a new, discreet form of social power and administration which is simultaneously and increasingly interventionist and yet 'enabling'. In other words, it is not simply oppressive nor exclusively determined by class or economic interest.

This emphasis on the *multiplicity* of historical events and 'discourses', out of which new programmes for training humans emerge has been developed in a number of directions (see, for example, Rose 1989). For example, John Bender (1987) considers how works of literature and art contributed to the way in which prison reformers designed their versions of new penitentiaries. Referring to contemporary novels by writers such as Daniel Defoe and to paintings by artists such as William Hogarth, he shows how art forms played a significant part in building reformist institutions, even to the extent of inventing new ways of forging selfhood as part of the penal process. And, drawing on Adam Smith's idea of the 'impartial spectator' as the agent of conscience, Bender links the realist novel to the robust reformist movements of the 1760s and 1770s and sees them reflected in the penitentiary architecture of the era.

> The penitentiary suspends the offender within a tightly specified topography of spectatorship which reproduces, as physical practice, an invisible masterplot that structures mental life in metropolital society... Citizens at large function, in imagination, as the beholders of penitentiary punishment, picturing themselves at once as the objects of supervision and as impartial spectators enforcing reformation of character on the isolated other... inspection is not so much a physical condition as a way of living in a transparent world. (p.228)

Demos (1996) describes changing penal policies in New England in the seventeenth century. The Puritans tended to use scorn and public humiliation, with sanctions such as the stocks and public floggings, which were designed to generate shame in the offender. Later, with the development of Protestantism, modes of punishment changed from public abasement to self-punishment, 'encouraged' by incarceration and isolation.

While the former strategy is likely to lead to a damaged self-esteem and withdrawal, the latter may promote feelings of guilt, remorse, a desire for reparation and to put matters right.

Such studies, whether historical or contemporary, may shed light on the implications of different penal polices for crime control and for the psychic adjustment of the offender. Recent work of this kind shows how it is possible to blend macrosociological data on crime rates and social policy with micro-sociological understanding of the nature and consequences of interactions between offenders, agents of social control and other professional practitioners. For example, in a recent paper John Braithwaite (1993)[3] argues for a 'reintegrative' response to offenders which avoids stigmatization:

> Stigmatisation is shaming which creates outcasts, where 'criminal' becomes a master status trait that drives out all other identities... where bonds of respect with the offender are not sustained. Reintegrative shaming, in contrast, is disapproval dispensed within an ongoing relationship with the offender based on respect, shaming which focuses on the evil of the deed rather than on the offender as an irremediably evil person, where degradation ceremonies are followed by ceremonies to decertify deviance, where forgiveness, apology and repentance are culturally important. (p.1)

SHAKING THE FOUNDATIONS: MARGINALIZING THE MORAL ORDER

We have illustrated some ways in which social theorists treat the moral emotions. With some notable exceptions (see Goffman 1959; Scheff 1990) these are formal and abstract treatments that deal with emotion in general terms. But why have sociologists had so little to say about the specificity of remorse, and even less about reparation? We have already referred to the traditional concern of social theory with the integration of structure and social action, whereby orderliness in social life is seen as a product of thought, reason and calculation. This banishes the emotions to the non-social or liminal domains of the 'unruly' or of the 'socio-biological'.

3   See also Braithwaite 1989.

Positivistic sociology, in its attempts to be 'scientific', to avoid value judgements and unobservable subjective phenomena, tended not merely to explain, but to explain away, the moral emotions. In so doing, it robbed them of authenticity and autonomy.

Subsequently, neo-Marxist schools of sociology reduced social definitions of morality to reflections of the interests of the ruling class, and private moral emotions to false consciousness. Meanwhile, other versions of 'critical theory' unleashed radical assaults on sociology's epistemology and philosophical foundations.

The implications of the new 'radical' thinkers for concepts such as remorse and reparation were indirect but fundamental. At one level, they challenged the bases of legitimacy of western societies, undermining the validity of established authority structures, legal systems, and social institutions such as family, church and education systems, which preserve and pass on traditional cultural and spiritual values. 'High culture' was denigrated and all aesthetic and moral criteria were devalued and debunked.

At another level, this assault encompassed a demolition of the idea of an integrated, universal self-identity. The overall result was a tendency towards an extreme relativism which brooked no limits to its iconoclastic assault on any previously established criteria for moral evaluation of phenomena such as good or evil, or of epistemological evaluation of truth or falsity.

Our argument is that extreme relativism rules out consideration of the deeper infrastructures which define evolved 'human-ness'. Here we mean something more than mental states. Rather, capabilities enacted in a social world: practices such as judging, evaluating, imagining, remembering, empathizing – in fact, the very constituents of morality and aesthetics.

One further feature of this self-destructive relativism is the absence of any concept of wrong-doing that does justice to the complexities of everyday life or which takes account of common-sense notions of harm, indignation, blame, remorse and measures for repentance, reconciliation and reparation (Rock 1979). This appears to fly in the face of inherent human experience. As Joanna North (1988) puts it:

> Any account which denies the existence of wrong, or which seeks to redescribe an act in terms outside the arena of moral discourse, is one which leaves no room for the possibility of forgiveness. (p.279)

EMBODIMENT AND EMPOWERMENT: TRANSCENDING DISCIPLINARY DIVISIONS

Such iconoclastic trends did not occur in isolation, or without concurrent thinkers putting forward alternative ideas. There are those who have suggested alternative foundations for value systems, postulating the possibility of some fixed reference points despite the swirling seas of extreme relativism.

In this concluding section, we draw on some of their work to indicate ways in which sociology can address morality and its implications for remorse by reconsidering the relationship between self and society and moving beyond the position of extreme moral relativism.

On the first of these issues, we refer to Norbert Elias (1978), a sociologist who has been somewhat neglected until recently. His broad sweep of history from the Middle Ages to the present day discusses the sociogenesis and psychogenesis of the 'civilized personality'. He defines the 'civilizing process' as one of pacification within states, the resolution of conflict by non-violent means, and a greater degree of self-regulation of their own behaviour by individuals. Although much of his research focuses on behaviour associated with norms of etiquette and courtesy, he suggests that these are not just superficial adjustments. Rather, citizens in 'civilizing' states experience actual changes in their personality structure, including a change in the balance of their emotional inclinations:

> We see people at table, we see them going to bed or in hostile clashes. In these and other elementary activities the manner in which the individual behaves and feels slowly changes. This change is in the direction of a gradual 'civilisation', but only historical experience makes clearer what this word actually means. It shows, for example, the decisive role played in this civilising process by a very specific change in the feelings of shame and delicacy. The standard of what society demands and prohibits changes; in conjunction with this, the threshold of socially instilled displeasure and fear moves; and the question of sociogenic fears thus emerges as one of the central problems of the civilising process. (p.xiii)

Elias presents us with one of the most successful attempts to transcend the simple dichotomy of self and society by showing the inseparability of social and psychic structures. The relevance of this approach for consideration of the phenomenon of remorse is that we do not have to see this moral emotion as a mere epiphenomenon, or effect of particular historical context. Instead, it may be an integral part of the formation of a social order both transcending, and embodied in, the people who inhabit it. According to Philip Abrams (1982) the book is:

> The most remarkable recent attempt to contain the social and the individual within a unified scheme of sociological analysis. (p.230)

On the second issue, writers such as Zygmunt Bauman (1993), who is heavily indebted to Emmanuel Levinas, suggest that there is a need to move forward from the dilemmas of extremely relativistic and in the end nihilistic views of morality, suggesting that it is:

The sociologist's task is to find out how it has come about that moral regulation has been 'decommissioned' from the arsenal of weapons once deployed in society's self-reproductive struggles. (p.3)

He suggests that moral impulses are an indispensable resource and must be harnessed and exploited, rather than merely suppressed and outlawed. However, the social management of morality is a complex, delicate and inherently ambivalent operation. Bauman argues that one must assume that moral responsibility is the first reality of the self, a starting point rather than a product of society. Moral responsibility is precisely the act of self-constitution. The outcome of such analysis, Bauman suggests, means that:

The kind of understanding of the moral self's condition which the postmodern vantage point allows is unlikely to make moral life *easier*. The most it can dream of is making it a bit more *moral*. (p.15)

We have tried to show how sociology may shed some light on ways in which moral emotions are formed and shaped by social processes; and how they may serve as mechanisms for the management of social relationships. These processes can be personally traumatic or benign, and socially destructive or integrative.

We have also contested sociological assaults on the very nature of morality. But if there are fundamental moral imperatives, then we cannot underestimate the significance of the moral emotions. We must recognize their importance, both for individual human beings and for the societies they inhabit. Recognizing the power that these emotions exert, we must use every relevant discipline to unravel the complex interplay of biological, psychological and social processes involved. This 'most dreadful' human sentiment of remorse, and possibilities for appropriate reparation, now need further interdisciplinary study if they are to be acknowledged and 'used' as constructively and humanely as possible.

CHAPTER 12

Un-doing

Social Suffering and the Politics of Remorse

Nancy Scheper-Hughes

This chapter does not pretend to offer an anthropology of remorse, a field which does not exist and which I have no intention of inventing here. The paucity of ethnographic references to remorse and forgiveness suggests either an appalling oversight by generations of anthropologists, or it could alert us to the modernist and western nature of the concepts under consideration. While anthropological references to vengeance, blood feuds, counter-sorcery, and witch-hunts are many, descriptions of individual or collective rituals of remorse and reparation are few indeed.

At the heart of this lacuna are the culturally specific meanings and experiences of 'basic' emotions – such as grief, rage, and remorse – often thought to be universally shared. Earlier generations of anthropologists invoked a shaky dichotomy between *guilt* and *shame* oriented societies (see Benedict 1946; Doi 1973; Lebra 1971; Piers and Singer 1967). The experience of deeply personal and internalized feelings of responsibility, guilt, and remorse – as distinguished from public spectacles of confession driven by more externalized social sentiments of blaming and shaming – were assumed to be weakly developed or absent in many non-western societies. Remorse presupposes the existence of a certain kind of western-civilized' or 'cultivated' self (see Foucault 1986; Elias 1978), a culturally produced 'self' that was acutely *self-conscious*, highly individuated, autonomous, reflexive, and brooding a prototypical Hamlet figure, if you will, overly preoccupied by a *guilty*, confessional conscience. Think, for example, of the overly scrupulous Irish Catholic conscience captured by James Joyce in his *Portrait of the Artist as a Young Man* and you have it.

Consider, however, the almost gleefully, shamelessly, *unrepentant* head-hunting Ilongot warriors of northern Luzon, Philippines, studied by Michelle Rosaldo (1980; 1983) and Renato Rosaldo (1984), and you have something very different. An older Ilongot man explained to Renato Rosaldo that the practice of severing and 'tossing away' a victim's head enabled Ilongot males to 'toss away' their anger following the death of a loved one. Instead of a 'mourning' complex of depression, inaction, guilt, resentful anger and remorse, the Ilongot ethno-psychiatry of mourning was built around an emotional complex of excitement, exhilaration, hyperactivity, and murderous, even, indeed, gleeful rage. The Ilongot 'self' is described as relatively undifferentiated, decidedly non-autonomous, and contained within an alternative moral/ethical system.

To Renato Rosaldo's perplexity his Ilongot informants denied any 'rational' basis for their guilt-free head-hunting practices. It was not motivated, for example, by ideas about social exchange such that one death (or one head) might cancel the death of another. No, head-hunting, Ilongots insisted, was about the enjoyment of it alone. Taking a stranger's head 'lightened' the weight of a personal loss, just as their head-hunting war songs made the Ilongot feel happy, calm, and at peace with the world. It took Rosaldo another decade and the tragic experience of his own wife's death in the field to overcome his cultural resistance to the Ilongot ethno-psychology of emotions. Following Shelly Rosaldo's accidental death, Ilongot emotions finally made sense to him, not because they conformed to a universal psychological script of mourning, but rather because he had absorbed a culturally distinct aspect of Ilongot ways of experiencing emotions and the self. The Ilongots' unforgiving – we could almost say remorseless – way of grieving became tragically available to him. Renato knew – or thought he knew – what it felt like to want angrily, gleefully, to take a head and to toss it away in order to toss off, as it were, the weight of profound grief.

Like Rosaldo, I, too, resisted for a very long time accepting at face value what impoverished northeast Brazilian women told me about their lack of grief regret, or remorse accompanying the frequent deaths of their young infants – deaths they sometimes aided and abetted by reducing or withdrawing food and liquids to babies seen as 'doomed' in any case. 'Infants are like birds', women of Alto do Cruzeiro said. 'Here today, gone tomorrow. It is all the same to them.' 'They die,' other mothers explained, 'because *they themselves wanted* to die, because they had no "taste", no "knack" for life'. 'We feel no remorse, only pity for the little creatures who die so young, before they have even let us know what kind of person they are.' In *Death without Weeping* (Scheper-Hughes 1992) I interpret the lack of grief and of maternal remorse for the over-production of a multitude of angel-babies in terms of a particular 'political economy' of emotions responding to a culture of scarcity and the constant anticipation of loss and premature death.

Still, a few isolated ethnographic examples of individualized remorse stand out. One is Colin Turnbull's (1962) account of the punishment and remorse of an Mbuti Pygmy hunter, Cephu, who violated the social mores concerning communal hunting and redistribution of game. Cephu cheated by running ahead of his band and capturing for himself some of the game just before the animals ran into the communal nets. Caught in act of cooking the purloined game in his hut,

Cephu was punished by banishment into the forest. Before two nights passed, however, the selfish hunter crawled back to the base camp, shamefaced, and repentant. He confessed his guilt, begged forgiveness, and promised to observe Mbuti ways. Consequently, Cephu was allowed to rejoin the small group.

And Jean Briggs (1970) has given us a moving account of her own experience of transgression and social ostracism by her Netsilik Eskimo 'family' following Jean's culturally inappropriate outburst of anger in the midst of a small scale society that had learned to survive the rigorous environment by repressing the expression of dangerously anti-social negative emotions. Once again, the value of open, honest, and direct emotional expression requires an autonomous individual-self that is lacking in a society where self and other are less highly differentiated. And so, like Cephu, Jean Briggs was forced to apologize for her immature and unruly outburst before she was fed from the communal store of scarce winter camp rations. But such examples of remorse and forgiveness are altogether rare in the anthropological literature.

So, rather than a review of a non-existent literature, I will offer, instead, an *anthropological reflection* on social suffering, remorse, forgiveness, and recon- ciliation, focusing on a single ethnographic instance: violence and recovery in the context of the new South Africa. I will begin with a reflection on the morally ambiguous task of 'making sense' of suffering: one's own and the suffering of others. How do survivors and perpetrators of individual, political, and structural violence later come to terms with what happened? What does it mean to be a victim/survivor? Whose pain is privileged? Whose suffering is ignored? How are memories and emotions structured and deployed in the various processes of recovery, especially in the personal narratives of those who suffered the violence and those who were the direct agents or passive collaborators to the violence?

I went to the Cape of Good Hope in 1993 to lose myself in a new anthropological fieldsite, following the publication of *Death without Weeping: The Violence of Everyday Life in Brazil,* which concluded more than a decade of research on love and death in the impoverished sugar plantations of northeast Brazil. I'd gone to South Africa to be where something good, beautiful, and hopeful was about to happen. But the approaching democratic elections that would sweep Mr Mandela and the ANC into power in a glorious display of popular victory were preceded by a final, desperate attempt of the National Party government's internal security forces to disrupt the transition. Meanwhile the PAC (Pan African Congress) and other militant groups were divided over the terms of the settlement being negotiated in Kempton Park and they held out for continuation of the struggle. Consequently, 1993–1994 turned into the worst year of political violence and deaths in more than a decade of undeclared civil war.

The day after we arrived in Cape Town in July 1993 three young men dressed in overalls and head-scarves burst into the evening service of the St James

Evangelical Christian Church in the white suburb of Kenilworth, bordering the University of Cape Town community where we had just settled. The men opened several rounds of ammunition and tossed nail-spiked hand grenades into the congregation of more than 400 worshippers while they were singing the hymn 'Come to the Garden'. In seconds 11 were dead and more than 50 were wounded and maimed. More might have died in the St James massacre (as it later came to be called) had a young man seated in the balcony not pulled out a revolver and fired back at the assailants who turned and fled from the church auditorium, escaping in a getaway car that had been stolen earlier that day in Khayalitsha – a sprawling black township containing nearly a million refugees from former apartheid designated homelands.

Barely a month later during an anti-government strike called 'Operation Barcelona', American Fullbright student Amy Biehl was dragged from her car in Guguletu township in Cape Town and stoned and stabbed to death by a jeering mob of radicalized students. The ring-leaders identified her as a white, a settler, and therefore, an enemy of African people. Then, on New Year's day 1994, a tavern in the student bohemian quarter of Observatory was attacked by PAC revolutionaries and four people were killed, two of them students at UCT, the third, Jose, an acquaintance of ours, the owner of a Portuguese seafood restaurant, *Machados*, where we often went to '*matar saudades do Brasil*'. Two of our three adult children were just down the street at another student hang-out when this, the 'Heidelberg massacre' took place. The image of the four frozen, startled faces of the victims – for I accompanied the state pathologist, Len Lerer, to the Salt River Mortuary for the autopsies and identifications by family and friends (see Scheper-Hughes 1994) – determined the focus of my work on democracy and violence.

But these much-publicized incidents of so called 'black-on-white' violence were exceptions to the general rule of 'white-on-black' violence, often carried out by paid or intimidated black collaborators. So overwhelming and 'numbing' were the daily statistics on black violent deaths that even the 'liberal' white press and the black medium newspapers recorded them only as anonymous 'body counts': 'Another 40 Bodies found on the East Rand'; 'Dozen Bodies removed from Gugulew in Weekend Casualties'; 'Nine Bodies found in Two Shacks Gutted by Fires in Khayelitsha', and so forth. Violent deaths were and today they remain primarily the legacy of Black South Africans.

Of course, many beautiful things also happened during that violent yet triumphal year. Immediately following the election, a celebratory, mood bathed all South Africans in a sea of good will. A sense of humour and vitality emerged and the intensely private, because still segregated, worlds of long hibernating white Capetonians opened into a newly fashioned public space. There were many reasons to celebrate in this land of terrible beauty. However, the legacy of the violence remains. The scars are deep and etched into the gutted and destroyed landscapes left by the apartheid state, in the empty spaces left by those who died in the political violence, and in the wounded bodies of those who survived the violence and chaos, but barely. A few observations from my field notes should suffice:

> You cannot avoid them for they are present at every political event. Father Michael Lapsley with his startling metal hooks where his hands should be … There he is mischievously lighting a young woman's cigarette (a magician's trick!) or, over there, skillfully holding the stem of a wine glass raised in a defiant toast … Once the shock leaves one wants to caress his gentle hook-hand, to stroke the ruptured, permanently discolored skin where his right eye once was, and to toast him, noble wounded warrior, with wine goblets raised high, clinking glass with metal and champagne with tears. And over there, with his back carelessly turned to the door, stands Albie Sachs with his handsomely lined face and his resonant soothing voice, the agnostics' theologian, dressed in his priestly robes, his favorite bright and bold dashiki, waving his phantom limb, to make a point. That ever-present missing piece is Albie's most expressive body part and he gestures forcefully with the freely waving sleeve, his sweet banner of liberty … Of thee, I sing, Albie. (Scheper-Hughes 1994)

MAKING SENSE OF SUFFERING

The problem with interpretive anthropology is that it is all about meaning in a world turned increasingly absurd. Devoid of any theological mediation we are destined, like Sisyphus, to collapse under the weight of our attempts to 'make sense' out of sense-less – or, to cite Immanuel Levinas (1986) – of *useless* suffering. In recent years an anthropology of suffering (see Kleinman, Das and Lock 1997) has emerged as a new kind of theodicy, a cultural enquiry into the ways that people attempt to explain the presence of pain, affliction, and evil in the world. At times of crisis, moments of intense suffering people everywhere demand an answer to the existential question: *Why me, oh God?* (Of all people?) Why now? The quest for meaning may be poised to vindicate an indifferent God, to quell one's self doubt, to restore one's faith in an orderly and righteous world. The one thing humans seem unable to accept is the idea of the world as deficient in meaning.

Accounting for one's own suffering is one thing. 'Making sense' of the suffering of the other is quite another and fraught with ethical quandaries, according to Levinas. This distinction becomes explicit following any collective tragedy – whether 'natural' or 'political' when the 'why me?' question becomes the 'why *not* me?, why was *I* spared? (and, by implication, why not the others?) as survivors try to account for their exemption, their saving grace.

Although the St James congregation are extremely faithful in their attendance, some regular worshippers did, of course, miss the Sunday service on that rainy evening in late July. A clerical worker had car trouble; a teacher was down with the 'flu; a university student grew impatient waiting in the rain for a friend to arrive, and she went home rather than disrupt the Sunday evening service after it had begun. Each one shared their thoughts with me about why God had chosen to spare them on that night, along with their doubts about whether it was a good or a bad thing to have been spared. 'You see', said Nadja, 'God was speaking very directly to us at that moment'. And for those present during the 90 second attack that changed their lives and transformed their understanding of the world forever, the challenge remained to make sense of the chequerboard pattern that killed some, injured so many others, and left the others physically unscathed.

Dawie Ackerman, who lost his wife in the massacre, has played over and over in his mind the moment that he walked into the church a few minutes after his wife and rather than disrupt Marita and the woman with whom she was sitting and chatting in the front left hand side pew, he quietly took his place several pews behind her. During an interview in February of 1998 he told me:

– Now, why didn't I take my seat next to my wife? Why didn't I interrupt the conversation and just take her firmly by the arm to sit beside me where she might have been safe? But I left her, instead, in the front line of the attack, one of the first to be killed … This was contrary to my nature which is to act quickly, so that when the attack happened you would think I would have been one of the first ones up there to try and stop it. But, obviously, I had no gun … and … well, I just fell down and hid beneath my pew, like everyone else. Which I don't have a problem with … but I wonder what would have happened if I had sat next to my wife? I think I would have jumped up and wrestled with the attackers or tried to take their gun or something. And now I'd be dead, too. But I didn't, I didn't – thoughts like these were always going through my mind at first. You would try to sleep and it would get to you …

But I came to realize that there was a reason why I did not die. I was protected through God's intervention. The two hand grenades that were thrown into the congregation just missed me. One exploded only three meters away and the other was about six meters from me. That is very close. People all around me were hurt, hit by shrapnel, some were sprayed with rifle bullets, some people sitting just behind me were killed by stray bullets. A man sitting on one side of me lost both his arms and his legs. I had to walk over several dead and wounded bodies to get to my wife. But neither the grenades nor the bullets caused me any damage. Not a bit of the shrapnel hit me. I was spared.

– So, why were you spared?

– First of all, to take care of my three children … But also, I believe that in the grand scheme of things there was another reason. I had to ask *why it was me*, a lead

Elder of the Church who was spared? Later on, when I started unpacking all of this, I had to accept that God had both chosen our church [for the attack] and He had chosen the individuals who survived to give testimony that would bring honor to Him. And, since the first moment of the attack, that has been the desire of my heart, to do that. *That* is the grander mission.

– What testimony did you give?

– An offer of immediate and unconditional forgiveness to our attackers. As a Christian I had to forgive them as Jesus forgave all sinners. And not only to forgive, but to bear no rancor against those who killed my wife. (Scheper-Hughes 1998)

Two weeks after the attack I had joined a few dozen church members at the large tea room above the auditorium following Sunday evening service. The massacre was still, of course, uppermost in everyone's mind. Their pastor, Bishop Reteif, had been leading the congregation through a series of theological reflections on the meaning of suffering. But their own independent interpretations were, paradoxically, both more mystical and more embodied than the intellectualized sermon 'Where was God?' that the Reverend had just delivered. Instead, they spoke among themselves with great intensity of a 'secret message' encoded in the attack. If only they knew what it was. 'We *know* God was trying to tell us something', said Marlene Sidreic. 'Only, the true meaning hasn't been revealed to us yet.' But Cynthia had a more direct interpretation: 'I believe God's message to us was that life is given, life is taken away. Live life fully, day to day. Be kind to those you love, cherish them now, for you never know if they will all be blown away tomorrow.'

Then, barely a week after the Heidelberg tavern massacre I attended two post-trauma therapy and healing sessions for several survivors held at the Anglican Church sponsored Center for Victims of Torture and Political Violence in Cape Town. All the survivors were, quite naturally, preoccupied with having so narrowly escaped death. 'I was in Cape Town', said an older woman, 'to celebrate my daughter's wedding. I almost celebrated her funeral instead.' But despite the heavy media coverage and the informed political commentary surrounding what was immediately labelled a 'senseless', 'meaningless' attack on 'innocent' soft targets during the late and extremely optimistic stages of political negotiations, all these survivors understood the attack as politically motivated.

'This is South Africa', said a white, former soldier. 'We knew something like this was going to happen sooner or later.' Another survivor, a young mixed-race 'coloured' man said: 'I live in a township and I understand the rage that lies behind this attack, and the feelings some young people have that the negotiations aren't going right, that things are not going to change their lives for the better.' A local hospital worker who lost a friend in the attack agreed. 'Every day I see the wounds of the townships that come into the emergency room. And I think to myself, how long can things go on like this? But even while attributing a larger political 'meaning' to the attack, the survivors saw themselves as mis-identified targets. *'Why did they go for us?' 'People of all colours come to this pub; we are not the enemy.'* And they doubted, even as they hung on to the hope that – as one participant put it – 'some good might come out of this in the end.'

The ability to turn bad into good is a sign of resilience and is necessary for healing, and it is immeasurably aided by strong religious faith and/or equally strong political convictions. Father Michael Lapsley, who in 1990 received a deadly letter bomb (disguised as a religious epistle) from some still unknown officials employed by the old South African government, has been able to say that he is a victor and not a victim of the apartheid state that tried to kill him. Each day, just by living, he defeats evil and death. Like some of the St James Church survivors (albeit survivors of a very different sort of violence) Father Lapsley believes he was never closer to God than in the almost transcendent moment of the evil blast that took away an eye and his hands: 'I sensed the presence of the Holy Spirit accompanying me and sustaining me', he told me in 1994. During a visit to Harlem's Canaan Baptist Church of Christ on 116th Street in Harlem less than three years after the bomb, he addressed the congregation:

> I stand before you as a sign of what apartheid has done, of the physical ruptures it has caused ... But I also stand before you as a sign of the power of God to heal, the power of love, of gentleness, of compassion. The power of light is stronger than the power of darkness, and in the power of God we shall be victorious. (Lapsley 1994)

The wounded body often becomes a template of individual and collective memory, both a map and a moral charter. In the St James Church tea room, Mrs K, one of the wounded, rolls back her turtle neck to reveal a large and inflamed wound covering her neck and shoulder where shrapnel was removed: 'Do you know what this means? she asks me. I shake my head dumbly. 'This means I belong to Jesus. I am His. This wound is precious to me. It has removed all my fears. Nothing can ever hurt me again. Let the savages return. I am ready for them for His mark is upon me. He owns me and what is left of my life is in His hands.' The woman's intensity frightens me. Suddenly I want to change the subject, even though, presumably, this *is* my subject.

Michael Lapsley gestures broadly with his metal hooks, referring to them as his 'entré' into the black community. 'These', he says, very nearly poking me in the eye, 'are the gold standard. They open many doors for me into South African township life.' Similarly, Justice Albie Sachs is as expressive with his phantom limb – the space where his right arm once was before it was ripped away in a car bomb blast – as Father Lapsley is with his hooks. Sachs (1990) has written a book that skillfully weaves his own personal recovery from that wound with the recovery of his wounded nation.

Still, there are many dangers and booby traps. For the quest to 'make sense' of suffering and premature death is as old as Job, and as fraught with moral ambiguity. This is as true for the anthropologist/witness as for the companions of Job. It is so for whoever demands a reason, an explanation for suffering, usually one that is compatible with one's convictions, religious or political.

Perhaps my anxiety with the all too human capacity for 'making meaning' out of untold suffering has its origins in my long-term immersion in the sugar plantation zone of northeast Brazil where mothers struggle daily to 'make sense' of the useless suffering and unnecessary deaths of a multitude of over-produced angel-babies, sacrificed to hunger and thirst, or what medical people fancily call protein-calorie malnutrition and dehydration. These deaths too, I have long maintained, are political deaths. Brave little unknown Brazilian soldiers lying in their unmarked graves. The women of the hillside shantytown appropriately named O Cruzeiro, Crucifix Hill, explained their infants' deaths not only as meaningful, but, necessary, in many cases. 'Why do so many infants die on the Alto do Cruzeiro?' Sister Juliana raised at a liberation theology 'base community' meeting, to which the women had a ready supply of answers: 'God takes them to save their mothers from much pain and suffering'; 'There is always a reason. If they lived, who knows, they might have grown up into thieves or murderers'; 'They die because they themselves want to die'; 'God takes them to punish us for the sins of the world'; 'They fly up to heaven to decorate the throne of God and to entertain the Virgin Mother'. I began to think of the little sacrificed angel-babies, some of whom were said to have died 'so that others – but especially their mothers – could live' in terms of René Girard's (1987) notion of the ritual scapegoat, the one who dies (like Jesus) to relieve the community of unbearable tension and guilt.

Just as the companions of Job taunt him to elicit an explanation for his suffering ('You must have sinned against God') the friends and relatives of those blameless people kidnapped and tortured during the Argentine 'Dirty War' insisted: 'You must have been *into something*'. Similarly, at the memorial service at the University of the Western Cape the day after Amy Biehl was stoned, her grieving friends and colleagues whispered conspiratorially among themselves, 'We don't want to blame her, *but Amy of all people should have known better!*' What was she doing driving her comrades home into Gugulew, a no-go zone, a war zone during those tense days?

But Job righteously and steadfastly refuses the temptation to self-blame, insisting that he was a just man. Albie Sachs who lost an arm to the anti-apartheid struggle insists that he and his ANC comrades suffered and died 'because we were good, not because we were bad'. So, too, Amy Biehl refused the judgement of her attackers and she approached their raised arms (smiling, even, I was told) saying,

'No, stop. You are mistaken. I am not a settler. I'm Amy, a comrade'. Amy's naive and possibly even presumptuous claim coming from her large, white smiling face may have enraged the angry young men even further. But, later, her words came back to haunt those who were ultimately convicted of her death. At his TRC (Truth and Reconciliation Commission) amnesty hearing, Ntobeko Peni ended his testimony with the following ambivalent statement of remorse: 'I feel sorry and very down-hearted, especially today [when I see that] I took part in a killing of someone who was on our side, someone we could have used to achieve our aims. Amy was one of those people who, in an international sense, could have worked for the country.' So Ntobeko did finally come to accept that Amy was a comrade, as she said.

The danger, Immanuel Levinas (1986) notes, of all theodicies, of all attempts to make meaningful the suffering of others, is the risk of normalizing and accepting the suffering and death of the other. In all theodicies – theological, philosophical, psychological, political, and anthropological – the arbitrary character of suffering and death is hidden. The companions of Job return to goad the hurt, the disappeared, the maimed, the dying: 'You must have been into something'; 'You must have neglected your religious [or political] obligations'; 'You yourself must have really wanted to suffer or die'; 'You death will serve as a lesson for the living'; 'Your wounds will serve as a sign, a beacon'. The endless search for meaning, the attempt to make sense of suffering has allowed people, Levinas writes, to blame sufferers for their own pain, to value suffering as penance for past sins or as a means to an end or as the price of sensitivity and consciousness, or, especially within the Christian tradition, as the path of saints and martyrs.

If my limited, lay reading of Levinas is correct, he is challenging us to consider the opposite: the existential 'meaningless' and 'the uselessness' of the suffering of the other. Suffering, Levinas writes, is pure undergoing. It is a blow against freedom, an impasse of life and being. It is evil and absurd. Any attempt to explain, to account for another person's suffering is, he suggests, the source of all immorality. While one may attribute meaning to one's own suffering, the only ethical way to think about the suffering of the other is to see it as irremediably evil and tragic.

And yet… I think of how often Irish mothers of fallen IRA soldiers and mothers in South African townships have consoled each other at political wakes and funerals with the firm belief that their 'martyred' children suffered and died purposefully and died well. The grieving mother of Amy Biehl, for example, whispered to me during a break in the trial of Amy's alleged killers in Cape Town: 'Don't you think there was something *destined* about Amy's death? Don't you think that for some reason, perhaps not known to us here and now, Amy had to die?' And Mrs Jeannette Fourie, who lost her daughter in the Heidelberg massacre, said that she thought that Lindy-Anne would have been proud to have given her life for the New South Africa. 'Even', I asked, 'in such an absurd and meaningless attack?' 'Yes,' she replied calmly. 'Even so. I really believe this.'

And I think, too, of Mrs Dolly Mphahlele of Tembisa township, the mother of 15-year-old Earnest, who was caught running with a street gang that had been terrorizing the community. When the young 'comrades' came looking for Earnest, Dolly knew that her son was as good as dead. She acquiesced and accepted as necessary the harsh 'codes' that governed township life during the final days of the anti-apartheid struggle. Dolly made only one request to the comrades: 'The one thing I won't stand for is fire on my son. *You can kill him if you must, but do not burn him.*' Her plea was ignored, however, and the next day Mrs Mphahlele buried the charred remains of Earnest. He, too, she implied, fell to the struggle that was transforming South Africa. It was a price a great many African mothers would have to pay. With the blood of their sons.

Later during the Biehl trial, I asked Linda to explain further what she had meant in saying that her daughter *had* to die. In the crypt of St George's cathedral, over a cup of Roibos tea, Mrs Biehl explained: 'There is something you need to know about Amy. She was so dedicated, an incredible high achiever, but in the end something always happened to check her, to trip her up. Perhaps she was ambivalent about her success. So I wasn't really surprised when I heard that she was murdered on the day before she was to leave South Africa ... In a way I was even prepared for it ... Amy was very competitive, a high diver and a marathon runner. The very last photo I have of her is a newspaper clipping showing Amy just as she came through the finish line in a [Cape Town] marathon. Her face is full of ecstasy, pain, exhaustion, and relief. I like to think that this is how Amy looked when she died in Guguletu, as if she was just breaking through another, her most difficult, finish line.'

One can only sympathize with Linda Biehl's desire to substitute an image of beauty and light in place of the brutal photos attached to Amy's autopsy reports. And, it must have summoned all of Linda Biehl's faith to refer to Amy as a 'martyr' in the tradition of Saint Stephen whose life was also taken in a battery of stones. It is a painful sort of accomodationist 'maternal thinking' that allows a mother – whether Dolly Mphahlele, Linda Biehl, or Jeanette Fourie – to accept the suffering and death of their own child as over-determined, as meaningful, and as necessary even, but their sentiments are redeemed by an accompanying life-saving refusal to condemn their children's youthful killers and the ability to see them as, one survivor put it, 'as children just like our own, children who under normal circumstances would have lead ordinary lives.' Another survivor of the St James massacre, who lost two family members, shared her moment of terror at the TRC amnesty hearings in Cape Town just before the young Pan Africanist Congress (PAC) militants walked through the door to take their place at the front of the room. 'I prayed to God for strength. And He helped me. Because I did not see three killers walk into that room. Instead I was allowed to see three young men who were carried away by the violence of the moment.'

Linda Biehl's simple faith in the idea of meaningful suffering allowed her to approach and to embrace the mother of one of her daughter's killers and at the TRC hearings publicly to forgive the young men who murdered her daughter and to refuse to stand in the way of their being granted political amnesty. Linda Biehl – along with a multitude of mothers, sisters, and wives in South Africa who are being called on to do the same – summoned her own and her family's tragedy to serve the larger cause of national reconciliation and healing.

While accepting the heightened ethical and theological sensitivity of Levinas toward establishing proper distance and respect to the suffering of the other – which should not be turned into an icon of idolatrous faith (like the small golden cross I wore at my throat for the first 25 years of my life) – who, in the end, would blame Mrs Dolly Mphahlele, Mrs Linda Biehl, Mrs Fourie and the countless victims of apartheid government sponsored violence, and the 'soft targets' of the retaliatory St James and Heidelberg massacres – and even their useless anthropologist – for the persistent search to find some meaning, some transcendent purpose, some beauty even in the suffering and deaths? Those meanings provide the smallest bit of consolation that are the first step in 'getting over' the past and reaching the other side.

GETTING OVER: REMORSE, FORGIVENESS, AND RECONCILIATION

As a very small girl 'in training' for my First Confession in preparation for First Communion, I was impressed by the story a nun told to our catechism class. It was about an old woman who went to her priest asking forgiveness for a sin of gossip that had harmed the reputation of a neighbour. The priest accepted the woman's expression of remorse, gave her 'conditional' absolution, told her to mend her ways, and gave her the following penance. He ordered the old woman to climb the belfry of the parish church where she was to cut a small hole in a feather pillow and then shake the feathers loose onto the streets below. Then she was told to go about the village collecting the feathers until she had enough to sew back into the pillow. 'But Father.' the woman protested, 'that would be impossible!' To which the good priest sadly replied: 'Yes, and so, too, is it impossible to *undo* the damage caused by malicious acts.'

Wise words but counter-intuitive to the received wisdoms of the day. For the romance with remorse and with reparation, memory, and healing – both the individual and the social body – has emerged as a master narrative of the late twentieth century as individuals and entire nations struggle to overcome the legacies of suffering ranging from rape and domestic violence (see Winkler 1995; Herman 1994) to collective atrocities of state sponsored dirty wars and ethnic cleansings (Weschler 1990; Suarez-Orozco 1987; Boraine, Levy and Scheffer 1994).

The psychologies of remorse, guilt, catharsis, and closure compete today with the theologies of reconciliation, forgiveness, and redemption in another version of what Philippe called 'the triumph of the therapeutic'. Michael Ignatieff has hit upon an appropriate generative metaphor for looking at the present contexts of national recovery: *getting over*. The words conjure up Biblical images of safe passage, of reaching the other side, and, finally, of *over-coming*. Just what needs to be 'gotten over' if South Africa and South Africans are to get safely to the other side? Is reconciliation possible without some kind of powerful, transcendental faith? Surely, as many have argued, a first step in the politics of reconciliation and forgiveness is knowledge-seeking, learning exactly what happened to whom, by whom, and why.

'I sometimes wonder', said Father Lapsley, 'who that man or woman was who typed my name on the envelope that was supposed to kill me. I wonder, what did they tell their spouses or children that night at supper time about what they did in the office that day? Either they are so dehumanized that they don't care or else they have learned to live comfortably with their guilt ... I don't want vengeance but I think that the names and faces of these people should be known.'

The official vehicle to facilitate individual and collective 'getting over' and liberating South Africa of the ghosts of its past is the TRC, the Truth and Reconciliation Commission. In hundreds of hearings around the country, more than 2000 victims of apartheid-era brutality have told their stories to the independent commission. A smaller number of perpetrators of the violence have come forward to confess the details of their attacks on civilians in exchange for political amnesty.

Those seeking truth in South Africa today do not want the partial, indeterminate, shifting 'truths' of the postmodernist which resemble the dissembling (and always described as) 'complex' truths and realities promoted by the old apartheid state. Instead they desire the single, sweet, 'objective' truth of the moralist, and with it a restored sense of wholeness and a taste of justice. But, as Albie Sachs has noted, South Africans are willing to settle for an agreed upon, a 'good enough' truth – a narrative that will at least place black and white South Africans, Afrikaners and English-speakers, Xhosas and Zulus, ANC and PAC members on the same map rather than living in different countries from each other.

There are, of course, many critics of the TRC 'process'. Some worry about the focus on the 'exceptional', the 'extreme', and on the 'gross' acts of human rights violation which runs the risk of obscuring or worse of normalizing the ordinary, daily, routine acts of apartheid's structural violence: the legal, medical, economic, bureaucratic, and commercial violations of human rights that alienated millions of

South Africans from their property, their homes, their families, their labour, their citizenship, and even from their own bodies.

Still others worry about the dangers of 'numbing' South Africans by exposure to images, televised almost daily, of the TRC's invented and routinized public ritual of feigned remorse and forced forgiveness. I recall a chilling scene evoked by anthropologist Michael Taussig when a few years ago he was visiting the capital of a South American country during a period of official truth – and soul-searching (Taussig 1989). He was directed to a local municipal office where documents were being filed by those who had been tortured during the previous regime. Taussig described the petty bureaucrats as seated along a bench behind a very long table. In front of each official stood a long line of ordinary – and some very poor and barefooted– people waiting their turn to testify to the suffering they had endured. They were asked to do so following the official form and set formula of questions. Each petitioner was given three or four minutes to answer the questions: *When were you abducted? Where were you taken? Were you beaten? tortured? On which parts of your body? What tools were used? What questions were you asked? How did you reply?* The officers might have been tax collectors. And so, the original torture was mimetically reproduced by a new structure of indifferent state interrogators.

Still others – the majority of ordinary South African whites I have spoken to in malls and shopping centres, in tea rooms and in public gardens, in office buildings and in hospitals, in private homes and large farm estates – worry about witch-hunting, scapegoating, and persecution. Indeed, a great many white people in South Africa still fail to get the point behind the TRC. So, time and again, I was told that if General Malan ordered these tortures or that massacre it was because he *had* to do it for the national security. Those who were detained, tortured, and killed were not 'innocent', after all, they were terrorists. And, I was reminded, there were border wars going on. Communists were poised to take over all of southern Africa.

As for the 'higher ups', their defences are well fortified. Mr Breytanbach, for example, a former Deputy Defence Minister who served in the old apartheid Secretary of Defence under both Presidents Botha and De Klerk, is now comfortably retired on a government pension and living out his days as a recovering heart transplant patient in a luxurious, well tended and secured gated community in Sun Valley, outside Cape Town. He remains unrepentant and willing to attribute the atrocities emerging daily through the TRC amnesty hearings to a 'few bad apples' in the old security and defence forces. I asked Mr Breytanbach his opinion of the TRC hearings:

– You were once in the Ministry of Defence. Do you think that your colleagues are getting a fair shake?

— Well, I don't think this [the TRC] is the right thing to do. Instead of reconciling us, it is making the divisions even bigger. The thing now is to join people together. Of course, I think, most people, even I — and I was Chairman of my party in the Orange Free State and in the Secretary of Defence for more than seven years — were unaware of what was going on. I was positively shocked out of my mind to hear of the … well, let's just call them atrocities, and that sort of thing. It gives me goosebumps. I just can't believe it. Some of the people standing up there [before the TRC] I know them well. You would never have thought that such things went on.

But I have a son in the police, and he was telling me going back all these years, 'Dad, you must look at some of these characters on the far right, the Afrikaner Weerstandsbeweging [The Afrikaner Brotherhood or AWB] and such.' He said the police were infested with them. A person who is not white, well these guys had no respect for him and eventually they had no respect for life itself. So, what is coming out there, well, it shakes me out of my mind every time.

I asked Mr Breytanbach if he watched the summary of the week's TRC proceedings produced by the SABC (South African Broadcasting Company) on Sunday nights.

— I watch it. I watch it with disgust, yah. But, you know, I sat in at all the top executive meetings of the Defence Force which is where all the decisions were taken. There was Magnus Malan, myself, and the whole Defence Council, all the generals and brigadiers and so on, and I swear to you that *never, ever* were these sorts of things discussed. OK. We said that we must try and achieve something in this area [i.e. torture] to get stability. But these characters went out and slaughtered people like cattle.

— Does that mean that discipline had broken down in the security forces?

— I wouldn't say that discipline had broken down so much as … If you read that book the *Sword and the Swastika* you can see what the Germans did in the past war to the Jews. It was so sickening, you know, I walked around the house for a few days after I read it. It left such an impression on me. You just can't believe it. And there, too, you find the same thing as happened here. It all boils down to a few individuals, a few rotten apples, small people sitting in big jobs who suddenly think that they can play God. Chaps like these had taken it on their own to do things such as they have done and to thinking that they can just 'remove' certain people. But nowhere and at no time were these things ever discussed or hinted at during the executive meetings.

— Do you believe that De Klerk and Botha did not know what was happening within their own forces?

– They must have known something. When I was a member of the Security Committee we were five people – the President, Mr Botha, General Malan, myself, Pik, and Bryon DePlussey, the Minister of Finance. They knew something because we kept asking for a lot of money for developing arms for the border wars and for the security problems at home. I think it was a case of people looking you in the eye and saying one thing while they go out and do another. As far as I am concerned these people are in for the highjump and let them go. I don't care..

– So you are opposed to amnesty then?

– No, amnesty is a good thing. If a man has something on his chest, he can come out and confess it and ask amnesty for it. So, I agree with that.

– Since all these atrocities were carried out in secret, now that things are coming to the light, what will happen to these men's private lives? I mean, for example, to a son watching his father on TV before the TRC amnesty hearings. Will he say, 'Dad, did you *really* do all those things?' What will it mean for those families?

– I don't know too much about that … But some of these characters have just disappeared. They have walked out and left their wives and kids. I know of one specific case in the Orange Free State where neighbours had to take up a collection and pay for food and rent for a family who was deserted by someone who couldn't stand to face the music. Finally, this family was so poor they had to move in with someone else's family. So, I can only imagine … but, then, remember you get some of those women in the AWB and you can't believe the things they still say. They are some of the worst ones. But I don't think there are very many of these real SS types. I have spoken to another girl whose husband was involved – who tortured and killed a lot of people, and she says that this part is worse for her than death itself. Kids at school point out her children and they say 'Your Daddy did this and this'. I often wonder how many of them have had mental problems around all this.

– What were the biggest surprises for you?

– [*Deep sigh!*] So many. What was going on at the Vlockplass [The organizing and training camp for the security police], this de Kock chap. He's unbelievable, a real monster. Some of these characters had access to accounts abroad with millions of rands that they used to do their dirty work. How did they get those funds? But the Vlockplass goings-on, that really shocked me, and the Biko thing. And this other hearing, the Kondile case now going on. The burnings of the bodies and all that. It is terrible. One just doesn't know. But, again, I would go back to the Nazi era. Pretty much the same thing happened there. People lost all sense of humanity and engaged in cold blooded murder. And, if you want to talk about atrocities, when I was stationed over there in Kenya it was during the Mau Mau massacres. On my off time I used to fly and I did some observations from the air. Once I found a small strip about halfway up Mount Kilimanjaro where you could land a small airplane. And from the air I saw farmers and cattle and small babies slaughtered. You can't sleep for months after seeing something that. And, if you go even today into KwaZulu-Natal and you will find similar massacres still going on. So, this whole thing is not clear cut. Both sides [i.e. blacks and whites] are to blame, and there is more to all this than politics … It's about power. They all want power. And total power corrupts totally.

– Do you believe that forgiveness and reconciliation is possible in South Africa?

– Yes, I am very optimistic. I have to be. I have a stake in this country. I have six adult children and they have no where else to go … But what really concerns me now is that the – let's call them the whites of the country, some not all of them, but a great many are beginning to think that there is no law and order in the country. When white people see these large number of so-called disadvantaged people marching down the street, breaking things, taking and stealing whatever they want, well, they become very negative. They think that there is no good policing any more. And they start to think, well if *these people* can get away with this, so we can, too. But I try to warn them not to lower their standards, to become like the bad ones …

In this extraordinary narrative, Mr Breytanbach both manages to deny and to assert his knowledge of, and responsibility for, the state-level atrocities, to attribute blame both above and below him, and to take comfort in the knowledge that the kinds of atrocities committed by the apartheid state are not unique to South Africa but have taken place before (as in Nazi Germany) and in other parts of Africa (as in Kenya during the Mau Mau massacres). And at the very end his discourse, the *real* 'bad guys' in this story turn out to be the 'disadvantaged' blacks who have no respect for law and order and who are corrupting the morals of white people. Like most whites I have encountered since 1992, Mr Breytanbach fails to recognize the enormous grace by which he and all white South Africans have been spared.

In light of the aberrant behaviours presently coming to light through the TRC, one is inclined to feel that perhaps the 'witch-hunting' metaphor is not such a bad trope. The apartheid state was filthy with 'witches' at all levels of power and authority and a little 'witch-hunting' could clear the air. Among its many horrors, the TRC has provided the world with unforgettable images of culture inverted and a world turned upside down. In comparison, so called 'black masses' never looked so benign.

The political assassinations were carried out by trained hit squads, acting – we now know through confessions delivered before the TRC – on explicit orders. Suspected 'terrorists' were abducted from their homes by police, blindfolded, kicked and beaten, and tortured in new, improved and creative ways, some of them similar to the 'toilet-plunger rape' technique used by New York City Police

Officer Volpe in the handling of a black suspect. What has come out of the halting, up-tight 'confessions' are images of the white South African 'national sport'-cum-family picnic, the 'brai' or barbeque, turned into a cannibalistic political ritual.

For example, at the TRC amnesty hearings in Pretoria several month ago, former police Hennie Gerber and Johan van Eyk told how they abducted, blindfolded, tortured and murdered a suspected PAC member, Samuel Kganakga. They took him to isolated rural setting, kicked and beat him, tied him up and hung his body upside down, pulled his trousers down and applied electric shocks to his private parts. Later they built a fire under his head to 'dry him out'. While Kganakga's fat splattered and sizzled over the fire, Jack Mkoma, a private guard and police accomplice was sent out to fetch brandy, vodka, and cold cans of soda which were passed around among the men in a signifying cannibalistic ritual of apartheid Afrikaner brotherhood.

No wonder so many family members of those tortured and killed by the police state have rejected the TRC imposed 'duty' to reconcile. 'I am not ready to forgive', the mother of Sidizwe Kondile, another victim of a police-orchestrated brai murder told me during a break in the TRC amnesty hearings for her son's murderers in Cape Town in February 1998. Father Michael Lapsley refers to 'cheap theologies ' of forgiveness and to his extreme discomfort with the idea of blanket amnesty, although he says that for the sake of the 'greater good' of the country – and for the nation to be able to close a chapter on the past, he accepts the TRC's version of exchanging full disclosure for *conditional* amnesty. And he has often expressed his resentment of those who seem to demand that he extend an instantaneous, unconditional, 'Christian' forgiveness toward his would-be assassins. And Michael notes how often his speeches and lectures are mis-heard by those who come up to him afterwards and thank him for being 'so forgiving' toward the people who sent him the bomb, although he has never once mentioned the word forgiveness (Worsnip 1996, p.134).

Albie Sachs (cited in Boraine, Levy and Scheffer 1994, pp.20–21) tells the story of his own failure to forgive, when, soon after he returned from exile, he was enjoying a night out at a jazz bar on Cape Town's waterfront. His private enjoyment was interrupted by a young, white man in a jacket and tie who approached Sachs' table and, in a thickly Afrikaner-accented English asked: 'Are you Albie Sachs?' Annoyed at the intrusion, Sachs replied brusquely, 'I am.' '*Verskoon my* [Forgive me],' the man said in Afrikaans, his voice almost drowned out by the drummers. Albie Sachs said nothing. Again, he repeated, '*Verskoon my*'. Albie tossed off the request with a somewhat callous, 'This lovely club is my forgiveness'. Later, he thought of things he might have said: 'Don't ask me for forgiveness – I was a volunteer in the struggle. I chose my fate. What about the millions of black South Africans who had no choice but to suffer and die under apartheid?' Still later, Albie Sachs confided (in a personal communication) 'What I probably should have done was embrace the young man and accepted his forgiveness. But I just couldn't. Not then.'

WITCHCRAFT AS POPULAR JUSTICE

Allow me, then, to play devil's advocate in suggesting that witch-hunting might not only be a fitting metaphor for the collective recovery and healing of South Africa, but to show the extent to which the South African Truth and Reconciliation Commission has incorporated certain aspects of traditional practices of popular justice into its curiously hybrid formulas and rituals.

Confession is, of course, a central dynamic in all witchcraft-believing societies (see Jeffreys 1952) from the Navajo and Pueblo peoples of the American Southwest, to highland New Guinea (Bercovitch 1989), to vast stretches of indigenous Africa (Douglas 1970), to the Bocage region of modern France to rural western Ireland. Conventional insight suggests that witch-hunts are aberrant and dysfunctional institutions based on the mobilization of 'primitive' projections with the identified 'witch' chosen as the surrogate ritual scapegoat who represents the group's worst collective nightmare. The processes of fact finding, guilt determination, the ritualized expressions of remorse and the demand for immediate, though often symbolic, reparation strike liberal, bourgeois sensibilities as weak, irrational, and unjust.

But a great many anthropologists (see, for example, Wilson 1951) working on the ground with witch-believing societies have challenged the western stereotype by showing the positive uses of witchcraft in restoring health to troubled communities. One thinks, for example, of the great meetings held by the South Fore peoples of highland New Guinea in the 1970s in response to an epidemic of paralyzing deaths from Kuru, a lethal slow virus that attacks the general nervous system (Lindenbaum 1979).

At these kibung gatherings, South Fore leaders sought to blame the epidemic on the malevolent acts of individual sorcerers who were asked to come forward at the mass meetings to express their guilt and remorse and to ask forgiveness. Kuru 'sorcery' and death seemed to be directed against local women, who died in great numbers.[1] Individual men came forward to express their remorse for the deaths of village women, *and* to acknowledge their hostility toward, and abuse of, Fore women which they believed was responsible for the epidemic. How could Fore men practise sorcery against their own sisters, wives, and daughters? How could

---

[1]   In actual fact, anthropologists working with the NIMH research virologist, Carlton Gadjeseck (who later received the nobel prize for his work on Kuru), attributed the women's particular vulnerability as being a result of Fore mortuary rites which required them to ingest the infected and presumably infectious brains of their deceased next-of-kin (see Lindenbaum 1979).

the Fore survive without women? the men asked rhetorically during the Kibung meetings. While to some observers the kibung might seem like a primitive witch-hunting ritual, to the medical anthropologist, Shirley Lindenbaum, the kibung seemed more like a hospital 'grand rounds' or a roundtable at the CDC (the Center for Disease Control) in Georgia.

The public confessions allowed Fore men, albeit in an inchoate way, to recognize their role in exposing women – as the objects of social discrimination – to practices which may have, in fact, exposed them to the virus. Denied an adequate source of food, Fore women sometimes supplemented their meagre diets by eating rats and cannibalizing the dead which exposed them to the virus. But more pertinent to our discussion here is the graphic illustration the kibung offers of a ritual of remorse and reparation. The kibung allowed the Fore to acknowledge and atone for a collective social sin: the mistreatment of women.

In South Africa the power of traditional Zulu medicine (see Berglund 1989; Nugubane 1977) resides in Sangomas (healer's) skill in identifying the social tensions, 'hard feelings' and anti-social hostilities that can congeal into sickness, misfortune, and death in the community. 'Witches' are asked to identify themselves, to come forward and to 'speak out' their 'bottled up' envy, hatred, and guilt. And a great many 'witches' do come forward. From their perspective, confessions are said to be a means of 'emptying themselves' of the burden of evil, and restoring feelings of lightness and emptiness which signify balance, health, and good relations.

Rarely, however, do such public confessions result in amnesty, of course, and even the most repentant 'witches' can be punished by fines, forced labour, and public floggings, not to mention the miscarriages of popular justice that can result in outbreaks of indiscriminate witch-hunting hysterias and witch-burnings, such as the much publicized spate of witch-hunts in Venda (see Minnaar and Payze 1992), the Northern Transvaal (see Niehaus 1997), and Soweto (see Ashforth 1996; Keller 1994) in the early 1990s. But these incidents are anomalies, while the more common and judicious applications of 'counter-sorcery' as a traditional form of popular justice are known to few outside the field of anthropology.

During the anti-apartheid struggle years, some of these older practices were transformed into newer institutions of popular justice including the people's courts, security committees, and discipline committees put into place by 'the comrades' in urban townships and squatter camps. People's courts meted out a rough sort of popular, revolutionary justice. Apologies and fines were levied for lesser infractions. More serious offences were punished through public 'spectacles' in which the lash – and less often the infamous necklace – predominated. At times, suspected or confessed police collaborators were punished or even killed as 'witches'.

But in my work in a new and desperately poor squatter camp outside Cape Town during 1993–1994 and during a return study in 1996 I was impressed by the generally responsible manner of those involved in community policing and administering the organs of popular justice. For example, in February of 1994 in Chris Hani squatter camp, several activist youths – members of the ANC and the PAC – intervened when an angry mob gathered around three local unemployed teenage boys who were caught stealing 400 rand from a local shebeen (see Scheper-Hughes 1995). The crowd wanted the boys burned (necklaced), but as the boys sat trembling a few youth leaders, waving the then draft ANC Bill of Rights, raised their voices in protest and argued for public whippings over the death penalty. The floggings – 50 lashings with a bullwhip – were laid on 'collectively' by several older men of the community.

I visited the boys following the flogging and they were not a pretty sight. Their eyes were dull with fever, they had trouble bending their legs to sit and had trouble urinating. The smallest, Michael B, scowled with pain and revenge. 'I'll kill them', he kept repeating of his floggers. But following the flogging incident, there were many open-air meetings in Chris Hani squatter camp at which the future of people's courts and popular justice were endlessly debated. Only one of the boys could not get over his anger and he was advised to leave the squatter camp and was given help in locating a new home. The other two boys accepted their punishment and they were reintegrated into the camp. Nothing more was said about their crime. One of them entered Xhosa initiation in the bush outside Franschhoek. The last time I saw him he was slathered with white clay and smiling broadly. He boasted that his circumcision 'cut' hurt very badly; it was much worse, he maintained, than his whipping.

The strength of these institutions of popular justice is that they are immediate, public, collective, face-to-face, and relatively transparent. They are based on traditional notions of *ubuntu* (an ethos of humanism based on collective values), and the power of shame within a context of codes of personal honour and dignity. I once attended an outdoor court meeting on a Sunday morning in 1994 held under a large tree in Chris Hani squatter camp. One of the petitioners to come before the community that morning had been accused by his neighbours of public drunkenness and disturbing the peace. The man sent a friend to represent him, explaining his absence as being due to a job he had to attend to that day. The friend was called to the front and read from a respectful letter of apology written by the man. The court of elder men and women listened attentively, conferred among themselves, and then gave their verdict the offender could not be forgiven until he appeared in person. The written apology was appreciated, but the man would still have to appear in front of those whom he had offended. He would have to 'face' them. Then the next case was heard.

Of course, popular justice and people's courts are vulnerable on many counts. They depend on volunteers and have a high turn-over following any criticism of their activities or decisions. And so, many township and squatter camp residents of good will are afraid to serve, fearing intimidation by relatives of those accused and/or punished, paving the way for 'strong men' with vigilante or police connections to usurp these roles. But on the whole these grassroots institutions operated judiciously. And, elements of both traditional and popular justice have made their way into the uniquely South African version of the late modern idea of the truth commission.

Like traditional witch-hunting and the people's courts which proliferated during the anti apartheid years, the TRC is not so terribly concerned with fact-finding and fact-checking and it relies more on the power of the dramaturgical moment: public enactments of suffering, confession, remorse, and forgiveness. Written testimonies and formal legalistic petitions are part of the TRC record and process, but these are never completely acceptable without an *appearance* by the petitioners in symbolic face-to-face encounters with their victims and survivors. The TRC places a high premium on apologies offered in person by the perpetrators who are asked to give 'eye contact' to those who were hurt and wronged. At the close of each amnesty hearing, the commissioners and trained 'briefers' expedite a 'closing' ritual, by inviting the survivors to come forward and address their former tormentors, raising with them any final, unanswered questions.

And so, Dawie Ackerman, who lost his wife in the St James massacre, came forward to tell the young men who killed his wife how he had been made to step over dead bodies in order to get to his wife, still sitting bolt upright in her front row pew, and how all the while he was hoping against hope, that Marita might just be shell-shocked but still alive, until he has finally crossed that endless expanse and reached her but just as he touches her back, her body rolls over and falls with a dull thud to the floor, her special Sunday clothes splattered with blood. Dawie continues, his composure now broken, his voice cracking and trembling with tears that have been, he said, a very long time – five years, in fact – in coming:

> I've never cried since I lost my wife other than to have silent cries. I've never had an emotional outburst till now. When … when Mr Makoma here [the young man who was 17 at the time he took part in the church attack] was testifying, he talked about his own tortures in prison, and that he was suicidal at times, but that he never once cried. I thought to myself – and I passed you [the TRC lawyer] a note, to please bring your cross-examination to an end. Because what are we doing here? The truth … yes. But then I looked at the way in which he, Makoma, answered you. All his anger … What on earth are we doing? And I thought that *he* cannot be reconciled.

Then, in a final and painfully wrenching scene Dawie Ackerman, now openly weeping, asked the three young applicants to turn their averted faces to look at him directly: 'This is the first opportunity we have had to look each other in the eye while talking. I want to ask Mr Makoma, who actually entered the church … my … wife was sitting at the door when you came in. [Dawie weeps and the words seem to be dragged from the roots of his shaking body]. She was wearing a long blue coat. *Please, can you remember if you shot her?*'

Makoma looks terrified, as if he is seeing Hamlet's father's ghost. He nervously bites his lower lip and slowly shakes his head. No, he cannot remember, neither Marita nor her long, blue coat. But all three young men apologized to Dawie. Makoma is the most affected: 'We are truly sorry for what we have done. But it was not intentional. It was the situation in South Africa. Although people died we did not do that out of our own will. It was the situation we were living under. And now we are asking you please, do forgive us.'

Dawie Ackerman *did* give Mr Makoma his forgiveness and he withdrew his formal, legal objection to the young men's receiving amnesty from the state. After the formal hearing, Ackerman and several other survivors, including Bishop Reteif, met behind closed doors in an arranged, private meeting with their attackers, each of whom walked around the table addressing each survivor in turn, shaking hands, and asking personal forgiveness.

Paul Williams, another victim of the St James Church massacre, who is partially paralyzed from a bullet lodged in the small of his back, said, 'I have now forgiven the one who shot me, unconditionally. I looked him in the eye and actually had a chat with him. It was a good experience for me. I saw that we could each forgive the other.'

– Each forgive the other? [I asked]

– You have to remember, that I am a coloured man and I know where these guys are coming from. I know how they were wronged and how even my own group [i.e. the mixed race population] turned away from their suffering.

Brian Smart was most struck by the ages of the PAC militants: 'They were only 17 years old, and I could relate to that. When I was 18 I was in the Air Force and sent to Cyprus in defence of the realm, if you like. The only difference between myself and them was that I was operating under a more controlled military order. So an incident like this [the massacre] would not have happened. But in their case the command structure was very weak and they had the normal soldier's ability to kill, just as I had.'

Mary Powers chimed in to say, 'I have been thinking about their parents, how it must have been so hard, you know, they were children. And maybe they had gone a way they didn't want them to go. Maybe they pleaded with them, but there were stronger forces at work. Or, maybe, they supported them. I don't know. But I am a mother, too, and I just feel for the parents.'

Bishop Reteif, who was not in the church until moments after the attack took place, and who subsequently suffered a great deal of pastoral survivor guilt (*Shepherd, why were you not keeping watch over your flocks by night?*) originally opposed the TRC and the granting of amnesty to 'terrorists'. His initial response to the massacre was to heroize the clergy and congregation and to criminalize the youth seen hardly as people but as 'instruments' of other evil forces. After the hearings the Bishop is contrite about the 'blindness' of his church to the suffering caused by the apartheid state. And, after actually meeting the young men he felt for the first time since the attack that he could carry on with his normal life. He said: 'Something like a weight has been lifted from my heart, something that would be hard for you to understand if you had not been a part of the TRC process yourself. Now, I finally understand why it [the TRC] was necessary to bring about healing in the end.'

Young Makoma, serving a 20+ year sentence for his part in the massacre, returned to Polsmor prison awaiting the result of his amnesty petition. The other two PAC applicants returned to the Defence Forces where they have been serving as soldiers since 1994, their trials pending the results of their amnesty pleas.[2] And while Dawie Ackerman, Bishop Reteif and other church members seem to have experienced a real catharsis through the TRC process, young Makoma has yet to find any such emotional relief. During an SABC media-arranged prison visit between Makoma and Dawie Ackerman's daughter, Leisel, the young man was asked how he felt upon seeing the graphic police photos 'of all the people and all the blood' at his amnesty hearing. He replied to the girl whose mother he had killed in the attack:

– Yah, I remember that OK. And I had feelings then. It was bad. But no matter how I feel now, at this moment, that what I did was bad, there is nothing which I can do. The people are dead. How I feel cannot change anything.

As a 'strong' and 'disciplined PAC militant Makoma still feels that all these emotional performances are unseemly and just a little bit beside the point.

CHANGES IN SPIRIT

Justice Albie Sachs (1998), himself a victim of apartheid terrorism, expressed the wish that there could be more 'felt emotion' by the perpetrators of political violence. He referred to those who seem unmoved by the TRC process, who (like

---

2   The Amnesty Committee of the TRC granted amnesty to the three PAC operatives involved in the St James Church Massacre on 11 June 1998.

P.W. Botha and Winnie Mandela) have refused the new history, and who remain frozen in the past.

But the TRC process has, in fact, opened up new emotional spaces where conversations and actions that were once impossible, even unthinkable, are now happening. The unlikely encounters between perpetrators and victims who are beginning to empathize with each other's situation is an extraordinary case in point. The first time a church member approached Makoma, soon after his arrest in 1993, he chased the young man (a divinity student), out of his cell, saying that he would send his 'comrades' out to get him. Less than five years later Makoma was both gracious and apologetic toward his visitors. And, after their arranged meeting, Leisel Ackerman was able to wonder, 'Will we ever see each other again? Could we possibly become friends?'

And I think of the ordinary Afrikaner couple with very concerned looks on their faces who approached me one day on the steps of St George's Cathedral in Cape Town (Archbishop Tutu's church). Where could they find the Bishop, they asked. 'Oh, he's a very busy man', I said. 'I'm sure he's not here now.' They both looked crestfallen.

– What did you want to see him about?

– We want to confess to the Truth Commission. We did not treat Black people very well and now we want to make a fresh start.

I explained that the was a very formal process 'with lawyers and official papers' and that it was meant for murderers and torturers and not for ordinary people who could have behaved better. But the real effects of the TRC will perhaps be felt in small ripple effects like these, and hopefully in various community circles where people, like this couple, might be able to meet with others in order to talk about just what happened to them, how they behaved, and how to set the record straight. This is what some of the churches and, in particular, Father Lapsley's 'Healing the Memories' forums are doing. At least some of these healing retreats are reserved for those who were neither official Victims nor Perpetrators, but ordinary people who were hurt, diminished, traumatized and/or compromised by the apartheid state and the violent struggle against it all the same. After the formal TRC has disbanded and all the counsellors return to business as usual, what will be needed still are a multitude of little TRCs, community based, for ordinary citizens who had to live through extraordinary times.

REDEMPTION

So I close, now, leaving you with the story of Hennie's redemption. Hennie is an acquaintance, an Afrikaner and a private security guard in Cape Town. During the year we first spent in South Africa in 1993, Hennie frequently dropped by our house to visit. I feared that either he was spying on us or that he had a special fondness for one of our adult daughters. But we tolerated his visits as patiently as we could. He seemed honestly curious and well-intentioned. I ran into Hennie in the streets of Cape Town during a spontaneous celebration of South Africa's having won the All-Africa Soccer Cup in February 1996. Hennie was very excited, almost emotionally overwrought, and he didn't know quite how to explain to me the magnitude and significance of that magical moment. 'Did you see the game?' he asked. I did, I said, on a big screen in a packed bar.

– Both goals?

– Yes, indeed.

– And did you see our President [Mr Mandela] right there out on the field?

– Yes.

– Can you possibly know what this means for us?

And without waiting for an answer, Hennie told me: 'It means we are not a hundred per cent bad. It means God is willing to forgive us. That He would give to us – of all people! – such great heroes! It is a sign that we are going in a good way now. We are not hated any more. Oh, how can I explain this? It's like before we were fat Elvis: sick, disgusting, ugly. Now we are like skinny Elvis: young, handsome, healthy. In the New South Africa we have all been reborn.'
  So be it.

Acknowledgments

Fieldwork was supported by a grant from Harry Frank Guggenheim Foundation (1996) and an Open Society Institute Fellowship (1997–1998). Writing was supported by a fellowship at the Institute on Violence, Culture and Survival of the VFH Center for the Humanities and Social Policy, Charlottesville, Virginia.

CHAPTER 13

Representations of Remorse and Reparation in Classical Greece

Douglas L. Cairns

Until recently, an essay on this theme would probably have started from the difficulty of investigating the concept of remorse in classical Greek, given the status of ancient Greek societies as shame-cultures. Remorse, on this view, is specific to guilt-cultures, in which the core of ethical evaluation is the agent's subjective interpretation of the intrinsic moral character of his own actions, and is of little importance in shame-cultures, where what matters is the construction placed upon one's conduct by other people. Fortunately, such a crude application of the shame-/guilt-culture antithesis has been decisively challenged: I have argued (Cairns 1993) that the original differentiae of shame- and guilt-cultures are of little practical use in the classification of real societies, while Williams (1993) and Gill (1996) have investigated in detail the intellectual history of these and other progressivist generalizations. The shame-culture/guilt-culture antithesis has its roots in a strategy of American self-definition which sought to elevate (an anti-historical and idealized version of) WASP cultural identity as a norm against which other cultures should be measured. At its heart stand assumptions regarding the superiority of post-Kantian models of the autonomous moral self which share the same project of using pre-modern, non-Western society as the contradictory of 'our' privileged, uniquely 'moral' outlook.

There is still room for disagreement as to the utility of a reformed antithesis between shame- and guilt-cultures,[1] but no sensible account will wish to retain the claim that part of the difference between the Greeks and ourselves lies in the former's lack of any internalized mechanism which might reject certain forms of conduct as unacceptable in themselves. Thus the fact that Greek ethical vocabulary is thoroughly pervaded by notions of honour and shame does not rule out a capacity for remorse. Remorse, I take it, is a species of regret over actions for

---

[1]   Cairns 1993, pp.45–7; Williams 1993, pp. 78–85; cf. Gill 1996, pp.66–7, 74–5.

which one considers oneself responsible, which one wishes one had not performed, and whose damage one would undo if one could. It thus has a natural association with the desire to make reparation. Some would specify that the responsibility that is necessary for remorse should be 'moral responsibility' for intentional harm, or distinguish remorse from guilt (e.g. in terms of their focus on one's acts *versus* one's self as agent); but it is my experience that people express remorse over actions for which they are merely causally responsible, and that remorse and guilt overlap to a great extent in popular usage.[2] Prescriptive definitions simply reflect 'our longing for a neater conceptual world than we in fact possess'.[3] Nor would I accept a sharp disjunction between guilt and remorse on the one hand and shame on the other; though we can distinguish shame from guilt in general terms, grey areas remain, especially where shame is a retrospective reaction to acts which one regards as breaches of one's own, internalized standards.[4]

Remorse is thus predicated upon responsibility, and holding people responsible for their actions is at the heart of the reactive attitudes in play wherever co-operation occurs.[5] Equally, remorse and its concomitant desire to make reparation (and elicit forgiveness) are fundamental strategies in the maintenance of co-operation – one accepts one's own responsibility while acknowledging the legitimacy of others' criticism, and thus declares oneself an acceptable moral interlocutor, ready to resume co-operation.[6] Some such strategy is to be expected wherever co-operation occurs, since all societies will demand that errant individuals demonstrate an awareness of the unacceptable nature of past behaviour and a willingness to co-operate in future. But remorse is not merely a strategy; as an emotion it has deep psychophysical roots; but like other emotions its specificity is not (or not only) that of its neurophysiological and/or visceral changes, but of its constitutive beliefs, its evaluative construction of experience in terms of a particular cognitive scenario. And whatever biological and cultural universality there may be in the emotional life of human beings, it is clear that scenarios and the beliefs in terms of which they are constructed may differ enormously from one society to another.[7]

We should thus expect to find evidence for the experience of remorse in our Greek sources, but be prepared to acknowledge that elements of similarity may be

2   Taylor 1985, pp.97–107, with Cairns 1993, pp.21–2.
3   Morris 1987, p.222.
4   Cairns 1993, pp.14–26; Williams 1993, pp.75–102, 219–23.
5   Strawson 1975.
6   Strawson 1975, pp.16–17, 22; cf. Williams 1993, p.90.
7   Social scientists tend to overestimate, evolutionary biologists to underestimate the significance of cultural diversity, but there is a growing consensus that unqualified cultural determinism is false; for recent, accessible contributions, see Carrithers 1992; Ridley 1996.

embedded in practices, concepts, and institutions very different from our own. As translations of 'remorse' Greek has several candidates: the common *metameleia* (lit. 'aftercare') covers both regret and repentance of culpable error; in *metanoia* (lit. 'afterthought') the cognitive aspect is to the fore, while the rare verb *metalgein* (to feel 'afterpain') highlights the affective aspect. But a survey of the semantics of these terms would not exhaust the search for representations of remorse, for that experience may be adumbrated periphrastically, or construed in other terms, whether in the language of 'conscience' common around the end of the fifth century BC, or in traditional language of honour and shame.

Plausible representations of remorse go back to the beginnings of Greek literature: to Hector's recognition that the failure which he regrets has left him open to reproach from those whom he has an obligation to protect (*Iliad* 22. 104–7),[8] Helen's bitter castigation of her own infidelity (*Iliad* 3. 173–6, 180, 6. 344–8), and Achilles' pain at having failed Patroclus (*Iliad* 18. 98–126). In classical Athenian drama, episodes which we should characterize in terms of remorse occur with relative frequency in unemphatic, 'ordinary language' contexts. In Euripides' *Andromache* (420s BC), the Nurse represents Hermione as suffering from intense remorse (she experiences 'afterpain', *metalgei*, 814, and recognizes that she has acted badly, 815) following reflection (*sunnoia*, 805) on the enormity of her attempt to have Andromache and her child put to death. Several passages of the comic poet, Aristophanes, equally depend for their effect on the audience's familiarity with the phenomenon: at *Wasps* 743–9 (422 BC) Philocleon's fellow-dikasts imagine him reproaching himself for his past mistakes,[9] and later in the same play (999–1002) Philocleon exploits the vogue for the term *suneidêsis* ('awareness', cf. Lat. *conscientia*) in a joke which represents the acquittal of a defendant as a breach of principle which no dikast could bear to have on his conscience. Aristophanes also gives us an episode of remorse construed in terms of *aischunê* ('shame') at *Knights* 1354–7 (424 BC). Demos hangs his head and shifts his feet uneasily because he is 'ashamed at his past mistakes'; his response has inhibitory and prospective (or self-protective) aspects, but the element of remorse is confirmed by the Sausage-Seller's attempt to assuage his anxiety with the reassurance that he was not to blame.[10] This coincidence of conscience, self-reproach, and inhibitory shame is demonstrated most subtly in Sophocles' *Philoctetes* (409 BC), where the plot turns to a large extent on the dilemma of Neoptolemus, who is forced, as a deep affinity develops between himself and his victim, painfully to confront the recognition that his deception of

8   Cairns 1993, pp.81–2, 145; cf. Gill 1996, pp.83–5.
9   Cf. Menander, *Epitrepontes* 888–900; Dover 1974, p.304.
10   On conscience and retrospective shame in other fifth-century contexts, see Cairns 1993, pp.291–305, 343–54.

the noble Philoctetes is incompatible with his own nature, and who eventually, when the promptings of shame can no longer be ignored, seeks to make good his offence by sacrificing his own interests in support of the man he has wronged. [11]

This is enough to demonstrate both that the Greeks were familiar with the phenomenon of remorse and that representations of that phenomenon need not be categorized as wholly distinct from standards of honour and shame. But we still need to reach some estimation of the salience of remorse in Greek culture. A fragment of the comic poet Diphilus (fourth century BC) illustrates the congruence of shame and remorse and accords them a value consonant with conventional modern assessments, when it asserts that retrospective, self-directed shame (*aischunê*), based on consciousness (*suneidêsis*) of base action, is a prerequisite for that shame/respect/inhibition before others that is the basis of ethical life (fr. 92 KA). [12] The expression recalls several maxims attributed to Democritus of Abdera (born c. 460 BC), in whose ethics the notions of conscience, obligation, and 'shame' (*aidôs/aischunê*) in one's own eyes seem to have been central. [13] Democritus insists on the value of self-respect as a deterrent to wrongdoing (B 244, 264 DK), and on that of retrospective shame at one's misdeeds as a precondition for progress (B 84 DK). This is in harmony with his one specific pronouncement on remorse as such (B 43 DK): 'repentance [*metameleia*] over shameful deeds is one's salvation in life'. Democritus is an important figure for his belief in moral progress through reform and for his explicit recognition of internalized mechanisms of conscience, and it is significant that he recognizes that such mechanisms may be rooted in the affective dispositions of shame, respect, and self-respect which are the traditional currency of Greek ethical discourse.

Democritus' stress on the sincere commitment to do good, based in affective states developed through socialization and education, is shared by the agent-centred ethical theories of Plato and Aristotle. The latter's ideal of perfect virtue has no room for retrospective shame, since this implies a disposition to do wrong (*Nicomachean Ethics* 1128b10–35); [14] hence remorse (*metameleia*) is characteristic not of the good, but of those who struggle and often fail to be good (*NE* 1150b29–31; *Eudemian Ethics* 1240b21–4; *Magna Moralia* 1211a40–b2). Yet Aristotle recognizes that one who possesses a sense of shame is in a better position to make progress than one who is deterred from wrongdoing by external sanctions alone (*NE* 1178b4–20), [15] and he allows the value of repentance

11   Cairns 1993, pp.250–63.
12   Dover 1974, p.222.
13   Cairns 1993, pp.363–70.
14   Cairns 1993, pp.414–19.
15   Cairns 1993, pp.424–5.

(*metameleia*) in distinguishing actions performed in ignorance which can and cannot be regarded as entirely involuntary (*NE* 1110b18–24).[16]

In Plato, questions of remorse and reparation arise most immediately in a penology which has its roots in the Socratic dictum that no one willingly does wrong and the conviction that injustice is a sickness of the soul analogous to bodily disease. Thus its expressed aim is 'cure' or reform.[17] The fullest account, moreover, encompasses a recognition that the response to an offence must also take account of the recompense due to the victim (*Laws* 862bc etc.);[18] thus through both reform and reconciliation the aim is reintegration of the offender into society.[19] We can therefore conclude that something like remorse or repentance is often presupposed. But while remorse may be implicit in the theory, it is disappointingly absent from the practical detail. We are probably justified in assuming that repentance is required of those curable heretics who undergo five years' re-education in the *sôphronistêrion* (*Laws* 908a–909a: sincere renunciation of heterodoxy is a requirement of release on a form of probation – recidivism to be punishable by death);[20] and the 'pardon' to be extended to perpetrators of involuntary homicide and homicide in anger once they have completed their required periods of exile (866a, 867e) might well, in the natural course of things, involve some expression of regret from the killer, but repentance only explicitly enters the picture in so far as the presence or absence of *metameleia* in one who has killed in anger affects the seriousness of the crime and the severity of the penalty.[21] Only here does the nature of the 'cure' depend on the presence or absence of remorse, and the point at which remorse makes a difference is not (explicitly) when it comes to the lifting of exile, but in the immediate aftermath of the offence.[22] Elsewhere it seems merely to be assumed that punishment of a traditional type will bring about the desired reform, with little effort to tailor the

---

16 For genuine remorse over unintentional action, see Herodotus 1. 45: Adrastus' profound distress and desire to be punished for unintentionally causing the death of his benefactor's son elicit (but are not assuaged by) Croesus' forgiveness. Other examples in Cairns 1993, pp.215–19; Williams 1993, pp.68–74; Gill 1996, pp.90–1.

17 *Gorgias* 477a–480d, 504b–505b, 507d (cf. *Protagoras* 324ac), where traditional methods of punishment are justified in reformative terms; but in *Laws* Plato explicitly declares his willingness to consider any form of treatment, not just the infliction of harm, if it will bring about the desired change in the offender (862d; cf. 862b–863a in general); see Mackenzie 1981; Saunders 1991.

18 Saunders 1991, pp.1, 144, and *passim*.

19 Saunders 1991, pp.50, 317, 352.

20 Saunders 1991, pp.157–8, 309–12, 317.

21 *Laws* 866d–868a with Saunders 1991, pp.155–6, 192, 225–31; at *Phaedo* 114a *metameleia* influences the fate of souls after death.

22 Neither class of offender is 'unjust' in the Platonic sense (homicide in anger is not fully voluntary); thus their injustice does not require 'cure', though they need to learn to control their anger (867c). But this is probably not the primary aim of the exile (Saunders 1991, pp.221–4).

remedy to the psychology of the offender, and in a number of cases the gravity of the offence itself is said to be adequate indication of the offender's 'incurability'.[23]

If a role for remorse is conceivable in Plato's penology, it is perhaps surprising that the topic is so scarce in the functioning legal system of Athenian democracy. Part of the explanation for this is that, where Plato's penology is broadly 'humanitarian', classical Athenian views are essentially retributive.[24] But there are also characteristic features of Athenian law which conspire to limit the extent to which remorse might feature in the legal process.[25] There was no distinction between civil and criminal law, and most cases had to be initiated by a private individual; an amateur prosecutor thus undertook to engage a defendant in a personal, adversarial struggle. State involvement in this process was low; there were no professional judges or advocates, and no cross-examination of witnesses or expert evaluation of evidence took place; witnesses demonstrated the power of a litigant's 'connections', and even statutory law was at the mercy of the litigants' rhetorical manipulation. Finally, the issue was decided by a large popular jury which received no legal guidance and had no opportunity formally to confer before reaching a verdict. These circumstances combine to make the trial a contest which the defendant has every interest in defending and every chance of winning, if he can persuade the dikasts to support him; this project is much less one of establishing one's innocence in terms of the 'facts of the case' than of convincing the representatives of the city-state that one does not deserve to be defeated by this opponent in this contest. There is thus little incentive (indeed little opportunity) for a defendant to plead guilty, hoping that his remorse will secure a more lenient sentence.[26] Since, moreover, there was no right of appeal against verdict or sentence, little use of imprisonment as a regular penalty, no probation, and no parole, clearly the circumstances in which remorse is relevant in modern penal systems do not obtain in the Athenian.

There are two areas of procedure in which a role for remorse is conceivable, though unattested. A man exiled for involuntary homicide had the opportunity to return, provided he could persuade the victim's relatives to grant him 'pardon'

23   Saunders 1991, pp.232–3, 251, 311–12, 317, 355.

24   Saunders 1991, pp.120–2.

25   Todd 1990 and 1993; Cohen 1995; cf. Dover 1974, pp.158–9, 292–5; Saunders 1991, p.123.

26   Aeschines' speech against Timarchus does refer to something like a guilty plea: Timarchus, accused of theft while holding elected military office, admitted the offence and (apparently) entered a plea in mitigation which brought a lighter penalty (1. 113). Aeschines assimilates this case, involving one of the procedures available to prosecute the misconduct of public officials, to the process by which some forms of common theft were dealt with, in which thieves who admitted their guilt were put to death, those who denied it sent for trial (cf. 1. 91; MacDowell 1978, pp.148–9); here, as in other cases, Athenian procedure provides a powerful disincentive to confession.

(*aidesis*).[27] This could have involved the exile's attempting to convince the relatives of his regret for the loss he had caused them; but the fact that the term for this institution is derived from *aidôs*, the emotion which protects one's own and acknowledges others' honour, suggests that, in origin, *aidesis* was a response to a form of self-abasement, analogous to supplication.[28] Certain cases required that the jury take a second vote to choose between penalties proposed by defence and prosecution in a brief post-verdict speech;[29] here there is room for representations of regret in a defendant who has, after all, been found guilty, but no evidence that anyone took advantage of this opportunity.

A few passages in the orators, however, bear directly on the topic of remorse. Pleading (c. 408 BC) before the assembly to be allowed to return from exile, Andocides argues that his previous error (*hamartia*) was entirely out of character and contrasts it with his present desire to make amends to the *dêmos*. In a sense he does repudiate his offence, but does so by means of a bizarre sophistry: while his body has persisted through time, his mind (*gnômê*, opinion, judgement) has changed; his previous *gnômê* was guilty, but his body was always innocent, and now houses a new, innocent *gnômê* (2. 24–5). The way in which this argument is both like and unlike what we should expect in similar circumstances suggests something of the unfamiliarity of a straightforward plea of remorse in Athenian legal and political contexts.[30]

The homicide speeches of Antiphon twice use the effects of a good *versus* a guilty conscience as an argument to invite the jury to infer the speaker's innocence from his confident demeanour.[31] These passages recognize that an offender might feel remorse, but the hypothesis of the remorseful offender which they exploit remains unrealized.[32] What one does find is the warning of the possibility of remorse on the part of the dikasts at condemning the innocent or acquitting the guilty.[33]

The paucity of evidence for remorse in Athenian court speeches is a function of their status as scripts in a 'social drama', in which participants in an often long-running dispute use the court as a means to establish their relative status in the citizen community.[34] Litigation at Athens thus belongs in the context of more general, extra-legal strategies of status-rivalry. Here, questions of reparation and

---

27   Heitsch 1984.

28   Heitsch 1984, pp.9–12.

29   MacDowell 1978, pp.253–4.

30   Saunders 1991, p.119.

31   Antiphon 5. 93, 6. 1; Cairns 1993, pp.348–50.

32   As it is in allegations of an opponent's lack of remorse (Lysias 3. 7, 10; 14. 29).

33   Antiphon 3. d. 9; 4. a. 4; 5. 88–9, 91–2; 6. 6; Gorgias B 11a. 36 DK; Lycurgus, *Leocr.* 146; Mackenzie 1981, p.110 n. 102; Saunders 1991, p.110; Cairns 1993, pp. 345–8.

34   Osborne 1985, pp.52–3; Cohen 1995, pp.23, 82, 87–118, 139, 186.

of adopting the correct attitude towards one's past actions can be important, but neither need be particularly associated with remorse. The position demanded of the agent, for example, *vis-à-vis* his/her past behaviour can be one of public demonstration of dishonour or unworthiness, such as Hecuba demands of Helen in Euripides' *Troades* of 415 BC (1025–8: Helen should go humbly in rags, trembling, her head shorn, manifesting modesty rather than shamelessness on account of her errors).[35] In the paradigm case of status-rivalry in Greek culture (the quarrel between Achilles and Agamemnon in the *Iliad*) Achilles certainly seeks a form of recompense from Agamemnon, but the medium through which he wishes his loss of honour to be made good is the non-material one of emotional distress: Agamemnon will not persuade Achilles until he pays back 'all the heart-rending *lôbê* [outrage]' (*Iliad* 9. 378–87);[36] he does not need the honour invested in Agamemnon's gifts, but will wait until the fulfilment of Zeus' plan reveals his true worth to all (9. 607–10). Thus Achilles demands a form of reparation which does not immediately turn on the requirement that Agamemnon – universally agreed to be in the wrong, even by himself[37] – should express his regret;[38] he requires not an apology as a prelude to forgiveness, but a public demonstration of the relative status of the two men.[39]

In these examples, as in our use of an offender's remorse as a sign of willingness to be rehabilitated, focus on one's offence and its implications is required, in order to indicate a readiness to play by the prevalent social rules. Displaying and demanding remorse is thus an important strategy in the maintenance of co-operation, but it is not the only such strategy. There is ample evidence that the Greeks, at all periods, were capable of remorse, and some Greeks recognized that emotion's moral significance. But the near-total absence from Athenian forensic oratory of the offender's remorse and desire to make reparation, which belongs with a tendency, in legal and extra-legal disputes, to place greater emphasis on questions of status than on acceptance of one's guiltiness *per se*, shows how the strategy of accepting the inappropriateness of one's actions can be construed very differently in different cultures, and how the demand for reparation can take forms other than the requirement to show remorse.

---

35   The attitude demanded resembles that forced upon adulteresses at Athens; see MacDowell 1978, p.125. More broadly, the penalty of *atimia* ('dishonour', loss of [certain] citizen rights) would in effect demand that the offender accept and demonstrate publicly his loss of stature.

36   Mackenzie 1981, pp.77–9.

37   2. 239–40, 377, 9. 104–11, 523, 13.107–15, 19. 85–6, 181–3. At 9. 372–3 Achilles assumes that Agamemnon knows he is in the wrong, but this is not enough to satisfy him.

38   Even when offering recompense at the quarrel's resolution, Agamemnon is careful *not* to apologize (*Iliad* 19. 78–144); he admits liability, but excuses himself from culpability in an exercise regularly regarded as a chapter in the history of ideas (Dodds 1951), but more readily explicable in terms of the politics of 'face'.

39   Mackenzie 1981, p.81.

CHAPTER 14

'Abhorring of Himselfe is a Remembering of Himselfe'

Cases of Conscience in the Universe of Shakespeare Plays

John S. Wilks

Shakespearean concepts of moral choice – conscience, remorse, reparation – intervene in a larger debate concerning the ethical status of man which became particularly acute in post-Reformation England. The great philosophical project of the Middle Ages had essentially been one of synthesis – the harmonizing of revelation with reason, of the categories of grace and nature: the effect of the Reformation was largely to fracture the epistemological coherence earlier achieved. The medieval achievement, essentially an absorption and Christianizing of Aristotle, was carried out by schoolmen such as Philip the Chancellor, Alexander of Hales but, above all, by the monumental *Summa Theologica* of Thomas Aquinas: the intellectual impulses brought to bear were ultimately towards the fusion of faith and reason. The theological aims of the Reformers, Luther and Calvin, were the opposite: the philosophical abasement of reason and the simultaneous elevation of faith were to shatter the ordered, rational cosmology of the old medieval world.[1] In the present state of literary scholarship, (though similarly fractured by postmodernistic wars of truth), most commentators would probably agree to situate Shakespeare's moral thinking at the intersection of these late-medieval/Reformation discourses. The following chapter will explore some of these informing discourses and then show how they illuminate Shakespeare's principle 'cases of conscience' as dramatized in *Richard III*, *Hamlet* and *Macbeth*.

---

[1]   The complex philosophical and theological currents of thought which extend from the Middle Ages to the Reformation and beyond have been charted by numerous scholars. See for example Little; New; Davies; Baker; Hoopes; Willey; Copplestone; Kristeller; Hillerbrand; Herndl; Wilks.

Aquinas' *Summa Theologica* had based itself on the premise that religion is intelligibly rational and reason fundamentally religious. The great principle of order is a series of rationally apprehensible effects predicated upon a divine cause: creatures exist, as Aristotle had suggested, to realize their particular natures after their own kinds; but this secular dispensation was authorized for Aquinas by revelation. The created world of scholasticism was therefore a God-centred teleology of purposive realization after the Aristotelian model; but man was accorded a special place in the scheme, since revelation had ordered him to a perfection beyond himself, and a participation in the divine nature (Aquinas, Part 2.1.Q.90–94). This elevation of reason and emphasis upon the divine sanction of natural law allowed, within the providentialist thesis, at least a conditional validity to the idea of individual freedom and responsibility.

The universe of Shakespeare's plays, still recognizably medieval in character, has inherently a legal basis: its moral axes are intelligibly rational, and it is permeated by a conception, scholastic in origin, of the natural law to which all creation is bound. In the individual, conscience (where invoked) functions as the internalized register of violations of this moral design, and a psychological witness of man's 'unnatural' dysfunction within it. By the same token, the reverberating concatenations in the world of nature that accompany such dysfunctions – ghosts, portents, the shroud of perpetual night in *Macbeth* – serve as theatrical metaphors for a breach in the legal ecology of the macrocosm.[2]

The scholastics, and their heirs in the Anglican casuistical tradition of the seventeenth century, posited a dual taxonomy to the moral faculty in man, which they perceived as operating according to a discursive logic very like that of scholasticism itself. Conscience itself was an ongoing function of the rational soul, a syllogistic dialogue between *synderesis* (the implicit register of natural law) and *conscientia* (the active witness, applying the universal propositions of the synderesis to particular cases).[3] *Synderesis* was considered an innate disposition of the reason, by which basic deontic premises (i.e. those implying ethical obligation or permissibility) could be known without intellection. Its dispositional tendency in turn implied that the human soul was appetitively inclined towards the good, that its ethical impulses could never be entirely extinguished. As Aquinas makes clear, it is the *conscientia* that is prone to error since evil may arise in the syllogism by which universal and deontic propositions are misapplied to mistaken conclusions (Aquinas, Part 1, Q. 79, Arts. 11–13).

2   The correlations between Elizabethan drama and Renaissance theories of cosmic order have been explored in a general sense by a number of commentators. See for example: Reese; Spencer; Tillyard; Farnham; Lovejoy; Craig; Bush; Danby; Curry.

3   Thomas Aquinas, *Debated Questions on Truth*, 16, 1 (Latin text in S. *Thomae Aquinatis, Opera Omnia*, vol. 22. *Quaestiones disputatae de veritatae*, Rome: *ad Sancta Sabinae*, 1972, 501–28) qtd. in Potts, p.122.

But if the utter extirpation of *synderesis* was impossible (since it was in virtue of its operations that the soul was considered rational) its operations could be impeded, and rationality vitiated therefore, where natural law premises were wilfully and habitually misapplied.[4] Amongst Shakespeare's characters, Richard III and Macbeth dedicate themselves to evil not because of a failure ultimately to recognize the good, but because of a degeneracy of mind on the whole wilfully determined. Thereafter, it is true, habitual and repeated violations could render the guilty conscience either insensitive (cognates: 'hardened', 'seared', 'cauterized') so that it falsely replicated the serenity of the good conscience, or precipitate its fall into despair ('desperata'), both of them deadly states because they undermined the coercive effects of the conscience, making it capable ultimately of judging 'evill good and good evill' (Jones, sigs.Aaa3–Aaa3v; Bourne, sig. C4; Dyke, sigs.D4–D4v; Perkins, pp.67–8). In this way, Macbeth's conscience becomes inured through 'hard use': only when he has 'supp'd full with horrors' can he say:

> I have almost forgot the tase of fears …
> Direness, familiar to my slaughterous thoughts,
> Cannot once start me. (V.v.9–15)

An equally insidious danger lay in the so-called 'doubting' conscience, which is almost certainly how any casuist would have construed Hamlet's dilemma. According to the Thomist tradition, the judgements of the conscience always possessed a binding force, even when misapplied to objectively evil courses. Hence arose what Gallagher calls the 'celebrated double bind' codified by Aquinas, according to which sin appeared in this state inescapable (Gallagher 1991, p.111). To act in doubt was to fail to eradicate potentially corrupting error, to remain vincibly ignorant of the moral premises implicitly known to the synderesis, and culpably ignorant of what ought therefore to be known. As Perkins, the pioneer of seventeenth century casuistry, puts it, 'Whatsover is done with a doubting conscience is a sinne … Whatsover thing is done in or with an erroneous conscience, it is a sinne … What is done against conscience though it erre and be deceived, it is a sinne in the doer' (Perkins, pp.41–2). Hamlet's delay, for so long the interpretative crux of the play, is partly attributable in this view to the unexpressed obligation to eradicate culpable ignorance, the kind of conscientious doubt induced by the ethical ambiguities inherent in the Ghost's command to revenge.

Much of the coercive authority of the conscience, its capacity to make 'cowards of us all' (*Hamlet*, III.i.85), lay in its power to induce the biting pangs of remorse. In the literature of seventeenth century casuistry the most salient

---

4   Aquinas, *Debated Questions on Truth*, 16.3, Discussion, qtd. in Potts, pp.128–9.

metaphors for the guilty conscience are either eschatological: the hellish Furies, the tormenting fiends and the never-dying worm of conscience, or forensic: the judge, the jailor, the hangman, the torturer. The possessor of an evil conscience, according to Robert Harris, endured the utmost conceivable agonies of mind, living out in anticipation the torture of hell-pains: thus the bad conscience:

> puts one to intolerable paines, it racks the memory, and makes it run backward twenty yeeres, as *Josephs* brethren, and *Aristocrates* in *Plutarch*, yea, it twinges for sinnes of youth, as Job complaines, it racks the understanding, and carries it forward beyond the grave, and makes it feele the verie bitternesse of death and hell, before it sees them; it racks the phantasie, and makes it see ghosts in men, Lyons in children, as it is storied of some. (Harris, sig.C3)

Whether remorse could lead on to reparation was, for seventeenth century casuists, filiated to the Augustinian logic of election and reprobation. To the elect, an evil conscience had an aspect of providential goodness, since its judgements were reformatory, a preparation for that spiritual conversion initiated in the mysteries of the divine will itself. In the *foro interno* of the conscience, according to Perkins's great pupil William Ames, the *'Judgement of repentance maketh void the judgement of punishment'* now and in the hereafter (Ames, sig.F4), and moreover could lead on to the unspeakable earthly bliss of the good conscience. Repentance, of course, was the essential condition of forgiveness. Thus Thomas Playfere testifies to the ultimately beneficent effects of a guilt-stricken conscience: of the contrite, he says, 'For this abhorring of himselfe is a recovering of himselfe: and the sooner hee repents in dust and ashes, the sooner he is freede from all his sinnes, and from all the punishments due to the same' (Playfere, sig.18). This is the remedy offered by Hamlet to his mother: 'Confess yourself to heaven' (III.iv.140), and, indeed, the object of the Duke's instruction to Juliet in *Measure for Measure*: 'how you shall arraign your conscience/And try your penitence' (II.iii.22–3). In fact, it may be averred that the theme of penitence followed by forgiveness, most fully worked out in the final comedies, is very close to the heart of Shakespeare's moral viewpoint.

However, for the reprobate, the evil conscience was an instrument of the execution of divine justice and their own perdition, since its torments induced only desperation and despair, themselves damnable states. As Ames puts it:

> *A Desperate Conscience* (fully representing all sinnes, together with their exceeding great and unpardonable guilt, and Gods fearefull wrath abiding upon Sinners ...) is Gods most powerfull meanes to torment the Reprobate; like unto a worme, that most sharply biteth and gnaweth their hearts for ever ... (Ames, sig.G3v)

The relationship between conscience and free will becomes increasingly vexed in the seventeenth century. As the quotation from Ames would suggest, conscience becomes as much an instrument as agent of man's moral destiny within a metaphysical universe which, following Luther and Calvin, has tilted perceptibly towards determinism. I have argued elsewhere that, whilst Shakespeare is not immune towards this tendency, the pervasive ingress of markedly voluntarist formulas of belief is more clearly demonstrable in the work of later Renaissance dramatists such as Webster and Ford, who represent a morally capitulated world where the function of conscience is simply to render inexcusable a compulsive degeneracy seen as humanly natural: Calvin's 'voluntary slaves' in action, 'bound by the fetters of sin' (Wilks; Calvin, 2.2.7). Although *Macbeth* seems uneasily poised within the spectrum offered by the 'unfree freedom' of a providentially ordered world, Shakespeare more typically tends to assume as a *datum* the possibility of moral autonomy within it. However, in the process he allows due weight to what would nowadays be called genetic and environmental factors: questions of birth, social custom and ingrained habit are seen as significant encroachments upon the effectiveness of the conscience freely to discriminate or register the moral status of action. Many of these questions are brought to bear in the representation of three major Shakespearean characters, Richard III, Hamlet and Macbeth, to a discussion of which I shall now turn.

Richard's case of conscience is complicated by the fact that his crippled body is quite intentionally constituted as the physical and theatrical sign of a signified moral condition. Because of this, Richard tends not only to be seen as a conventional villain but also as artistically unintegrated: an otherwise remorseless psychopath whose fifth-act recognition that crime does not pay is psychologically implausible, no more than an unmotivated gesture paid to the play's ideological underpinnings as Tudor propaganda. According to this argument, there is no psychological continuity between the monster who throughout mocks conscience, and the man who, in the babbling dreams of the eve of Bosworth, is finally mocked by it. However, the theme of repressed guilt runs as a leitmotif throughout the play, especially in the conscience-stricken colloquy between Clarence's murderers and in the terrible dreams that afflict Clarence and Richard on the eve of their deaths. All these testify to the extent to which the warning voice of conscience, however ruthlessly suppressed, would inevitably give way to its accusing voice. As the casuist would put it: 'There is a warning conscience, and a gnawing conscience. The warning conscience commeth before sinne: The gnawing conscience followeth after sinne. The warning conscience is often lulled a sleepe: but the gnawing conscience waketh her againe' (Smith, sig. Ggg3v).

That Richard's conscience is in this way defective (rather than absent) is shown by Shakespeare's concern to suggest its origins in emotional deprivation and a classically delinquent childhood. His mother's horrified reaction to his birth, their mutual antipathy, the 'Tetchy and wayward infancy', the 'wild and furious schooldays' (IV.iv.169–70), all contribute to the famous opening soliloquy, in which Richard extenuates and justifies his choice of villainy in terms of his natural and acquired disadvantages:

> And therefore, since I cannot prove a lover
> To entertain these fair well-spoken days,
> I am determined to prove a villain … (I.i.28–30)

The soliloquy suggests, in short, not only the freely-willed suppression of conscience 'Dive thoughts, down to my soul' (I.i.41), but also in its self-justifying logic, a mind not wholly at ease with its own inclinations. Although for much of his subsequent career in slaughter, Richard's conscience remains hidden by the hysterical self-assertion, the contempt for his victims, the intoxicated zest for histrionics that are all part of the stage persona of the 'Machiavel', it continues to erupt in the 'timorous dreams' (IV.i.84) reported by his queen and in the hastily-repressed compunction over the murders of the princes in the Tower:

> Uncertain way of gain! But I am in
> So far in blood that sin will pluck on sin;
> Tear-falling pity dwells not in this eye. (IV.ii.65–7)

On the eve of Bosworth, Richard's hitherto self-confident ego begins to disintegrate; the conscience, its warning functions 'hardened' into 'security', now recoils upon him, multiplying his villainies in a 'thousand several tongues' as the ghosts of his victims accuse him, thronging to the 'bar' in an apocalyptic vision of judgement (V.v.147,153). True to the pathology of the evil conscience, it now induces the terrors of desperation, which Richard, like Macbeth, can only flee by plunging self-destructively into battle. Of course the didactic necessities of history required that Richard be unequivocally beyond reparation. Hence, even his final courage at Bosworth is seen as a species of theological despair into which the 'reprobate' conscience drives him, and for which he must be damned, since upon his unredeemed degeneracy rested in large measure the claims of the Tudor settlement.

Hamlet's predicament is in complete contrast, for he is a man upon whom is imposed the hard necessity of action in a world so overwhelmingly flawed by the ambiguities of evil, that the principles of well-doing and any absolute certainty as to integrity of motive, are alike rendered obscure. In so far as he must act, there exist at the same time serious impediments to action of both an internal and external nature; but one powerful inhibition is his conscientious doubt, intermittently recognized, as to the ethical status of the action he is called upon to accomplish. For Hamlet's dilemma is that he reviles and despises his incestuous and murdering uncle, which excites in him the baser motive of a bloody but private revenge; at the same time this course is apparently sanctioned by heavenly mandate, together with obligations incurred by Hamlet's heir-apparent duty to execute public justice in the public interest. Apparently sanctioned – but for his conscience, as casuists would have testified, that is pre-eminently the question. Aquinas had warned that sin committed through an error of conscience is almost invariably mortal, except in cases of factual mistake. And yet in the terms of Thomistic analysis, Hamlet's responsibilities seem exacerbated still further because they are governed by two contradictory deontic premises: that the heavens ought to be obeyed, and that man shall not kill.

Thus Hamlet remains paralyzed in the grip of this dilemma, the implications of which he only partly perceives, vacillating between the state of doubt and error in the conscience according to the ebb and flow of his passions, all of which derives from that original failure in reason to discern what Aquinas calls the 'ultimate good' (Aquinas, Part 2.1, Q.77, Art.1). Restrained by the dispositional light of his *synderesis*, Hamlet does not know why what he feels bound to do by conscience and duty still remains undone. This hypothesis allows us to appreciate, not only the origin of that curious reversal of values which permits in Hamlet the apparently remorseless destruction of Ophelia, Polonius, and Rosencrantz and Guildenstern ('They are not near my conscience', V.ii.59): but also to explain the paradox by which a prince, whose intention is palpably to destroy evil, nonetheless comes so preposterously to further it.

At the end, a dying Hamlet kills the guilty Claudius, thus cleansing the state of what was 'rotten' in it, and wins through to a putative redemption in which 'flights of angels' will sing him to his rest (V.ii.312). What has changed, put succinctly, is the quality of his motive: returning from England, he seems to abandon the passionate purpose of a private revenge which before had blinded his reason and conscience, and submits his will to what he sees as the shaping ordinance of providential justice, tempered both to exact its punishment on Claudius and accept his own death, should that also be decreed (V.ii.165–709).

An oblique fatalism seems to invest Macbeth, in a world even more profoundly suffused by the ambiguities of evil. The opening incantation of the Weird Sisters, 'Fair is foul and foul is fair' (I.i.10) symbolizes at the outset both the deep moral equivocation at the heart of this world, and the fatal inversions of value that precipitate Macbeth's downfall. This mysterious ambivalence extends to the prophecies themselves: that their partial truths are consecutively revealed as fact confirms Banquo's intuition that the Sisters are 'instruments of darkness' (I.iii.122), and invites the suspicion that Macbeth is foredoomed from the start. At the same time, Macbeth apparently confers upon the prophecies their only power to destroy him and proceeds upon moral choices freely made, and in defiance of his conscience, to embark deliberately and unnecessarily upon an evil course. In fact he draws all the unnecessary inferences: that chance will not crown him without Duncan's murder; to endow the augury 'beware Macduff' (IV.i.87) with a fateful certainty by the needless slaughter of his family; and finally to yield himself up to Macduff by abandoning his castle. Indeed, one source of the play's philosophical profundity lies in its ability to dramatize the tenuous division between the free act and the determined one (Sanders 1968, p.282). But it is also true that whatever original freedom Macbeth possesses is gradually circumscribed by the predictions which co-opt his will: which nurse into being the germ of ambition, infect and impair his conscience, debilitate his reason, and collapse the moral categories so that 'nothing is but what is not' (I.iii.140–1).

Set against Macbeth's ambition is, of course, his conscience. Though often compared to Richard, Macbeth is no monstrous psychopath; on the contrary, his conscience provides the most terrifyingly eloquent commentary on its own violation in the whole of literature. Whether in its warning or accusing voices, it is a harrowing witness to the corrosive effects of evil upon the psyche. Before the murder of Duncan, Macbeth's conscience registers a moral squeamishness so acute that we are made to feel that were it not for the fatal constellation of external factors – the glorious victory, the installation of the heir-apparent Malcolm, his wife's urgings – it might have prevailed upon his will and passions. In the aftermath, his conscience transmutes into accusing mode, excoriating him with terrible dreams and lacerating remorse. But as his career in slaughter accelerates, so his reason becomes increasingly corrupted. Whilst moral insights are still fitfully supplied by the *synderesis*, they become fatally perverted and misapplied in the treacherous paralogic of a will seeking to habituate itself to evil. He knows that reparation is available to him, that like the traitor Cawdor, he might '[confess] his treasons' and 'set forth/A deep repentance' (I.iv.5–7). He knows the further murders of Banquo, Fleance and Macduff's family to be an outrage upon law and conscience; yet he deludes himself that the anodyne to conscience lies in the utter extirpation of its natural-law precepts.

But the peace that Macbeth finally attains, though it secures him from racking torments and spectral visions, is of the kind well known to casuists as 'carnal security' – in which state the '*reprobate minde*' 'judgeth evill good, and good evill' and the conscience thus '*seared*' registers no 'feeling or remorse' (Perkins, p.68). The weary indifference with which he receives the news of his wife's death – 'She should have died hereafter' (V.iv.16) – testify to a kind of *rigor mortis* of the soul, a callousness to human pain or pity. By the end, his life is emptied of positive value: the past and future amount to a dreary continuum, a meaningless tedium of successive tomorrows stretching to the grey horizon of time and eternity. This is the ultimate tragedy of Macbeth as, in staring stonily across the void of his own moral annihilation, he recognizes its terrible cost in the cancellation of his own humanity.

In sum then, the intellective and rational nature of the conscience as formulated in the Renaissance enabled its operations to be described in terms of a syllogism in which the natural law intuitions of the *synderesis* were actualized in the *conscientia* and applied therein to particular cases. Moreover, the act of moral discrimination takes place in a variably conditioned moral ethos, but one which centres responsibility firmly in man: Shakespeare's tragic heroes act according to a free will counselled by a conscience which is in turn dispositionally oriented towards the ultimate good. Thus Richard rationalizes his depravity in terms that show it to be a choice freely undertaken, whilst Hamlet's conscientious scruples are subjected to a recurrent process of intellection whose moral co-ordinates are, if not immediately clear, at least philosophically unconfined. In Macbeth, the axes of free will versus fore-ordination are held in less auspicious counterpoise, rendering more oblique that slippery slope whereby a man may consign himself, by destruction, to an involuntary doom.

The case of Hamlet is unique as a study of the doubting or erroneous conscience; also unique is its artistic documentation of an instance of reparation unheralded by any obvious signs of remorse. The syndrome of the warning and accusing conscience is fully complete only in Macbeth; the former is wilfully repressed in Richard; the latter afflicts both equally; but in either mode, it is characteristically livid with the kind of visions and appalling sights that afflict both individuals. In neither case can remorse lead on to reparation, since the terminal convulsions of the seared conscience and the inverted categories of the reprobate mind can lead only to desperation and theological despair.

CHAPTER 15

Kierkegaard and Remorse

Remorse is an Existential Concern

Bjarne Jacobsen and Alice Theilgaard

INTRODUCTION

Søren Kierkegaard (1813–1855)

1813 was the year in which Søren Kierkegaard was born in Copenhagen. It was also the year in which the Danish state became bankrupt, after an exhausting war lasting six years with the English. He describes his entrance into this world in his characteristically ironic and metaphorical style:

> *When so many other mad notes were put to circulation. And my existence seems best to be compared with such a note. There is something with me, as if I was something great, but due to the mad devaluation of the currency, I am only valid for a little.* (V, A, 3 (our translation[1]))

The question of human value is a general theme in the life and authorship of Kierkegaard, and he is convinced that the value ought to have a transcendent foundation. Only by relating to a value beyond human existence is basic human equality obtainable. This is one of the essential reasons for his publishing approximately half of his work under pseudonyms. By letting pseudonyms carry the responsibility, he hoped that his writings would intensify the reader's focus on the meaning, or rather meanings of the text, because those works written under fictitious names are not confined to one meaning. Assisted by sharp psychological analyzes, he puts forward the question of the meaning of life. A proper answer to this question is first offered in the second part of the Kierkegaardian canon. This does not follow the pseudonymous writings, but was published concurrently. Those parts of the writings known as 'Christian edifying discourses', carry his own name.

---

1 Direct quotations from Kierkegaard are printed in italics and are in Hong and Hong's translation, unless otherwise stated.

As his authorship is stamped by irony, so it appeared that the destiny of his writings also became ironic. Kierkegaard says about his first two works, a pseudonymous one, and one published in his own name, respectively:

With my left hand I passed Either-Or *to the world, with my right* Two Upbuilding Discourses, *but everyone – or almost everyone grasped with their right hand after the left hand.* (vol. 18, p.91 (our trans.))

The pseudonym-authorship which Kierkegaard almost disclaims – *there is not a single word of my self* (vol. 10, p.286 (our trans.)), and for which he does not want to be quoted (vol. 10; p.287 (our trans.)) – is first and foremost appealing to the readers' attention. In this chapter we also grasp the left hand of the author, who in a biographical sense lived a relatively simple life which is easy to survey, though his mind was passionately occupied by the few events filling his life: the father, the engagement to Regine Olsen – and the breaking of it – his fight with the press (The Cosar-discord) and his showdown with the Danish State Church. He grappled with problems – or perhaps only with a single problem – which, in his own terms, constituted the nerve in his whole production.

After my death (that is my comfort) no one will find in my papers a single item of information of what has essentially filled my life. Neither will he find the script in my mind which explains everything, and which often makes what the world would call trivial, yet which has enormous significance to me. But when I withdraw the explanatory secret note, it is reduced to insignificance. (IV, A, 85 (our trans.))

Kierkegaard and the Concept of Remorse

It has been Kierkegaard's destiny – as a great but not very accessible thinker and writer – to lend his name to many thoughts and viewpoints which would have been foreign to the Danish theologian and philosopher himself. Although the present chapter does not pretend to do justice to Kierkegaard, we hope that he does not entirely disappear in our attempt to apply his thoughts in a psychological context.

The Danish word for remorse is *anger*[2], of Old Norse origin, covering the meaning both of grief and harm. The etymological root of the word is *ang* (narrow), and is akin to *angst* (dread and fear) and also related to Latin *angor*: oppression of spirit.

'Remorse' is not a psychological term and it appears very rarely in psychological literature, but Kierkegaard's understanding of the word has profound psychological implications. One of the difficulties when reading

---

2   Both the words *remorse* and *repentance* are covered by the Danish word: *anger*. Kierkegaard also sometimes uses the word *ruelse* linked to the English word *rue*.

Kierkegaard is his idiosyncratic application of words and concepts. He does so without defining the words anew, which obviously creates great problems for the translator, when one tries to be as true as possible to his particular verbal style.

It is in practice valid for all of Kierkegaard's central concepts that they mutually elucidate each other. Therefore, it is very difficult to break into his text-corpus and lay claim to a single concept, without either accepting the total Kierkegaardian conceptual universe or running the risk of violating the way in which a chosen concept has taken shape in his texts. We are aware that space clearly does not permit a true 'unpacking' of Kierkegaard's terminology, but in the following we try to present his conceptual view of remorse.

Remorse relates to Kierkegaard's theory of stages of life's way as a borderline-phenomenon between the ethical and the religious. It refers to his distinction between the internal and the external, between recollection and remembering.

Furthermore, the concept of remorse is related to his spiritual view of man, to Christianity, indeed to Kierkegaard's total understanding of man. The question is not whether the remainder of his concepts constitute a Kierkegaardian-inspired analysis of the concept of remorse, but rather where the limit should be drawn, and where the essential interface is.

In order to speak of remorse in a meaningful way three conditions have to be considered:

(1) Man must be free. If man, like a flower or a dove, is spun in a causal interlacing pattern, it is meaningless to speak of remorse. Only if an act both could and could not be performed, may we refer to remorse.

(2) Man must live in time, and time must live in man. If the past cannot offer itself in the now with all its strength and meaning, then we cannot truly speak of remorse.

(3) Finally man has to relate to value; only if the act concerned can be seen in the light of good and evil, right or wrong, can it be a question of remorse.

All three conditions are essential aspects in the anthropology of Kierkegaard, of his philosophical and theological view of man, which cannot be separated from his psychological outlook.

MAN AS FREEDOM – POSSIBILITY AND NECESSITY

Kierkegaard operates with a trichotomy of man: a soul, a body, a spirit, *and the spirit is the self. But what is the self? The self is a relation that relates itself to itself, or is the relation's relating itself to itself in the relation* (1980, p.13 (orig. 1849, p.73)).

Thus there is both a relation and something in this relation, which relates to the relation. Kierkegaard sees this as a relation between possibility and necessity (ibid.). While the necessity is the inevitable, including the past which we cannot alter, the possibility comprises everything which might be different, not least the future. The self is this confrontation between the possible and the necessary, and not only the confrontation, but it is also that the person confronts himself with these categories. The disparity should not be united (*forenes*) in a third, but come to an agreement (*enes*) in a third. *The synthesis is unthinkable, when the two do not agree in the third. This third is the spirit* (vol. 6, p.137 (our trans.)).

This relating to one's own disagreement is freedom. *The self is freedom. But freedom is the dialectical aspect of the categories of possibility and necessity* (1980, p.29 (orig. 1849, p.87)).

Kierkegaard's concept of freedom should not be confused with free will. Freedom is not an ability with which man is endowed, which enables him to do as he pleases with the multitude of existence. Existence itself is a possibility, even if this possibility does not contain other than necessity. Kierkegaard is very precise, when he states: *For freedom, the possible is the future, and the future is for time the possible* (1980, p.91, in R. Thomte's trans. (orig. 1844, p.179)).

MAN IN TIME, TIME IN MAN – TIME AND ETERNITY

Time is an essential aspect in the Kierkegaardian anthropology: to be human is to be conscious of time. As man is determined by the possible and the necessary, so is he also defined by the eternal and the temporal.

Time is the infinite succession (vol. 6, p.174 (our trans.)). Time is a constant stream without any past, present and future. Or rather, more correctly: time's past, present and future are only imaginary.

We can step outside time and consider it in its different phases, but time itself does not provide a foothold, where past, present and future exist. It means that man is able to survey time and attend to the right time (in time). But for that reason, time does not become momentous for the individual, which is also expressed in the phrase: killing time.

The eternal is not a temporal category. Eternity is not something which is longer than temporality, for were it longer, then it would only be a longer temporality. Eternity is the category in which time reflects itself, and thereby becomes temporality. The tangent of eternity and time *is* the moment (= *øjeblik*, a moment of special nature), and this moment ought to have a special name: *The fullness of time* (vol. 6, p.22 (our trans.)).

Time is thus not a stream which will eventually lead us to eternity. No, time is the medium through which eternity allows itself to be created in the moment, so that time becomes eternally valid and thereby turn into an inner temporality.

Temporality first comes into being the moment I am able and have courage to let time assume eternal importance. If it is beyond my power, time and habit are ready to take over.

> *When authenticity in seriousness is acquired and kept, then there is succession and repetition; as soon as authenticity fails to come in repetition, then habit is there.* (vol. 6, p.229 (our trans.)).

The effort to escape from time is an everyday phenomenon because it implies constant, self-centred worry and concern for existential security (Nordentoft 1972, p.499f).

THE MEANING OF LIFE

Existential philosophers and psychologists are often flapping in their own net. This is especially the case when they have been unable to find out what life is pointing to, at the same time as they have tried to work out the human basis by perspicacious analysis. The analysis shows that something exists, but is unable to say why and for what, it exists. They present the question, but are unable to answer it.

Camus shows the consequences, when he states that without the answer it is just as good to blow the fire in the crematorium as consecrate one's life to nursing the leprous. Evil and virtue are capricious (Camus 1951, p.11 (orig. 1950)). The directions to act crumble away, and the question, naturally, has to be directed to life itself. Why not do as recommended by one of Kierkegaard's figures (vol. 2, p.32): to go down into the grave while participating in a funeral, because all that remains is a row of empty years.

Whereas philosophers often attempt to solve the problem, there is a tendency among psychologists to assume that the meaning of life for each individual is a given (van Deurzen 1988, p.7). Alternatively, they try to avoid the problem by neglecting the question (Yalom 1989, p.12).

As for us, we should like to emphasize the importance of the question as well as the answer, although we recognize that psychological concepts do not bring us closer to a concrete answer to the meaning of life.

Kierkegaard's formal answer rests on the assumption that man is created by something higher:

> *The human self is such a derived, established relation, a relation that relates itself to itself and in relating itself to itself relates itself to another.* (1980, p.13f (orig. 1849, p.73))

There is no doubt that this 'another' for Kierkegaard is the Christian God. In the formal definition, quoted above, when he uses the word 'another' it has the purpose of underlining its universal validity.

In his relation to himself man must relate to something which is not in himself, and which can act as a line of direction. Value is thus given 'outside' and 'before' man. It is important to note that it is not the value as such to which man should relate, but in as much as man relates to himself, shall he relate to the value. And how deeply this value is implanted and thus accessible to the individual – and consequently not of public concern – is demonstrated, when Kierkegaard recommends one to throw away the Bible (IX, A, 442). This, in his opinion, is in the way of 'Christendom'.[3] Kierkegaard's dialectic is here shown at its most ferocious, which, however, calms down when he comes to describe his faith and love.

REMORSE

Remorse arises when the self in freedom chooses itself and its story in relation to the Other – the value of man.

> Now he discovers that the self he chooses has a boundless multiplicity within itself in as much as it has a history – a history in which he acknowledges identity with himself ... this history contains painful things, and yet he is the person he is only through his history ... This makes him uneasy, and yet it must be so, for when the passion of freedom is aroused in him ... he chooses himself and struggles for his possession as for his salvation, and it is his salvation. He can give up nothing of all this, not the most painful, not the hardest, and yet the expression for this struggle, for this acquiring is – repentance. (1987, part II, p.216 (orig. 1843)).

Remorse thus cannot do its work without having dread as its companion, and therefore many people avoid feeling remorse. By understanding one's life in relation to the external, by conceiving it by the lifeless rationality of modernity, dread is diminished. Guilt does not appear in the consciousness of the individual. Man develops a rule of shrewdness by which he becomes unsurpassed in the act of making excuses for himself – instead of repenting. Life turns into a light and irrelevant 'retreat' without remorse and consciousness of guilt.

Remorse and Forgetting

Man is then torn between the possibility of becoming himself and losing himself. While remorse is the relating by which one possesses the painful side of one's own history, the forgetting is the relating by which one avoids one's own painful story.

---

3   Kierkegaard makes a sharp distinction between Christendom and Christianity. Whereas Christendom is the teaching which Jesus also exemplified in his own life, Christianity is the teaching which Jesus also drained from existential meaning. Through the whole body of his work Kierkegaard criticizes modern man in that he acquires the doctrine of the Bible without attributing the least existential meaning to it. His attack against the state church and its ministers – whom he found responsible for this development – became more and more implacable throughout the 1850s.

To forget – this is the desire of all people, and when they encounter something unpleasant, they always say: If only I could forget. (1987, part I, p.293 (orig. 1843))

But to forget does not imply that the forgotten has disappeared or been put to rest. It only means that man does not direct his will and his attention towards the forgotten, and *in an unguarded moment it often surprises a person with the full force of the sudden* (vol. 2, p.271 (our trans.)). It is evident that Kierkegaard here has anticipated Freud's idea of the unconscious. But what is it that is forgotten?

It is not necessarily merely the factual, but the atmosphere, the ethos which gives significance and meaning to the event. The very event may well live on in consciousness, at the same time as the specific mood and atmosphere connected with the event is forgotten.

Memory is immediate. Recollection is reflected (vol. 7, p.8 (our trans.)). Kierkegaard differentiates between the concepts of *memory* (*hukommelse*) and *recollection* (*erindring*) with regard to these two aspects of remembering. And he goes so far as to say that *memory* acts as a repressing agent in relation to *recollection*, the latter housing the significant and valuable. *What is remembered is also forgotten* (vol. 7, p.17 (our trans.)). This is of decisive importance in relation to the phenomenon of remorse, because remorse is a recollection of guilt (vol. 7, p.19), which may be disturbed or eliminated by memory.

Every external interference runs the risk of bringing the repentant to forget guilt. Thus repentance is a recollection of guilt.

From a purely psychological point of view, I really believe that the police aid the criminal in not coming to repent. By continually recounting and repeating his life experiences, the criminal becomes such an expert at rattling off his life that the ideality of recollection is driven away. (1988, part I, p.14 (orig. 1845))

By-Ways of Remorse

Man may avoid remorse, but remorse and guilt may also run wild and thus be maladaptive.

Despair over Sin

Sin is the violation of the good – a violation of value with which man relates. 'Despair is sin.' (vol. 15, p.159 (our trans.))

The potentiation in the relationship between sin and despair over sin could be described as the break with the good, and the break with remorse. (vol.1 5, p.160 (our trans.))

When despairing of sin, man yields and submits to it. It is an attempt to give a holding to sin. (ibid.)

We recognize such contemporary concepts as sociopathy and psychopathy, but Kierkegaard understands them as an inner struggle between good and evil. Through human evolution evil and sin have gained ground to such a degree that man can neither cope nor have courage to face them. On the contrary remorse tends to be disregarded, and the individual hardens himself by becoming obdurate. Kierkegaard makes a comparison with a hot-air balloon which ascends by throwing ballast overboard. He who despairs over his sin by throwing the good overboard becomes lighter, even though he strips the self to the extent that he has not the least to live by – as a result of this manoeuvre (ibid.).

Insane Remorse

Even in remorse a longing for sin may be hidden. (III, A, 85 (our trans.))

Remorse grasps sin in search of freedom, though it cannot overcome it. Such 'insane' remorse does not give up the struggle as it does in 'despair over sin'. *Remorse is reduced to a possibility in relation to sin, in other words, remorse cannot abolish sin; it can only grieve over it* (vol. 6, p.199 (our trans.)).

And while remorse is grieving over sin, sin proceeds. Remorse discovers the consequence of sin, but is unable to prevent it and looks instead on it as a punishment. Sin intends with the acceptance of remorse to reproduce itself. Remorse has gone insane (vol. 6, p.200 (our trans.)).

Mad remorse has a part to play in all forms of vice: aggression, jealousy and intemperance of every kind.

> *The individual may repent of his anger, and the deeper he is, the deeper is his remorse. But the remorse may not set him free; in that he is mistaken. The occasion arrives; dread has already discovered it, every thought quivers, and dread bloodsucks the power of remorse and shakes its head. It is as if the anger has already won, in that it has already had the foreboding of the crush of freedom which is reserved for the next moment. The moment arrives. Anger wins.* (vol. 6, p.200f (our trans.))

Kierkegaard states that this remorse cannot be stopped by *words and figures of speech* (vol. 6, p.200 (our trans.)). Nordentoft (1972, p.367) has pointed to a parallel: Freud's idea of the importance of a guilty conscience for the patient's resistance toward restoration to health.

Temporal Remorse

While the two previous categories demonstrate the fallacy of remorse, the next two are 'incomplete'.

The most 'incomplete' form Kierkegaard describes as that of the 'Philistine'. In this case the individual regretfully acknowledges his fault in order hastily to overcome it: *The sudden remorse will gather all the bitterness of grief in one sweep – and then along* (vol. 11, p.24).

Kierkegaard presents a parable by describing a criminal who accepted his punishment in sincerity; after he had served his sentence, he moved to a foreign place in order to leave his misdemeanours behind him by doing good deeds. One day, however, an acquaintance from the past appeared, and despair took over, *precisely because the remorse had been forgotten* (ibid.).

Immature Remorse

There are different forms of remorse, which do not free the repentant (vol. 11, p.25 (our trans.)):

(1) The one where the repentant continually writhes under his guilt and become exhausted in his daily work; then the remorse is immature

(2) The one where a tiring worry does not leave consciousness, the knowledge of wasted time; there the remorse is immature

(3) The one where the good deed has not been frank and open, because remorse keeps the personality in its guilty conscience; there the remorse is also immature.

From an ethical perspective remorse is paradoxical. For the ethic claims the deed, and where no action has taken place, or when the act has gone wrong, repentance is necessary. But in the moment I repent, I am prevented from acting. True remorse must thus come to an understanding with the freedom of the individual in order not to become its own contradiction.

True Remorse

When living ethically one has to stay in life all the time; when remorse is experienced one cannot stay in life, because one has to look back and cannot, therefore, live in the present. This is to commit a new sin by breaking the continuity. In true remorse temporary cessation also occurs, but it is an interruption, *which sets the continuity* (VII-1, A, 141 (our trans.)). And the set continuity is the inner story. As the person in the moment after the awakening of freedom chooses what he finds right, thus in remorse he also chooses the story which cannot be otherwise. This remorse is neither a blatant nor a conspicuous event, but a quiet, inner and painful taking over of one's self.

It is not a quick and effective by-pass to innocence, but a quiet, daily worry. Thus remorse does not let go its hold on the individual, but becomes a part of him. Paradoxically, remorse also forms the basis for the subsequent healing of the personality, which is neither a specific developmental phase nor something related to a certain age. Such healing, therefore, is the existential emerging of one's self, and this is the ever present possibility for every adult human being.

Man is embedded in time and outside time he is nothing. If you try to collect yourself outside time (outside temporality), you are nothing. *For what else is remorse other than that which looks back – although it hastens the movement to what is ahead* (vol. 6, p. 23 (our trans.)).

REMORSE AND REPARATION

Thus far, it will have appeared that Kierkegaard's concept of remorse is not reserved for a small selected group which the modern tabloid press might describe as ' hardboiled criminals'. Remorse addresses everybody. The criminal has the advantage over the common citizen in that his guilt has become visible, while it is often the latter's destiny to spend his life with the illusion that he is raised above guilt as well as guiltlessness, *for in the crowd of people one does not become guilty, when one is innocent* (vol. 7, p.23 (our trans.)).

> *Let others complain that the times are evil. I complain that they are wretched, for they are without passion … [People's] desires are staid and dull, their passions drowsy; they perform their duties, these mercenary souls … they think that even though the Lord keeps ever so orderly an accountbook, they can still manage to trick him a little. That is why my soul always turns back to the Old Testament and to Shakespeare. One then still feels that those who speak are human beings; there they hate, there they love, there they murder the enemy … there they sin.* (1987, part I, p.27f (orig. 1843))

The wretched, the passionless, the scheming can be helped by remorse. We have to suppose that Kierkegaard would not look with mitigating eyes on modern and postmodern society, but that he is more likely to insist on the importance of remorse: for the individual who himself does not feel the need to repent, and for him whose personality necessitates remorse.

However, the concept of remorse has been largely ignored by modern psychology, and Kierkegaard's particular interpretation is hardly known. This may be due to the fact that his concept of remorse is not therapeutically orientated. It cannot be a therapeutic task to induce the experience of remorse. It cannot be evoked at the command of an other. At best an individual could be given time and space for remorse to develop.

It is also obvious that Kierkegaard's concepts of *Freedom, Time* and *Value* do not correspond with the way in which they are understood today. While freedom at present is understood as the right to act freely, for Kierkegaard the concept implies the capacity to be free. Whereas today time is something which we 'manage', for Kierkegaard it was something one existed in or into which one came into being. Nowadays values are not necessarily stable. In Kierkegaard's terminology they imply a question of *striving to be worthy of one's self.*

In modern culture man is 'liberated'. One of the aims of psychotherapy is to liberate an individual from the restrictive legacy of the past. The flexibility which man has developed in order to survive in the most varied conditions makes the experience of remorse 'foreign' – as man is 'foreign' to himself.

Mersault, in the novel by Camus, *The Stranger*, lives this fragmented life, where nothing is of significance. By coincidence he commits murder. The judge asks him if he repents of his deed. 'I thought carefully and answered, that I probably did not really feel remorse, but rather was annoyed by the deed' (1972, p.78 (orig. 1942)).

Remorse puts the individual in the innermost contact and the greatest connection with the surrounding world (vol. 3, p.223 (our trans.)). But does the world yield? Does it disappear? Or does it offer itself in new seductive forms which compromise my freedom? Thoughts such as these exemplify Kierkegaard's way of expressing the desperate fear of emptiness which is the haunting hallmark of modern man. *For life does not begin now with nothing, and if I cannot repent of the past, then freedom is a dream* (1987, part II, p.239 (orig. 1843)).

CONCLUDING UNSCIENTIFIC POSTSCRIPT

As we stated in the introduction, we are fully aware of the difficulties in trying to present Kierkegaard's views of remorse. This is due not only to the limits of space, but also because his psychological thoughts are often formulated in a dialectic and paradoxical way at a very high level of abstraction and in a terminology foreign to our time. Kierkegaard himself comments as follows: *only insofar as they constitute elements in the realization of the idea I had, but which in an ironical way I was exempted for realizing* (1987, part I, p.xii).

In conclusion, we wish to re-emphasize that, if we accept Kierkegaard's concept of remorse, we concomitantly have to approve of a great part of his conceptual universe. But this appropriation will also enable us to perceive the concept with more nuances than is generally the case in psychological literature. The reason for this is that Kierkegaard shapes the concept in relation to the personality, i.e. who repents before the event to be repented. Remorse is thus in its basic form an existential dimension in every individual; it is not possible to imagine an individual (except perhaps Jesus) for whom the question of remorse will not be topical. This basic delineation of remorse enables Kierkegaard to understand the psychological conditions which compel the individual despairingly relating to remorse; to despair over sin and insane remorse. He is able to analyze remorse in its undeveloped forms, temporal remorse and immature remorse. He demonstrates how the remorselessness of modern man should be considered dialectically in relation to true remorse. The question of remorse will always be existential. When an individual does not repent, this lack of repentance should be seen in relation to a wish not to repent – to avoid his own existence. Kierkegaard's understanding of remorse is thus different from the concept which first and foremost stresses the event calling for repentance or the very act of repenting. A forced or urgent request to repent – whether it originates in the individual himself or whether it comes from outside – will prevent the individual from attaining true remorse. Remorse is an existential concern.

References

Abel, G.G., Becker, J.V., Cunningham-Rathner, J., Rouleau, J., Kaplan, M. and Reich, J. (1984) *The Treatment of Child Molesters*. Available from SBC-TM, 722 West 168th Street, Box 17, New York, NY 10032.

Abrams, P. (1982) *Historical Sociology*. Shepton Mallet: Open Books.

Ainsworth, M. (1982) 'Attachment, retrospect and prospect.' In C.M. Parkes and J. Stevenson-Hinde (eds) *The Place of Attachment in Human Behaviour*. London: Routledge.

Ames, W. (1639) *Conscience with the Power and Cases Thereof*. n.p.

Aquinas, T. (1921?-32) *The Summa Theologica of St Thomas Aquinas*. Trans. the Fathers of the English Dominican Province. 2nd ed. 22 vols. London: Burns, Oates and Washburne.

Ashforth, A. (1996) 'Of secrecy and the commonplace: Witchcraft and power in Soweto.' *Social Research*, Winter 63, 4, 1183–1233.

Austen, J.L. (1961) 'A plea for excuses'. In J.L.Austen, *Philosophical Papers*. Oxford: Oxford University Press.

Baker, H. (1952) *The Wars of Truth: Studies in the Decay of Christian Humanism in the Earlier Seventeenth Century*. Cambridge, MA: Staples Press.

Bauman, Z. (1993) 'Introduction: Morality in modern and postmodern perspective.' In *Postmodern Ethics*. Oxford: Blackwell.

Bendelow, G. and Williams, S.J. (eds) (1998) *Emotions in Social Life: Critical Themes and Contemporary Issues*. London: Routledge

Bender, J. (1987) *Imagining the Penitentiary: Fiction and the Architecture of the Mind in Eighteenth-Century England*. Chicago: University of Chicago Press.

Benedict, R. (1946) *Chrysanthemum and the Sword: Patterns of Japanese Culture*. Boston: Houghton Mifflin.

Bercovitch, E. (1989) 'Moral insights: Victim and witch in the Nalumin imagination.' In G. Herdt and M. Stephen (eds) *The Religious Imagination of New Guinea*. New Brunswick: Rutgers University Press.

Berglund, A.I. (1989). 'Confessions of guilt and restoration of health. Some illustrative Zulu examples.' In *Culture, Experience and Pluralism: Essays on African Ideas of Illness and Healing*. Department of Anthropology, University of Upsala, Sweden: Upsala Studies in Cultural Anthropology.

Bicknell, J. (1983) 'The psychopathology of handicap.' *British Journal of Medical Psychology 56*, 167–178.

Blanck, P.D. (ed) (1993) *Interpersonal Expectations: Theory Research and Applications*. Cambridge: Cambridge University Press.

Bluglass, R. and Bowden, P. (eds) (1990) *Principle and Practice of Forensic Psychotherapy*. Churchill Livingstone.

Blum, L. (1980) *Friendship, Altruism and Morality*. London: Routledge and Kegan Paul.

Boraine, A., Levy, J. and Scheffer. R. (eds) (1994) *Dealing with the Past: Truth and Reconciliation in South Africa*. Cape Town: IDASA.

Bourne, I. (1623) *The Anatomie of Conscience*. London.

Boyle, J. (1977) *A Sense of Freedom*. London: Pan Books.

Braithwaite, J. (1989) *Crime, Shame and Reintegration*. Cambridge: Cambridge University Press.

Braithwaite, J. (1993) 'Shame and modernity.' In *British Journal of Criminology 33*, 1.

Braithwaite, J. and Mugford, S. (1994) 'Conditions of successful reintegration ceremonies: Dealing with juvenile offenders.' *British Journal of Criminology 34*, 2, 139–171.

Briggs, J. (1970) *Never in Anger.* Cambridge, MA: Harvard University Press.

Broad, C.D. (1930) Five Types of Ethical Theory. London: Routledge and Kegan Paul.

Burkitt, I. (1997) 'Social relationships and emotions.' In *Sociology 31* 1, 37–55.

Bush, D. (1939) *The Renaissance and English Humanism.* Toronto: University of Toronto Press.

Cairns, D.L. (1993) *Aidôs: The Psychology and Ethics of Honour and Shame in Ancient Greek Literature.* Oxford: Oxford University Press.

Calvin, J. (1953) *Institutes of the Christian Religion.* Trans. Henry Beveridge. 2 vols. London: James Clark.

Camus, A. (1970) *Oprøreren.* København: Gyldendals Uglebøger (orig. 1950).

Camus, A. (1972) *Den fremmede.* København: Gyldendals Bekkasinbøger (orig. 1942).

Carlisle, Rt. Hon. Lord of Bucklow (1988) *The Parole System in England and Wales. Report of the Review Committee.* Cm 532. London: HMSO.

Carrithers, M. (1992) *Why Humans Have Cultures: Explaining Anthropology and Social Diversity.* Oxford: Oxford University Press.

Christie, N. (1977) 'Conflicts as property.' *British Journal of Criminology 1977*, 17, 1–15.

Cohen, D.J. (1995) *Law, Violence, and Community in Classical Athens.* Cambridge: Cambridge University Press.

Cooley, C. (1922) *Human Nature and the Social Order.* New York: Charles Scribner's Sons.

Copplestone, F. (1963) *A History of Philsophy.* 4 vols. London: Burns, Oates & Washburne.

Cordess, C. and Cox, M. (eds) (1996) *Forensic Psychotherapy: Crime, Psychodynamics and the Offender Patient.* London: Jessica Kingsley Publishers.

Cox, M. (1986) 'The "holding function" of dynamic psychotherapy in a custodial setting: a review.' *Journal of the Royal Society of Medicine 79*, 162–164.

Cox, M. and Theilgaard, A. (1994) *Shakespeare as Prompter.* London: Jessica Kingsley Publishers.

Craig, H. (1936) *The Enchanted Glass.* New York: Oxford University Press.

Creighton, S. and King, V. (1996) 'Parole and release.' In *Prisoners and the Law.* London: Butterworth.

Curry, W. C. (1959) *Shakespeare's Philosophical Patterns.* Baton Rouge: Louisiana State University Press.

Damrosch, S.P. and Perry, L. A (1989) 'Self-reported adjustment, chronic sorrow, and coping of parents of children with Down syndrome.' *Nursing Research, 38* (1), 25–29.

Danby, J.F. (1949) *Shakespeare's Doctrine of Nature: A Study of King Lear.* London: Faber & Faber.

Davies, D.H. (1970) *Worship and Theology in England.* 5 vols. London: Oxford University Press.

Deigh, J. (1996) *The Sources of Moral Agency: Essays in Moral Psychology and Freudian Theory.* Cambridge: Cambridge University Press.

Demos, J. (1996) 'Shame and guilt in early New England'. In R. Harre and W.G. Parrott (eds) *The Emotions: Social, Cultural and Biological Dimensions.* London: Sage Publications.

Deurzen-Smith, E. van (1988) *Existential Counselling in Practice.* London: Sage Publications.

Dodds, E.R. (1951) *The Greeks and the Irrational.* Berkeley and Los Angeles: University of California Press.

Doi, T. (1973) *The Anatomy of Dependence.* Tokyo: Kodansha.

Dolan, B. (1995) 'The attribution of blame for criminal acts: relationship with personality disorders and mood.' *Criminal Behaviour and Mental Health 5*, 41–51.

Douglas, M. (ed) (1970) *Witchcraft Confessions and Accusations.* ASA Monographs, No. 9. London: Tavistock.

Dover, K.J. (1974) *Greek Popular Morality in the Time of Plato and Aristotle.* Oxford: Basil Blackwell.

Dyke, J. (1624) *Good Conscience: Or a Treatise shewing the Nature, Meanes, Marks, Benefit and Necessity Thereof.* London.

Elias, N. (1978) *The Civilising Process: The History of Manners.* English translation. Oxford: Basil Blackwell.

Erikson, E.H. (1956) 'The problem of ego identity.' *Journal of the American Psychoanalytic Association* 4, 56–121.

Erikson, E.H. (1965) 'Eight ages of Man.' In *Childhood and Society.* London: Pelican.

Eysenck, H.J. (1960) 'Symposium: The development of moral values in children. The contribution of learning theory.' *British Journal of Educational Psychology 30,* 11–21.

Eysenck, H.J. and Eysenck, S.B.G. (1991) *Manual of the Eysenck Personality Scales (EPS Adult).* London: Hodder & Stoughton.

Farnham, W. (1936) *The Medieval Heritage of Elizabethan Tragedy.* Berkeley: University of California Press.

Fazio, D.R., Kroner, D. and Forth, A. (1997) 'The attribution of blame scale with an incarcerated sample.' *Criminal Behaviour and Mental Health,* 1, 153–164.

Ferguson, E (1997) 'Sculptor, Writer, Killer.' *Observer,* 23 February.

Foucault, M. (1977) *Discipline and Punish: The Birth of the Prison.* English edition. London: Allen Lane.

Foucault, M. (1986) *The Care of the Self.* New York: Vintage.

Foulds, G.A., Caine, T.M. and Creasy, M.A. (1960) 'Aspects of intro-punitive expression in mental illness.' *Journal of Mental Science 106,* 599–610.

Frank, A.W. (1995) *The Wounded Storyteller: Body, Illness and Ethics.* Chicago: The University of Chicago Press.

Freud, S. (1896a) 'Extracts from the Fleiss papers: Draft K: The neurosis of defence.' *Standard Edition of the Complete Psychological Works of Sigmund Freud,* Vol. I, 220–228. London: The Hogarth Press and the Institute of Psycho-Analysis.

Freud, S. (1896b) 'Extracts from the Fleiss papers: Letter 71.' *Standard Edition of the Complete Psychological Works of Sigmund Freud,* Vol. I, 263–266. London: The Hogarth Press and the Institute of Psycho-Analysis.

Freud, S. (1906) 'Psychoanalysis and the establishment of the facts in legal proceedings.' *Standard Edition of the Complete Psychological Works of Sigmund Freud,* Vol. IX, 103–114. London: The Hogarth Press and the Institute of Psycho-Analysis.

Freud, S. (1913) 'Totem and taboo.' *Standard Edition of the Complete Pscyhological Works of Sigmund Freud,* Vol. XIII, 1–162. London: The Hogarth Press and the Institute of Psycho-Analysis.

Freud, S. (1916) 'Some character types met with in psychoanalytic works (iii) Criminals from a sense of guilt.' *Standard Edition of the Complete Psychological Works of Sigmund Freud,* Vol. XIV, 332–333. London: The Hogarth Press and the Institute of Psycho-Analysis.

Freud, S. (1917) 'Mourning and melancholia.' *Standard Edition of the Complete Psychological Works of Sigmund Freud,* Vol. XIV, 237–258.

Freud, S. (1923) 'The Ego and the Id.' *Standard Edition of the Complete Psychological Works of Sigmund Freud,* Vol. XIX, 3–66. London: The Hogarth Press and the Institute of Psycho-Analysis.

Freud, S. (1925) 'The economic problem of masochism.' *Standard Edition of the Complete Psychological Works of Sigmund Freud,* Vol. XIX. London: The Hogarth Press and the Institute of Psycho-Analysis.

Freud, S. (1933) 'New introductory lectures on psycho-analysis.' *Standard Edition of the Complete Psychological Works of Sigmund Freud,* Vol. XXII, 3–182. London: The Hogarth Press and the Institute of Psycho-Analysis.

Freud, S. (1937) 'Analysis terminable and interminable.' *Standard Edition of the Complete Psychological Works of Sigmund Freud,* Vol. XXIII. London: The Hogarth Press and the Institute of Psycho-Analysis.

Freud, S. (1957) 'On the history of psychoanalytic movement. Papers on metapsychology and other works.' *Standard Edition of the Complete Psychological Works of Sigmund Freud,* Vol. XIV. London: The Hogarth Press and the Institute of Psychoanalysis.

Freud, S. (1961a) 'Civilization and its discontents.' (originally published 1930 [1929]). In *Standard Edition of the Complete Psychological Works of Sigmund Freud,* Vol. XXI, 59–148. London: The Hogarth Press and the Institute of Psycho-Analysis.

Freud, S. (1961b) 'Dostoevsky and Parricide' (originally published 1928). *In Standard Edition of the Complete Psychological Works of Sigmund Freud,* Vol. XXI, 175–194. London: The Hogarth Press and the Institute of Psycho-Analysis.

Frith, U. (1989) *Autism: Explaining the Enigma.* Oxford: Blackwell.

Gaita, R. (1991) *Good and Evil: An Absolute Conception.* London: Macmillan.

Galaway, B. and Hudson, J. (eds) (1996) *Restorative Justice: International Perspectives.* Amsterdam: Kugler Press.

Gallagher, L. (1991) *Medusa's Gaze: Casuistry and Conscience in the Renaissance.* Stanford: Stanford U.P.

Gilbert, P., Pehl, J. and Allan, S. (1994) 'The phenomenology of shame and guilt: An empirical investigation.' *British Journal of Medical Psychology 67,* 23–36.

Gilson, E. (1955) *History of Christian Philosophy in the Middle Ages.* London: Sheed & Ward.

Gill, C. (1996) *Personality in Greek Epic, Tragedy, and Philosophy: The Self in Dialogue.* Oxford: Oxford University Press.

Girard, R. (1987) 'Generative scapegoating.' In *Violent Origins: Ritual Killing and Culture Formation.* Stanford: Stanford University Press.

Goffman, E. (1959) *The Presentation of Self in Everyday Life.* New York: Anchor Books.

Goleman, D. (1995) *Emotional Intelligence: Why it can Matter more than IQ.* London: Bloomsbury.

Gough, H.G. (1960) 'Theory and measurement of socialization.' *Journal of Consulting Psychology 24,* 23–30.

Gudjonsson, G.H. (1984) 'Attribution of blame for criminal acts and its relationship with personality.' *Personality and Individual Differences 5,* 53–58.

Gudjonsson, G.H. (1990a) 'Cognitive distortions and blame attribution among paedophiles.' *Sexual and Marital Therapy 5,* 183–185.

Gudjonsson, G.H. (1990b) 'Psychological treatment for the mentally ill offender.' In K. Howells and C. Hollin (eds) *Clinical Approaches to Working with Mentally Disordered and Sexual Offenders.* Issues in Criminological and Legal Psychology, No. 16. Leicester: British Psychological Society, 15–21.

Gudjonsson, G.H. (1992) *The Psychology of Interrogations, Confessions, and Testimony.* Chichester: John Wiley & Sons.

Gudjonsson, G.H. (1994) 'Psychological vulnerability: Suspects at risk.' In D. Morgan and G. Stephenson (eds) *Suspicion and Silence. The Right to Silence in Criminal Investigation.* London: Blackstone Press Ltd, 91–106.

Gudjonsson, G.H. (1995) ' "I'll help you boys as much as I can" – how eagerness to please can result in a false confession.' *Journal of Forensic Psychiatry 6,* 2 333–342.

Gudjonsson, G.H. (1997) 'Crime and personality.' In H. Nyborg (ed) *The Scientific Studies of Human Nature. Tribute to Hans J. Eysenck at Eighty.* Oxford: Elsevier.

Gudjonsson, G.H. and Bownes, I. (1991) 'The attribution of blame and type of crime committed: data for Northern Ireland.' *Journal of Forensic Psychiatry, 2,* 337–341.

Gudjonsson, G.H. and Bownes, I. (1992) 'The relationship between attribution of blame for criminal offences and the reasons why suspects confess during custodial interrogation.' *Journal of the Forensic Science Society 32,* 209–213.

Gudjonsson, G.H. and Petursson, H. (1990) 'Homicide in the Nordic countries.' *Acta Psychiatrica Scandinavica 82,* 49–54.

Gudjonsson, G.H. and Petursson, H. (1991a) 'The attribution of blame and type of crime committed: transcultural validation.' *Journal of the Forensic Science Society 31,* 349–352.

Gudjonsson, G.H. and Petursson, H. (1991b) 'Custodial interrogation: Why do suspects confess and how does it relate to their crime, attitude and personality?' *Personality and Individual Differences 12,* 295–306.

Gudjonsson, G.H., Petursson, H., Sigurdardottir, H. and Skulason, S. (1991) 'The personality of Icelandic prisoners: some normative data.' *Nordisk Psykiatrik Tidsskrift 45*, 151–157.

Gudjonsson, G.H. and Roberts, J.C. (1983) 'Guilt and self-concept in "secondary psychopaths".' *Personality and Individual Differences 4*, 65–70.

Gudjonsson, G.H. and Roberts, J.C. (1983) 'Guilt and self concept in 'secondary psychopaths".' *Personality and Individual Differences, 4*, 65–70.

Gudjonsson, G.H. and Roberts, J.C. (1985) 'Psychological and physiological characteristics of personality-disordered patients.' In D.P. Farrington and J. Gunn (eds) *Aggression and Dangerousness.* Chichester: John Wiley & Sons, 81–101.

Gudjonsson, G.H. and Singh, K.K. (1988) 'Attribution of blame for criminal acts and its relationship with type of offence.' *Medicine, Science and the Law 28*, 301–303.

Gudjonsson, G.H. and Singh, K.K. (1989) 'The revised Gudjonsson Blame Attribution Inventory.' *Personality and Individual Differences 10*, 67–70.

Gunn, J. and Taylor, P. (eds) (1993) *Forensic Psychiatry, Clinical, Legal and Ethical Issues.* Oxford: Butterworth Heinemann.

Haley, J. (1996) 'Crime prevention through restorative justice: Lessons from Japan.' In B. Galaway and J. Hudson (eds) *Restorative Justice: International Perspectives.* Amsterdam: Kugler Press.

Hanson, R.K., Cox, B. and Woszczyna, C. (1991) 'Assessing treatment outcome for sex offenders.' *Annals of Sex Research 4*, 177–208.

Harding, J. (1982) *Victims and Offenders: Needs and Responsibilities.* London: Bedford Square Press.

Harding, J. (1989) 'Reconciling mediation with criminal justice.' In M. Wright and B. Galaway (eds) *Mediation and Criminal Justice.* London: Sage Publications.

Hare, R.D. (1975) 'Psychopathy.' In P.H. Venables and M.J. Christie (eds), *Research in Psychophysiology.* New York: John Wiley & Sons, 325–348.

Harre, R. (ed) (1986) *The Social Construction of Emotions.* New York: Basil Blackwell.

Harris, R. (1630) *Sixe Sermons of Conscience.* 2nd ed. London.

Heider, F. (1958) *The Psychology of Interpersonal Relationships.* New York: John Wiley & Sons.

Heitsch, E. (1984) *Aidesis im attischen Strafrecht.* Akademie der Wissenschaft und der Literatur, Mainz. Abhandlungen der geistes- und sozialwissenschaftlichen Klasse, 1. Stuttgart: Franz Steiner Verlag.

Herman, J. (1994) *Trauma and Recovery.* New York: Basic Books.

Herndl, G.C. (1970) *The High Design: English Renaissance Tragedy and the Natural Law.* Lexington: University of Kentucky Press.

Hildebran, D. and Pithers, W.D. (1989) 'Enhancing offender empathy for sexual-abuse victims.' In D.R. Laws (ed.), *Relapse Prevention with Sex Offenders.* New York: Guilford Press.

Hillerbrand, H.J. (ed) (1968) *The Protestant Reformation.* London: Macmillan.

Hollins, S. (1985) 'Families and handicap.' In M. Craft, D.J. Bicknell and S. Hollins (eds) *Mental Handicap. A Multidisciplinary Approach.* London: Baillière Tindall.

Hollins, S. and Grimer, M. (1988) *Going Somewhere. People with Mental Handicaps and their Pastoral Care.* London: SPCK.

Home Office (1969–1994) *Reports of the Parole Board for 1968 to 1994.* London: HMSO.

Hood, R. and Shute, S. (1993) *Parole in Transition: Evaluating the Impact and Effects of Changes in the Parole System.* Oxford: Centre for Criminological Research, University of Oxford.

Hood, R. and Shute, S. (1995) *Paroling with New Criteria.* Oxford: Centre for Criminological Research, University of Oxford.

Hooper, J, (1997) 'From bloody crime to charity.' *Guardian,* 1 February.

Hoopes, R. (1962) *Right Reason in the English Renaissance.* Cambridge, MA: Harvard. University Press.

Hough, M. and Moxon, D. (1985) 'Dealing with offenders: Popular opinion and the views of victims.' *Howard Journal* 24 (3): 160–75.

Hyler, S., Reider, R., Spitzer, R.L. and Williams, J. (1987) *Personality Diagnostic Questionnaire*. New York: New York State Psychiatric Institute.

Ignatieff, M. (1977) 'Digging up the dead.' *The New Yorker*, 10 November, pp.85–93.

Inbau, F.E., Reid, J.E., and Buckley, J.P. (1986) *Criminal Interrogation and Confessions. Third Edition*. Baltimore: Williams and Wilkins.

Irving, B. (1980) *Police Interrogation. A Case Study Of Current Practice*. Research Study No. 2. London: HMSO.

Jeffreys, M.D.W. (1952) 'Confessions by Africans.' *Eastern Anthropologist 6*, 42–57.

Jones, W. (1635) *A Commentary upon the Epistles of St Paul to Philemon, and to the Hebrewes*. London.

Joyce, J. (1986) *Ulysses: The Corrected Text*. Originally published 1922. New York: Vintage Books.

Juni, S. (1991) 'Remorse as a derivative psychoanlaytic construct.' *American Journal of Psychoanalysis 51* (1): 71–81.

Keller, B. (1994) 'Apartheid's grisly aftermath: Witch burning.' *New York Times*, 18 September.

Kemp, E. and Mitchell, K. (1997) *The Mysteries: A New Version by Edward Kemp for the RSC Production by Katie Mitchell. Part 1: The Creation. Part II: The Passion*. London: Nick Hern.

Kennedy, H.G. and Grubin, D.H. (1992) 'Patterns of denial in sex offenders.' *Psychological Medicine 22*, 191–196.

Kernberg, O.F. (1992) *Aggression in Personality Disorders and Perversions*. New Haven and London: Yale University Press.

Kierkegaard, S. (1968) *Papirer [Papers]*. Vol. I–XIII. København, Gyldendal. References are made to volume, group and number, for instance: IV A 75.

Kierkegaard, S. (1962) *Samlede værker*, 3rd edition. København: Gyldendal.

Kierkegaard, S. (1843) Vol. 2: *Enten-Eller*. Første del. København. *[Either/Or. Part 1]*.

Kierkegaard, S. (1843) Vol. 3: *Enten-Eller*. Anden del. København. *[Either/Or. Part 2]*.

Kierkegaard, S. (1844) Vol. 6: *Begrebet Angest*. København. *[The Concept of Anxiety]*.

Kierkegaard, S. (1845) Vol. 7: *Stadier paa Livets Vei*. Første del. København. *[Stages on Life's Way. Part 1]*.

Kierkegaard, S. (1846) Vol. 10: *Afsluttende Uvidenskabelig efterskrift*. Anden del. København. *[Concluding Unscientific Postscript]*.

Kierkegaard, S. (1847) Vol. 11: *Opbyggelige taler i forskellig Aand*. København. *[Upbuilding Discourses in Various Spirits]*.

Kierkegaard, S. (1849) Vol. 15: *Sygdommen til døden*. København. *[The Sickness Unto Death]*.

Kierkegaard, S. (1859) Vol. 18: *Synspunktet for min forfattervirksomhed*. København. *[The Point of View for My Work as an Author]*.

Kierkegaard, S. (1980a) *The Concept of Anxiety*. Trans. by R. Thomte. New Jersey: Princeton University Press.

Kierkegaard, S. (1980b) *The Sickness unto Death*. Trans. by Hong and Hong. New Jersey: Princeton University Press.

Kierkegaard, S. (1987) *Either/Or* Parts I and II. Trans. by Hong and Hong. New Jersey: Princeton University Press.

Kierkegaard, S. (1988) *Stages on Life's Way* Part I. Trans. by Hong and Hong. New Jersey: Princeton University Press.

Klein, M. (1957) 'Envy and gratitude.' *The Writings of Melanie Klein, Vol. 3*. London: The Hogarth Press.

Klein, M. (1975) *Love, Hate and Reparation*. London: The Hogarth Press.

Kleinman, A., Das, V. and Lock, M. (eds) (1997) *Social Suffering*. Berkeley, California: University of California Press.

Kristeller, P.O. (1961) *Renaissance Thought: The Classic, Scholastic and Humanist Strains*. New York: Harper.

Lapsley, M (1994) 'South Africa: The end and the beginning are near.' *Metro Exchange* 9, 1, January.

Lebra, W. (1971) 'The social masochism of guilt and shame: The Japanese case.' *Anthropological Quarterly 44*, 241–255.

Leplanche, J. and Pontalis, J. B. (1988) *The Language of Psycho-Analysis.* (First published 1973.) London: Karnac.

Levinas, I. (1986) 'Useless suffering.' In R. Cohen *Face to Face with Levinas.* New York: State University of New York Press.

Lewis, H. (1971) *Guilt and Shame in Neurosis.* New York: International University Press.

Lindemann, E. (1944) 'Symptomatology and management of acute grief.' *American Journal of Psychiatry 101*, 141–148.

Lindenbaum, S. (1979) *Kuru Sorcery.* California: Mayfield Press.

Little, D. (1970) *Religion, Order and Law: A Study in Pre-Revolutionary England.* Oxford: Basil Blackwell.

Louden, R. (1992) *Morality and Moral Theory.* Oxford: Oxford University Press.

Lovejoy, A.O. (1936) *The Great Chain of Being.* Cambridge, MA: Harvard University Press.

Loza, W. and Clements, P. (1991) 'Incarcerated alcoholics' and rapists' attributions of blame for criminal acts.' *Canadian Journal of Behavioural Science, 23,* 76–83.

Lykken, D.T. (1957) 'A study of anxiety in sociopathic personality.' *Journal of Abnormal and Social Psychology 55,* 6–10.

MacDowell, D.M. (1978) *The Law in Classical Athens.* London: Thames and Hudson.

Mackenzie, M.M. (1981) *Plato on Punishment.* Berkeley and Los Angeles: University of California Press.

Marks, I.M. (1965) *Patterns of Meaning in Psychiatric Patients. Semantic Differential Responses in Obsessive and Psychopaths.* London: Oxford University Press.

Marshall, T. and Merry, J. (1990) *Crime and Accountability: Victim/Offender Mediation in Practice.* London: HMSO.

Marshall, W.L. (ed) (1990) *Handbook of Sexual Assault: Issues, Theories, and Treatment of the Offender.* New York: Plenum Press.

Marshall, W.L. and Barbaree, H.E. (1990) 'Outcome of comprehensive cognitive- behavioural treatment programmes.' In W.L. Marshall (ed) *Handbook of Sexual Assault: Issues, Theories, and Treatment of the Offender.* New York: Plenum Press

Matza, D. (1964) *Delinquency and Drift.* New York: Wiley.

May, S. (1997) 'Overcoming morality: A study of Nietzsche's ethics.' PhD dissertation, University of London.

McDonald, P. (1996) 'The Chatterton Lecture on Yeats and Remorse'. Unpublished lecture given at the British Academy, London. 31 October 1996.

Mead, G.H. (1934) *Mind, Self and Society.* Chicago: University of Chicago Press.

Mealey, L. (1995) 'The sociobiology of sociopathy: An integrated evolutionary model.' *Behavioral and Brain Sciences 18,* 523–599.

Megargee, E.I. (1966) 'Undercontrolled and overcontrolled personality types in extreme antisocial aggression.' *Psychological Monographs 80,* 611.

Meyer, M. (1994) Introduction to Ibsen, H, *Plays, 3.* London: Methuen.

Minnaar, A. De V.D. Offringa and Payze, C. (1992) *To Live in Fear: Witch Hunting and Medicinal Murder in Venda.* Pretoria: Human Sciences Research Council.

Morris, A. and Maxwell, G. (1993) 'Youth justice in New Zealand: A new paradigm for making decisions about children and young persons who commit offences'. *Commonwealth Judicial Journal 9,* 4, 24.

Morris, H. (1987) 'Nonmoral guilt.' In F. Schoeman (ed.) *Responsibility, Character, and the Emotions.* Cambridge: Cambridge University Press.

Mosher, D.L. (1966) 'The development of multitrait-multimethod matrix analysis of three measures of three aspects of guilt.' *Journal of Consulting Psychology 30*, 25–29.

Murdoch, I. (1970) *The Sovereignty of Good.* London: Routledge and Kegan Paul.

New, J. F.H. (1964) *Anglican and Puritan: The Basis of Their Opposition, 1558–1640.* London: A & C. Black.

Ngubane, H. (1977) *Body and Mind in Zulu Medicine.* London: Academic Press.

Niehaus, I. (1997) *Witchcraft, Power and Politics: An Ethnographic Study of the South African Lowveld.* Johannesburg, University of Witwatersland, Department of Social Anthropology.

Nordentoft, K. (1972) *Kierkegaards psykologi.* København: G.E.C. GAD.

North, J. (1988) 'The politics of forgiveness.' In R. Scruton (ed) *Conservative Thoughts: Essays from the Salisbury Review.* London: Claridge Press.

OED (1971) 'Remorse.' *Oxford English Dictionary, Compact Edition.* New York: Oxford University Press.

Olshansky, S. (1962) 'Chronic sorrow: a response to having a mentally defective child.' *Social Casework 43*:190–193.

Osborne, R. (1985) 'Law in action in classical Athens.' *Journal of Hellenic Studies* 105, 40–58.

Osgood, C.E., Suci, G.J. and Tannebaum, P. (1957) *The Measurement of Meaning.* Urbana, IL: University of Illinois Press.

Parkes, C.M. (1972) *Bereavement: Studies of Grief in Adult Life.* London: Penguin.

Parole Board (1997) Report of the Parole Board for 1996/7. London: The Stationery Office.

Peay (1989) Tribunals on trial.

Perkins, W. (1966) 'A Discourse of Conscience'. In Thomas F. Merrill (ed) *William Perkins 1558–1602, English Puritanist: His Pioneer Works on Casuistry.* Nieuwkoop: Nieukoop B. De Graaf.

Piers, G. and Singer, M. (1967) 'Shame and guilt: A psychoanalytic and cultural study.' *American Lecturer in Psychiatry.* Springfield, ILL. Thornon.

Pincus, L. and Dare, C. (1978) *Secrets in the Family.* London: Faber and Faber.

Pinker, S. (1994) *The Language Instinct.* New York: W. Morrow and Co.

Playfere, T. (1611) *Hearts Delight (The Power of Praier. The Sickmans Couch).* London.

Potts, T.C. (1980) *Conscience in Medieval Philosophy.* Cambridge: Cambridge University Press.

Reese, M.M. (1961) *The Cease of Majesty.* London: Edward Arnold.

Reeves, H. (1984) *The Victim and Reparation.* London: NAVSS.

Reif, P. (1966) *The Triumph of the Therapeutic.* New York: Harper.

Richards, D. (1971) *A Theory of Reasons for Action.* Oxford: Oxford University Press.

Ridley, M. (1996) *The Origins of Virtue.* London: Viking Penguin.

Robertson, J. (1989) *Separation and the Very Young.* London: Free Association Books.

Rock, P. (1979) 'Another common-sense conception of deviancy.' In *Sociology* 14, 75–88, January.

Rosaldo, M. (1980) *Knowledge and Passion: Ilongot Notions of the Self.* Cambridge, MA: Harvard University Press.

Rosaldo, M. (1983) 'The shame of the head hunters and the autonomy of the self'. *Ethos 11* 3, 135–51.

Rosaldo, R. (1980) *Ilongot Head Hunting 1883–1974.* Stanford, California: Stanford University Press.

Rosaldo, R. (1984) 'Grief and a head hunter's rage: On the cultural construction of emotions.' In S. Plathner and E. Bruner (eds) *Text, Play and Story,* pp.78–195. Washington DC: American Ethnological Society.

Rose, D. (1991) 'Lifer refused parole escapes "in total despair".' *The Observer,* 6 October. London.

Rose, N. (1989) *Governing the Soul: The Shaping of the Private Self.* London: Routledge.

Rosthal, R. (1967) 'Moral weakness and remorse.' *Mind 76*, 576–79.

Salter, A. (1988) *Treating Child Sex Offenders and their Victims.* London: Sage.

Sanders, W. (1968) *The Dramatist and the Received Idea.* Cambridge: Cambridge University Press.

Saunders, T.J. (1991) *Plato's Penal Code: Tradition, Controversy, and Reform in Greek Penology.* Oxford: Oxford University Press.

Schalling, D. (1978). 'Psychopathy-related personality variables and the psychophysiology of socialization.' In R.D. Hare and D. Schalling (eds) *Psychopathic Behaviour: Approaches to Research.* Chichester: John Wiley & Sons, 85–106.

Scheff, T. (1990) *Microsociology: Discourse, Emotion and Social Structure.* London: University of Chicago Press.

Scheper-Hughes, N. (1992) *Death without Weeping: The Violence of Everyday Life in Brazil.* Berkeley: University of California Press.

Scheper-Hughes, N. (1994a) Field notes – February.

Scheper-Hughes, N. (1994b) 'The last white Christmas: The Heidelberg pub massacre.' *American Anthropologist* (December), 96, 4, 1–28.

Scheper-Hughes, N. (1995) 'Who's the killer? Popular justice and human rights in a South African squatter camp.' *Social Justice 22,* 3 Issue 61, Fall, 143–64.

Scheper-Hughes, N. (1998) Field notes – February.

Shilling, C. (1997) 'Emotions, embodiment and the sensation of society.' In *Sociological Review 45* 2, 195–219.

Schneiderman, L. (1988) 'Two types of remorse in psychotherapy.' *Psychotherapy Patient 5* (1–2), 135–145.

Shakespeare, W. (1991) *The Complete Works.* Gen. eds Stanley Wells and Gary Taylor. Oxford: Oxford University Press.

Sigurdsson, J.F. and Gudjonsson, G.H. (1994) 'Alcohol and drug intoxication during police interrogation and the reasons why suspects confess to the police.' *Addiction, 89,* 985–997.

Sinason, V. (1986) 'Secondary mental handicap and its relationship to trauma.' *Psychoanalytic Psychotherapy 2,* 2, 131–154.

Smith, H. (1592) *The Sermons.* London.

Smith, A. (1759) *The Theory of Moral Sentiments.* In: D. Raphael and A. Macfie (eds) (1976) edition. Oxford: Clarendon Press.

Snaith, R.P., Constantopoulos, A.A. and McHuffin, P. (1978) 'A clinical scale for the self-assessment of irritability, anxiety and depression.' *British Journal of Psychiatry 132,* 164–171.

Snyder, M. (1976). 'Attribution and behaviour: social perception and social causation.' In J.K. Harvey, W.J. Ickes, and Kidd, R.F. (eds) *New Directions in Attribution Research.* Vol. 1. Hillsdale, N.J: Erlbaum.

Sobsey D. (1994) *Violence and Abuse in the Lives of People with Disabilities: The End of Silent Acceptance?* Baltimore: Paul H. Brookes.

Solomon, R.L., Turner, L.H., and Lessac, M.S. (1968) 'Some effects of delay of punishment on resistance to temptation in dogs.' *Journal of Personality and Social Psychology 8,* 233–236.

Spencer, T.B. (1943) *Shakespeare and the Nature of Man.* New York: Cambridge University Press.

Strawson, P.F. (1975) 'Freedom and resentment.' In *Freedom and Resentment and Other Essays.* London: Methuen.

Stroebe, M.S., Stroebe, W. and O'Hansson, R. (1993) *Handbook of Bereavement: Theory, Research and Intervention.* Cambridge: Cambridge University Press.

Suarez-Orozco, M. (1987) 'Children in the dirty war.' In N. Scheper-Hughes (ed) *Child Survival.* Dordrecht, The Netherlands: D. Reidel.

Taussig, M. (1989) *The Nervous System.* New York: Routledge.

Taylor, G. (1985) *Pride, Shame, and Guilt: Emotions of Self-Assessment.* Oxford: Oxford University Press.

Taylor, G. (1996) 'Guilt and Remorse.' In R. Harre and W.G. Parrott (eds) *The Emotions: Social, Cultural and Biological Dimensions.* London: Sage Publications.

Tennent, G. (1990) 'The Parole Board.' In R. Bluglass and P. Bowden (eds) *Principles and Practice of Forensic Psychiatry.* Edinburgh: Churchill-Livingstone.

Thalberg, I. (1968) 'Rosthal's notion of remorse and irrecovability.' *Mind 77,* 288–89.

Tillyard, E.M.W. (1943) *The Elizabethan World Picture.* London: Chatto & Windus.

Times Literary Supplement (1993) 'My duties – to myself.' 13 August.

Todd, S.C. (1990) 'The purpose of evidence in Athenian courts.' In P.A. Cartledge, P. Millett, and S.C. Todd (eds), *Nomos: Essays in Athenian Law, Politics, and Society.* Cambridge: Cambridge University Press.

Todd, S.C. (1993) *The Shape of Athenian Law.* Oxford: Oxford University Press.

Torrance, T.F. (1969) *Space, Time and Incarnation.* Oxford: Oxford Unversity Press.

Tricomi, A.H. (1974) 'The Aesthetics of Mutilation in *Titus Andronicus.*' *Shakespeare Survey 27,* 11–19.

Turnbull, C. (1962) *The Forest People.* New York: Simon and Schuster.

Umbriet, M. (1994) *Victim Meets Offender: The Impact of Restorative Justice and Mediation.* Monsey, NY: Willow Tree Press.

Utting, D. (1991) 'Sentenced for Life.' *The Guardian,* 30 October, London.

Vanier, J. (1985) *Man and Woman He Made Them.* London: Darton, Longman and Todd.

Walker, N. (1991) *Why Punish?* Oxford: Oxford University Press.

Webster's Third New International Dictionary of the English Language, Unabridged. (1986) Chicago: Encyclopaedia Britannica Inc.

Wentworth, W. M. and Ryan, J. (eds) (1994) *Social Perspectives on Emotion.* Greenwich, Conn.: JAI Press.

Weschler, L. (1990) *A Miracle, a Universe: Settling Accounts with Torturers.* New York: Viking.

Whitehead, B.D. (1993) *Atlantic Monthly.* April. Quoted in M. Phillips (1996) *All Must Have Prizes,* p.246. London: Little, Brown and Company.

Wilks, J.S. (1990) *The Idea of Conscience in Renaissance Tragedy.* London and New York: Routledge.

Willey, B. (1964) *The English Moralists.* London: Chatto and Windus.

Williams, B. (1993) *Shame and Necessity.* Berkeley and Los Angeles: University of California Press.

Wilson, M. (1951) 'Witch beliefs and social structure.' *American Journal of Sociology 56,* 4, 307–313.

Winkler, C. (1995) 'Rape attack: Ethnography of the ethnographer.' In *Fieldwork Under Fire,* pp.155–185. Berkeley: University of California Press.

Winnicott, D.W. (1964) *The Child, the Family, and the Outside World.* London: Pelican.

Wolfgang, M. (1966) *Patterns in Criminal Homicide.* New York: John Wiley & Sons.

Worsnip, M. (1996) *Michael Lapsley: Priest and Partisan.* Melbourne: Ocean Press.

Wright, M. (1982) *Making Good: Prisons, Punishment and Beyond.* London: Burnett Books.

Wright, M. (1991) *Justice for Victims and Offenders.* Buckingham: Open University Press.

Wynne, J. (1996) 'Leeds mediation and reparation service: Ten years' experience with victim offender mediation.' In B. Galaway and J. Hudson (eds) *Restorative Justice: International Perspectives.* Amsterdam: Kugler Press.

Yalom, I.D. (1989) *Love's Executioner and Other Tales of Psychotherapy.* London: Bloomsbury.

Yeats, W.B. (1950) *The Collected Poems.* London: Macmillan & company

Zehr, H. (1990) *Changing Lenses: A New Focus for Crime and Justice.* Scottdale, PA: Herald Press.

CASES CITED

Regina v Secretary of State for the Home Department and the Parole Board, Ex parte Powell. *The Times Law Report,* December 13, 1996.

Regina v Secretary of State for the Home Department and the Parole Board, Ex parte Zulfikar. *The Times Law Report,* July 26, 1995.

Thynne, Wilson and Gunnell v The United Kingdom. *European Human Rights Reports* (1990), 666–699.

The Contributors

Michael Borgeaud is Senior Lecturer in Health Studies, University of North London.

Douglas Cairns is Senior Lecturer in Classics at the University of Leeds.

Caroline (Baroness) Cox is Chancellor of Bournemouth University, formerly Director, Nursing Education Unit, Chelsea College.

Murray Cox was consultant Psychotherapist at Broadmoor Hospital from 1970 until 1997. He was an Honorary Member of the Institute of Group Analysis and of the Danish Society for Psychoanalytic Psychotherapy, and an Honorary Research Fellow of The Shakespeare Institute, University of Birmingham.

James Gilligan is Clinical Lecturer in the Department of Psychiatry of the Cambridge Hospital, Harvard Medical School.

Gisli Gudjonsson is Reader in Forensic Psychology at the Institute of Psychiatry, University of London.

John Harding is Chief Probation Officer of the Inner London Probation Service.

Sheila Hollins is Professor of Psychiatry of Learning Disability at St George's Hospital Medical School, University of London and Consultant Psychiatrist in Wandsworth Community Health Trust.

Andrew Horne is Consultant Forensic Psychiatrist at Broadmoor Hospital.

Bjarne Jacobsen is Assistant Researcher at the University of Copenhagen.

His Honour Henry Palmer was Regional Chairman of South Thames Mental Health Review Tribunal from 1993 to 1998, and is a retired Circuit Judge.

Nancy Scheper-Hughes is Professor and Chair of the Department of Anthropology at the University of California, Berkeley, where she directs the doctoral programme in Medical Anthropology.

Leslie Sohn is Honorary Consultant Psychotherapist at the Academic Forensic Department at The Maudsley Hospital, and at Broadmoor Hospital.

Alice Theilgaard is Doctor of Medical Science and former Professor of Medical Psychology at the University of Copenhagen, and an Honorary Research Fellow at The Shakespeare Institute, University of Birmingham.

Alan Thomas is Lecturer in Moral Philosophy at the Department of Philosophy, King's College London.

David Tidmarsh, former Consultant Forensic Psychiatrist at Broadmoor Hospital and Psychiatric Member of the Parole Board of England and Wales.

Cleo Van Velsen is consultant Psychotherapist at The Maudsley Hospital.

John Wilks is Professor of English Literature at Okayama National University, Japan.

Subject Index

Author Index

Abel, G.G., Becker, J.V., Cunningham-Rather, J., Rouleau, J., Kaplan, M. and Reich, J. 91
Abrams, P. 143
Ainsworth, M. 99
Ames, W. 182
Aquinas, T. 180, 181, 185
Ashforth, A. 164
Austen, J.L. 24

Baker, H. 179
Bauman, Z. 143, 144
Bendelow, G. and Williams, S.J. 135
Bender, J. 140
Benedict, R. 145
Bercovitch, E. 163
Berglund, A.I. 164
Bicknell, J. 96
Blanck, P.D. 137
Bluglass, R. and Bowden, P. 15
Blum, L. 130
Boraine, A., Levy, J. and Scheffer, R. 156, 162
Bourne, I. 181
Boyle, J. 107
Braithwaite, J. 113, 141
Braithwaite, J. and Mugford, S. 113
Briggs, J. 147
Broad, C.D. 130
Bush, D. 180

Cairns, D.L. 171–175, 177
Calvin, J. 183
Camus, A. 193, 198
Carlisle, Rt. Hon. Lord of Bucklow 51
Carrithers, M. 172
Christie, N. 112
Cohen, D.J. 176, 177
Cooley, C. 137
Copplestone, F. 179
Cordess, C. and Cox, M. 15
Cox, M. 27
Cox, M. and Theilgaard, A. 17

Craig, H. 180
Creighton, S. and King, V. 51
Curry, W.C. 180

Damrosch, S.P. and Perry, L.A. 96
Danby, J.F. 180
Davies, D.H. 179
Deigh, J. 128, 130, 131
Demos, J. 141
Deurzen-Smith, E. van 193
Dodds, E.R. 178
Doi, T. 145
Dolan, B. 87, 88, 89
Douglas, M. 163
Dover, K.J. 173, 174, 176

Elias, N. 143, 145
Erikson, E.H. 41, 100
European Human Rights Reports 56
Eysenck, H.J. 90
Eysenck, H.J. and Eysenck, S.B.G. 91

Farnham, W. 180
Fazio, D.R., Kroner, D. and Forth, A. 85
Ferguson, E. 108
Foucault, M. 140, 145
Foulds, G.A., Caine, T.M. and Creasy, M.A. 91
Frank, A.W. 97
Freud, S. 36, 39, 63–66, 73, 93
Frith, U. 103

Gaita, R. 133
Galaway, B. and Hudson, J. 111
Gallagher, L. 181
Gilbert, P., Pehl, J. and Allan, S. 90
Gill, C. 171, 175
Girard, R. 153
Goffman, E. 141
Goleman, D. 99
Gough, H.G. 89
Gudjonsson, G.H. 83–85, 87–91, 93, 94, 102
Gudjonsson, G.H. and Bownes, I. 86–88, 90, 91

Gudjonsson, G.H. and Petursson, H. 86, 88, 90, 91
Gudjonsson, G.H. and Roberts, J.C. 65, 89, 91–93
Gudjonsson, G.H. and Singh, K.K. 83–86, 88, 91
Gudjonsson, G.H. Petursson, H., Sigurnardottir, H. and Skulason, S. 89
Gunn, J. and Taylor, P. 15

Haley, J. 112
Hanson, R.K., Cox, B. and Woszczyna, C. 55
Harding, J. 111
Hare, R.D. 91
Harre, R. 136
Harris, R. 182
Heider, F. 83
Heitsch, E. 177
Herman, J. 156
Herndl, G.C. 179
Hildebran, D. and Pithers, W.D. 29
Hillerbrand, H.J. 179
Hollins, S. 96
Home Office 59–60
Hood, R. and Schute, S. 54
Hooper, J. 107
Hoopes, R. 179
Hough, M. and Moxon, D. 111
Houseman, A.E. 13–14
Hyler, S., Reider, R., Spitzer, R.L. and Williams, J. 89

Ignatieff, M. 157
Inbau, F.E., Reid, J.E. and Buckley, J.P. 90
Irving, B. 86

Jeffreys, M.D.W. 163
Jones, W. 181
Joyce, J. 43
Juni, S. 96

Keller, B. 164
Kemp, ? and Mitchell, ? 12
Kennedy, H.G. and Grubin, D.H. 55
Kernberg, O.F. 65
Kierkegaard, S. 15, 189–199